'John Tusa has an extraordinary range of experience across so many fields, starting as a presenter on *Newsnight* and including a long period as Managing Director of the Barbican. This depth of experience informs his analysis of the way that bureaucratic organizations need creative, sometimes combative mavericks to break their conventions. "Bright sparks", as he calls them, are often not popular; however, they can be the people who bring in the best new ideas.'

Sir Charles Saumarez Smith, former Secretary and Chief Executive,
Royal Academy of Arts

'This is a delightful book. The case studies remind us that pioneering entrepreneurs exist just as much in the arts as they do in business – indeed there is lots here that business leaders can learn from. A bit of luck, a lot of passion, and clear vision can achieve great things.'

Lord Vaizey, former Minister of Culture

'John Tusa is not only an acute observer of organizations and inspirational individuals – he's also a gripping storyteller who makes you keep turning the pages.'

Lucasta Miller, biographer and critic

'This book is a must-read for all those who have a vision and who are willing to take a risk. John Tusa, through a collection of excellent stories from a long life, charts a pathway through rejection, innovation and challenges, never forgetting that governance is at the core of achieving success.'

Dr Harry Brunjes, Chair, English National Opera & London Coliseum

'*Bright Sparks* brings together what makes things happen in a variety of cultural and other worlds. It's moving, funny and original, and pays tribute to those who won't take no for an answer. I loved it all, but what nearly made me weep was the story of Shakespeare in Gdańsk, an almost impossible triumph in difficult circumstances – and a real celebration of those who brought it to fruition. The book is un-putdownable – fascinating, energizing, and inspiring.'

The Baroness Neuberger DBE

'In this seminal book, John Tusa discusses how to turn a brilliant idea into reality. He uses a number of real-world examples of success and interviews the key figures who made it happen. From it all emerges a profound insight into how creativity can be implemented.'

Lord Chris Smith, Master of Pembroke College Cambridge,
and former Secretary of State for Culture

'Time and again in these richly detailed case studies one meets inspirational innovators with clarity of vision, determination and daring along with enough pragmatism, insistent belief and careful thinking to handle challenges. *Bright Sparks* provides through vivid examples a healthy dose of reality and a wealth of inspiration for anyone aspiring to bring to life a dream or innovation. It is full of examples of the rough journeys taken outside comfort zones and often against a myriad of headwinds to create a lasting impact. A fascinating read full of insights as well as wise words of advice. Stepping off the precipice into the previously unknown of any new project is a potentially scary prospect, but these pages reassure that others have taken the plunge successfully in various disciplines and directions, with helpful lessons to be found.'

Victoria Robey OBE, Founder and Director, UK Music Masters

OTHER BOOKS BY JOHN TUSA

Conversations with the World
A World in Your Ear
Art Matters: Reflecting on Culture
Engaged with the Arts: Writings from the Front Line
Pain in the Arts
On Creativity: Interviews Exploring the Process
The Janus Aspect: Artists in the Twenty-First Century
Making a Noise: Getting it Right, Getting it Wrong in Life,
the Arts and Broadcasting
On Board: The Insider's Guide to Surviving Life in the Boardroom

WITH ANN TUSA

The Nuremberg Trial
The Berlin Blockade

JOHN TUSA

BRIGHT SPARKS

How Creativity and Innovation Can Ignite Business Success

BLOOMSBURY BUSINESS
LONDON · OXFORD · NEW YORK · NEW DELHI · SYDNEY

BLOOMSBURY BUSINESS
Bloomsbury Publishing Plc
50 Bedford Square, London, WC1B 3DP, UK
29 Earlsfort Terrace, Dublin 2, Ireland

BLOOMSBURY, BLOOMSBURY BUSINESS and the Diana logo are trademarks
of Bloomsbury Publishing Plc

First published in Great Britain 2023

A catalogue record for this book is available from the British Library

Library of Congress Cataloguing-in-Publication data has been applied for

ISBN: 978-1-3994-0240-8; eBook: 978-1-3994-0239-2

2 4 6 8 10 9 7 5 3 1

Typeset by Deanta Global Publishing Services, Chennai, India
Printed and bound in Great Britain by CPI Group (UK) Ltd, Croydon CR0 4YY

To find out more about our authors and books visit www.bloomsbury.com
and sign up for our newsletters

To Bright Sparks who refused to become Damp Squibs

CONTENTS

ACKNOWLEDGEMENTS

I could not have written this book without the detailed and enthusiastic co-operation of so many friends and former colleagues. They are an exceptional collection of outstandingly gifted individuals. I am fortunate to have known and worked with them. They told me things I did not know, suggested ideas I had not thought of and put right many facts, dates and judgements. They were patient and generous with my core thesis. Above all, they gave their time, support and friendship. In the course of research, I was able to revive several deep and valued relationships. It made the business of writing pleasurable and personally rewarding. I could not be more grateful to them all.

During the course of writing, I received warm hospitality from Sally Stewart and her family in Crieff and from Graham Sheffield and Julia Glawe in Worcester. I learned a lot and enjoyed a lot.

My research was greatly assisted by the devotion of certain individuals to establishing and keeping alive the facts surrounding the projects in which they played a part.

Ian Richardson's personally and painstakingly assembled BBC World Service Television timeline is an essential part of the historical record. He created it over several years without support from BBC History and occasionally in the face of actual resistance from BBC Public Affairs.

Tim Williams' only slightly less formal chronology of the MPM Project is just as essential and certainly unique. I relied heavily on both, as will future historians. Tim's personal archive of MPM should not be lost to history.

Fiona Cushley has kept a treasure trove of MPM publications and kindly made them available.

Sheila Colvin lent me the all-important 1983 Edinburgh Festival Yearbook for John Drummond's pioneering Vienna 1900 festival. Far more than a catalogue, the essays inside by John Drummond and Professor Peter Vergo provided essential insights into the philosophy behind that unique festival. Professor Vergo also identified a precious Secession souvenir that was given to John Drummond after his festival directorship.

Di Lashmore passed on valuable personal documents from the estate of Bob Lockyer, himself the legatee of John Drummond.

Shoshana Stewart arranged for me to see foundation documents from the early years of the Turquoise Mountain Foundation. Marshall Marcus played a similar role in making available the annual brochures of the European Union Youth Orchestra over a 40-year period. I am deeply grateful to them both.

David Morton and Elena Cook gave me subtle and wise observations about politics in the former Soviet Union as it morphed into the new Russia.

I am particularly grateful to Professor Boika Sokolova for drawing my attention to the extraordinary story of Professor Jerzy Limon and the Gdańsk Shakespeare Theatre. Professor Sokolova then helped with my approaches with Mrs Justyna Limon. She generously entertained me in Gdańsk, arranged an amazing series of meetings with key participants and opened the facilities of the theatre. It was an unforgettable and highly productive weekend.

I could not have worked and written as I did without the speedy, efficient, timely and super-intelligent transcription of the interviews by Kate Foot.

I have been supported and encouraged throughout by Ian Hallsworth, Allie Collins and the entire Bloomsbury Business editorial, production, marketing, communication and sales teams. They have been tirelessly efficient in a seemingly effortless way. And nice with it.

This is the first book I have written which has not had the guiding editorial mind, hand and eye of Annie Tusa applied to it. I have no doubt that it would have been better under her firm but loving scrutiny. She would have improved but in the end, I trust, would have approved.

Introduction

From time to time, any one of us has, or thinks we have, a big idea, a great new project, a fantastic scheme. It feels good, life is filled with the shiny optimism of new opportunity, sure success, bright horizons of achievement. For the overwhelming majority, the 'big idea' rapidly dissipates — often that same morning — or does not survive the first critical encounter and examination. Almost always the idea is simply not good enough, not original enough, not coherent enough to survive that pleasing flash-in-the-pan moment which turns out to be just that — a flash in a pan, momentarily dazzling but entirely transitory and wholly insubstantial. But it probably felt good for those precious few moments when we kidded ourselves that we did indeed have the next new big idea in our hands! Don't feel bad about it. This small, sad tale of self-delusion is part of the human comedy, that array of experiences shared by the overwhelming majority of our fellow human beings. It is not unique. Your failure is not special. Mine is the same.

What *is* special is that a very small number of people with a big idea really do have one. Better still, they turn the idea into reality. Even better, the experience of reality confirms the validity of the idea. Something extraordinary will have happened. How did it happen? Why did it succeed? And by whom was it managed?

There is an important connected question. Why are people frightened of the original idea? Why are so many organizations and institutions alarmed by them, threatened even? Why are organizations so incapable of creating the precise type of environment in which the truly original can be conceived, can flourish and can finally deliver?

This book addresses these questions through seven studies of new ideas, new ways of leading, new ways of working and shows how they were turned into reality. The book looks at the whole picture of innovation and creation, including: where did the ideas come from? How were they realized? What were the personalities involved? What obstacles did they face? How did they change as they evolved? Why were they opposed or rejected? What did they lead to and what lessons can be drawn from their success?

There is nothing abstract about the activity of innovation and creativity. Every idea comes from a human being. So who are the people who have both Big Ideas and possess the determination, the skills, the vision to turn them into reality? Are they special, are they particular, are they just peculiar? Do they need to be all three? The path between the first idea and the final project is long, complex, detailed and filled with obstructions, disappointments and failures. Those who possess vision need not be those who can turn vision into actuality. The handful of true originators manage both functions because both are needed: they *dream* but they also *do*. Those who handle both are vanishingly rare – they do exist, and should be nourished.

What kind of people are they? How much of the maverick must they have inside them, how much of the lone wolf but also how much of the truly inspirational leader? This is a heady mix, seldom found but uniquely required if the demands of true innovation are to be realized. These seven studies explore a range of creators with little in common except a stubborn determination to turn a vision into an actuality. It is the very variety of the types who fall into the small category of the true 'original' which make them fascinating. There is no apparent formula for originality, no set temperament where it brews, where it ferments. If originators seem to share certain qualities, they appear to spring from behaviour rather than the intellect. Both are needed; the exact mix varies from person to person.

Beware! Such attributes do not belong only to extraordinary individuals. Sometimes, the realization of the idea into the practical is achieved by a small group of people united, perhaps unexpectedly, by a shared belief in the importance of the idea. The occasional existence of a group who develop a shared response to an idea adds riches and complexity to understanding the process of innovation. It is possible for a group to own an idea and make it actual. A group may behave as a leader.

How does one capture the mercurial quality of this process? I turn heavily to eyewitness accounts and analysis from those with a record of innovation and originality at all levels. What were the ingredients that created the alchemical mix of the different? How much was based on system and analysis, how much on hunch and experience? How much came from the bright spark, how much turned on sheer luck? Did they depend on moments of inspiration followed by the application of steady pragmatism? What are the innovators like to work with and to work for? Do they command loyalty or must they demonstrate it first? Does each case study point to different routes to success in innovation? Can it involve groups united in the pursuit of an idea or project? How different will the dynamics of such group activity be, or do they share elements in common?

Perhaps above all, what can be learned from them? Are the examples of the success of the originals a rebuke to the ossification and rigidities of established organizations with their systems, structures, rules and methods? Why is there so little space for the working of the original in the wider world? In truth, who can afford to miss out on such innovations? Doesn't every great organization need their own in-house, if not house-trained, innovator? Each case study also throws light on a time, a period, an organization and a professional culture that was challenged to change and often actively resisted the challenge. This will also be a cultural history showing how the idea of daring to innovate, to be original, emerges and can flourish in a wide variety of disciplines ranging from international development to global news, to distance learning, cultural leadership and programming. As a result, the book has a wide international scope – from social and cultural transformation in the former Soviet Union to economic development in Afghanistan to musical co-operation throughout the European Union to cultural programming from Edinburgh to the British Council worldwide to global satellite television news and editorial journalistic innovation.

A personal footnote: this book may appear to be a hybrid. It *is* a hybrid, deliberately, inevitably so. It studies, describes and analyses people. That represents the biographical element, the objective ingredient. It does so on the basis of my considerable personal engagement; the autobiographical element, the subjective ingredient. Does this matter? It cannot be wished away nor would I wish it to be. I describe things that I saw, people that I know, events that I took part in. I believe it to be a source of witness, strength and insight. It is also about institutions, how they react to people and ideas beyond the borders of their own rules and conventions. Sometimes their failure to adapt, even to recognize the novel, the daring, the innovative are glaringly revealed. Why are they not regretted more?

I have been close to those involved in these case studies – sometimes personally close, often professionally close. I have seen them at work and at play. Acutely aware of the dangers of such proximity distorting, perhaps softening, my judgements, I believe that the advantages of my depth of knowledge, my inside-outside perspectives more than outweigh an occasional inevitable lack of pure objectivity. But these are not in any sense my stories, they are theirs. I apologize for none of it.

There is a further element involved. I examine not only the actions of significant individuals, I attempt to unpick how and why they acted and behaved as they did. Mood, motivation, morals all play a large part in explaining what happened, what was achieved. It adds a further dimension to the intentional hybridity of the book, the psychological. Is there a category to which it belongs? Why not Psychobiography?

I have also balanced my own views by the essential inclusion of judgements and observations from those who have a broader, closer range of perspectives about the people and events described. Taken together, I believe that we present a rich mosaic of description and assessment of the work, the characters, the achievements, the foibles, the setbacks, the failures of the originals. They exist to surprise us and they certainly deserve a close look – I believe this book offers such a look.

'A Passion Organization': The Turquoise Mountain Foundation, 2005–11

Featuring interviews with:

Will Beharrell, Deputy CEO, Director, Community Programming, 2006–11

Richard Dwerryhouse, Country Director, Jordan 2018–present

Lyse Doucet, BBC International Correspondent

David Loyn, BBC Correspondent Afghanistan, Visiting Senior Fellow, War Studies Department, King's College London

Jemima Montagu, Director, Cultural Programming, Turquoise Mountain Foundation

Tamim Samee, Trustee, Turquoise Mountain Foundation

Rory Stewart, former Deputy Governor in southern Iraq; Managing Director, Turquoise Mountain Foundation 2016–2018

Shoshana Stewart, Chief Executive, Turquoise Mountain Foundation, 2008–11; President from 2021

Tommy Wide, Country Manager Afghanistan, 2012–14; Managing Director, Turquoise Mountain Foundation, 2014–16

The ancient city of Herat lies in the far west of Afghanistan. Iran is closer than Kabul, the Iranian influence almost tangible. Its skyline is filled with the domes of the Friday mosque, magnificently blue- and gold-tiled. Over there, the remaining towers of Queen Farhad Shah's once-magnificent madrassa. A little outside the centre, the Sufi shrine of Gazurgah, the local saint. At Herat's heart is the fortress, Bala Hissar (Arg), brick-built, massive ramparts at least a kilometre square with a few decorative areas of the original vividly coloured tiling still remaining on some of the towers. Here, the great names of medieval history from Alexander the Great onwards stopped, fought, usually destroyed, sometimes built and moved on. The air is thick with dust from the surrounding plains and the remembered echoes of ancient war, conquest and epic encounters. Here, the centuries lie closely packed, never remote in our awareness and understanding.

A strange meeting took place in January 2002. The Taliban had recently been defeated by Western forces; a new government had been in place in Kabul for just two weeks. A whiff of normality was in the air. There are two versions of the meeting which was held in the only hotel in Herat then authorized for foreigners, the Mowafaq.

In his book, *The Places in Between*, about his ambitious mid-winter walk to Kabul through the mountain snows, Rory Stewart describes how he got up that morning and dressed in traditional Afghan clothing: long *shalwar kemis* shirt, baggy trousers, Chitrali cap and brown *patu* blanket wrapped around his shoulders. He sat down at a breakfast table with some journalists. One of them, Vaughan Smith, former Grenadier Guards officer-turned-freelance cameraman, had worked in Afghanistan for a decade: 'Are you leaving this morning?' he politely enquired. 'I hope so,' replied Rory. 'And are you really going to walk to Kabul through Ghor?' continued Vaughan

Smith, knowing that it was the mountainous, snow-blanketed route. 'Yes,' said Rory and ate six fried eggs to stock up on protein. 'Good luck,' Smith tersely observed.

That meeting is rather differently described by the long-time BBC correspondent in Afghanistan, David Loyn. He recalls: 'This rather thin, gangly Brit appeared at our breakfast table one day, having heard people speaking English. We thought, "He's a bit of an idiot" when we first encountered him. He was very affable, wearing *shalwar kemis*, and then we realized what he was doing. It seemed to be completely barmy but he was very resolute. He had literally torn out the pages from Nancy Dupree's 1970 guidebook, this blue-covered guidebook that everybody had of Afghanistan, with a very rudimentary map. He was going to head east across some of the toughest country in Afghanistan towards the Minaret of Jam. We had a meal or two with him and then he disappeared off into the hills and we thought we'd never see him again. We thought that was it, he would never be seen alive.'

Loyn's worst fears were nearly realized. Rory almost perished in the mountain snowdrifts, saved only by the instinctive ministrations of his devoted dog, Babur. Having set out to walk to Kabul by the direct, snowdrift-filled mountain route in winter, Rory spent no time in Kabul itself on arrival, as he states in his book. It was the walk that mattered, it seemed, not the destination. Yet scarcely four years later, he returned to the Afghan capital for a project that would turn out to be almost more extraordinary, albeit in a wholly different way, than his life-threatening walk. What brought him back?

For almost four years after his walk, Kabul and Afghanistan had no place in Rory's plans. He cut a romantic, public figure. He had been deputy governor in two provinces in southern Iraq during the Iraq War, based in Basra. There, he formed a police force and even organized elections. At the then Prince Charles' suggestion, he set up a vocational training school. This added up to quite a record. Not surprisingly, journalism wanted him, television wooed him, publishers courted him. He could do them all and do them well. What glittering path would he follow? Rory's priority inclined to a return to his basic trade, diplomacy, and he applied for the British Embassy in Belarus. Unencumbered by family and children, shrewdly keeping his private relations remote from public view, few young men in their early thirties had so much to choose for their future as he did.

Events then offered an accidental and decisive turn. During his undergraduate years at Oxford, Rory had been drawn to the attention of the then Prince of Wales as a suitable summer tutor for the young Princes, William and Harry. Clearly, Charles formed a good impression and kept him in mind as a promising person. During 2005, the Prince had been hosting the Afghan President, Hamid Karzai, in London. Karzai was much taken with the Prince of Wales' School of Traditional Arts. Surely Afghanistan needed one too? Keen to help, Prince Charles despatched Rory on a fact-finding visit to Kabul.

Despite having, on his own admission, only a 'general romantic interest in the history of Afghanistan but no academic interest', or at least only extending to reading 'a few jolly books about Central Asia', Rory travelled to Kabul in December 2005 to oblige the Prince but in a very sceptical frame of mind about the possibility or the relevance of the project. After five days of meetings with government vocational schools, aid agencies and cultural organizations, he decided that focusing on traditional crafts would not work, though he thought the woodcarving of very high quality. What Afghanistan needed, he concluded, was plumbers and electricians. In fact, there were plenty of them, flooding in from Pakistan to earn a living. His report to the Prince and President Karzai would be both short and disappointing. Then chance stepped in.

Three days before returning to London with nothing to offer but fine words and negative conclusions, Rory happened on a corner of the Old City of Kabul which he had never previously entered, Murad Khane. As he recalls, 'I discovered this extraordinary sequence of courtyard houses that were on the verge of total collapse, filled with banana boxes, goats, being used to store strange bits of junk from the bazaar. I began to wonder whether it might not be possible to combine the idea of training traditional crafts with saving this part of the old city before it vanished.'

It was an imaginative and daring piece of synthesis that was entirely Rory's responsibility. From this moment, like it or not, his was the vision that would finally shape the project: 'I'd been asked by the Prince of Wales and President Karzai to go and look at the crafts. They were Prince Charles' personal priority, historic buildings less so. It was my own personal enthusiasm for that part of the old city – I was just entranced by how both fragile and beautiful it was. Maybe I could use the extraordinary political capital of having the President on side if I put his traditional crafts training school in the centre of the old city. I could essentially defy anyone to demolish it. I was slightly wickedly using the traditional crafts idea as a way of regenerating this community and this area.'

There was a long way to go. Rory returned to Kabul in January 2006. He was accompanied by a recent acquaintance, an Arts Council England officer involved in cultural promotion, Jemima Montagu. She told Rory that he was a diplomat, he knew nothing about cultural regeneration and he should get such advice from her. For the first time in this story but not the last, Rory bought in skills and knowledge he lacked himself.

Jemima's recollection of that January visit is as off-putting as it could be: 'It was pouring with rain in Afghanistan. We were there for about three days. The rain in Kabul means it's just mud everywhere, just muddy streets, small backs of taxis with no effective windscreen wipers. Everything is a deluge, you can't see a thing. We turned up in Murad Khane, walked around. It didn't even have streets at that point, it was just a dump. My photographs from that weekend we used for a very long time because we got the one of the goat standing on the roof of part of the Great Serai (a once-important building). Rory could see the possibility of something where I saw an awful lot of wheelbarrows. It wasn't just about clearing out rubbish, about restoring that building, it was about the whole community around it. We learned along the way how much of a community development project it needed to be. And to believe in it when everyone else said, "This is a dump, this is a shithole."'

This alternative perspective is crucial to understanding what Rory was to achieve in the coming years. He was undaunted. Where Jemima saw mere rubbish, he saw promise and potential. In doing so, he both took risks and displayed enormous cheek, or *chutzpah*, depending on your point of view. In the pouring rain and clogging mud of January in Kabul, he took a huge gamble. And why not? The only alternative would have been to concede failure at the first setback. Instead, he went on the offensive: 'I very grandly went in to see various ministries, representing myself as a sort of personal emissary from the Afghan President and the Prince of Wales on the basis of not a great deal. I got them to sign great memorandums of understanding. I cobbled together a map of that part of the old city and I presented in this document that we were going to restore this part of the old city. We requested the Afghan government to protect it in exchange for the investment we were going to bring in. In a fit of enthusiasm, various officials in the Ministry of Urban Development signed and I went off with it.'

Rory now had a fancy document, vague political endorsement but lacking any real legal standing to restore part of old Kabul.

More to the point, he had no money to do the restoration, to set up a traditional crafts school or anything else in his vision. Above all, he had no idea how any part of the project might actually be carried out or paid for. Back in London, he explained his rather embarrassing dilemma to his patron. The Prince of Wales suggested that he write a proposal on what could be done in Afghanistan and present it to key donors. The Prince then offered to host a dinner to engage anyone who might be interested in backing the project.

Rory sold these potential supporters a dream of restoring the centre of the old city in Kabul. He was acutely aware that his dream was based on the scribbled fruits of two weeks in the city, with no money, no staff, no planning, just a simple belief that it was the right thing to do. His eloquence and articulation of a vision must have been persuasive. Conjuring the vision may have been the more intense because he still did not see himself as actually being involved in delivering it.

As the result of his lobbying, two 'very generous individuals' who had read his proposal committed US$ 2 million for the first year. For a moment, Rory may have thought he had done what Prince Charles had asked him to do: research a project in Kabul, define its scope and purpose, sell the idea to a few influential backers, go back to dreaming of the Embassy in Belarus. Life was not that simple. Prince Charles said to Rory: 'Would you mind *awfully* going back to Kabul and getting it all started?' How do you refuse a prince?

Still, Rory was less than halfway committed to whatever the project might be. It was one thing to fall in love with the remains of the old city of Kabul. Now he had to face the enormity of the reality: 'The whole of the centre of the site was a pile of plastic bags, collapsed walls, mud, brick and goodness knows what else, with dogs and goats all over the top of it. Some of these were building rubble on top of which garbage had accumulated. You could in effect walk over these piles of garbage, over people's walls into their courtyard houses.'

It still remains remarkable that anyone could have seen through the piles of rubbish and believed that something precious, valuable, genuine and worthwhile could be found in it, then made out of it. Rory returned to Kabul in February 2006 on a very limited basis: he would be an unpaid volunteer, without contract for just three months. Thereafter, things began to take over.

The first office was a backroom in a tailor's shop. Someone loaned him a driver. With a sixth sense of how the world works, Rory named him the 'logistics manager', his very first employee. The tailor's brother appeared, said to be an engineer with years of working for the United Nations. Would it be a good idea to start by clearing the rubbish from the old city, suggested Rory? 'Engineer' as he was always called thereafter replied, 'Come tomorrow morning and see what happens.' A hundred Afghans armed with wheelbarrows and shovels paraded, then started to assault the accumulated, impacted layers of rubbish. 'Engineer' Hedayatullah was at the core of the project for a decade. He was Rory's second employee. A friend of a friend recommended an Afghan with a background in security. He was also an accountant. Fifteen years later, Ajmal Samimi is still finance manager. One of Rory's qualities was to give and to receive loyalty. Was this an essential part of his appeal, for appeal he certainly had?

There was a key moment in his three-month 'volunteering' commitment when Rory became committed in a perhaps unexpected way. The originally promised US$ 2 million had been crucial but longer-term funding was vital. Towards the end of February 2006, Italian government officials were invited to visit the site. For Rory, it was a moment of realism: 'The Italian government representatives were just horrified – it looked to them like such a filthy, decrepit sort of slum that they could see no point in the thing at all. This convinced me that I really needed to finish a building, show what a building could look like, if I was to have any hope of getting anyone else to support us.'

Though he might not have known it, from this moment of brutal practicality, Rory was head over heels in a project that he could never have conceived, had he set out to plan it coherently and systematically. Any consultant would have rejected the project out of hand. In orthodox assessment, they would have been right. That is one paradox of the creation of what became the Turquoise Mountain Foundation.

The other relates to Rory himself. He was, perhaps always will be, the ultimate loner. Only such a character would set out to walk across much of the Middle East and the subcontinent because he found meaning in walking, observing, noticing, thinking, meeting and talking. But this loner was also very gregarious; he was not isolated or selfish in his isolation. How could he be as a former diplomat? If being a loner was part of his make-up, so too was leadership. He was also a Pied Piper who attracted others by dint of his past and the strength of his vision for the future.

The group who were to form a loyal core of key workers and supporters for years to come were a striking lot. It was like iron filings attracted to an irresistible magnetic core. Rory and his exploits were the magnet. They came one by one. Will Beharrell had had a literary interest in Central Asia from the age of 17. After a degree in Arabic and Persian, he was fascinated by Rory's book. A mere 20-minute conversation with him was enough to get Will on the plane to Kabul, aged just 25. Will's sensible, practical friends objected.

'They said, "Do you know anything about this chap? Where are the contracts? What are you doing and how much are you getting paid?" I hadn't thought of anything so I went out not knowing very much at all, but perfectly open-minded and willing

15

to do whatever I could. And I thought, "What do I pack? What do I wear?" I put on an old tweed jacket that I had for formal occasions. I landed in Kabul, was able to speak a few words of classical Persian, which I think made me the object of ridicule. And started from there.'

Will Beharrell later became Rory's deputy – a grand name for following Rory around and following up action points after meetings. Another arrival was Tommy Wide, also an Arabist. He too was seduced after reading Rory's *The Places in Between* as he wondered what to do with his own life post getting a degree: 'Afghanistan had been on my radar for a while. I looked up Rory online and I read an article that he was setting up this thing called "Turquoise Mountain". This was in its very early days. And I thought, "God, that sounds absolutely brilliant. So many things I'm interested in – foreign cultures, language, arts and culture." I wrote to the Turquoise Mountain website and almost immediately got a response back from Rory's then deputy Will Beharrell, who said, "Well, I'm coming to Oxford soon, why don't we meet?".'

Not that Tommy Wide, like Beharrell, didn't have voices in his ear warning him off the impulsive decisions of a young man. Such as his father: 'He thought the TM website was really bad, the whole thing seemed so implausible. He was convinced it was some kind of front and that I was getting myself involved in something that it was unwise for a 23-year-old to be involved in. My dad was very sceptical of the whole enterprise and of Rory. That was an initial warning flag for me, that I should check that everything was what it seems.'

If Rory himself was not overtly aware of Tommy's doubts, he set many of them at rest by doing what he instinctively did – taking a walk and taking Tommy with him on his very first day in Kabul. Tommy recalls: 'We walked from where we were living all the way to a restaurant. And I just thought this is remarkable. I thought Kabul would be blast walls and armoured cars. There was this guy, just stepping out into the street and taking me with him. I was after all a volunteer, duty of care and all that. And this man said, "Look, this is the way we do things. We walk everywhere and talk to people as we go." So what really struck me from the beginning was just the kind of courage and chutzpah involved.'

Rory Stewart probably would not have put it in these words, but that walk with Tommy Wide through Kabul streets summed up what would become crucial parts of the culture of the organization that he was steadily setting up. It would always be in touch with the place, with the people. Those were its values. Tommy was to stay with Turquoise Mountain in many guises for a decade.

Shoshana Clark, a 26-year-old eighth-grade teacher in Harlem and Boston, showed up in Kabul with a friend because she wanted a year off from teaching in September 2006. Once there, she volunteered to work for Turquoise Mountain. She got a free room in exchange. For the rest?

'What I thought I was doing, I have no idea – I thought I was exploring Afghanistan. There were a lot of volunteers around in the office, it was chaos, with five or six Afghan staff and five or six computers. They weren't connected to each other. I decided to be helpful and made a computer network of some sort with Aziz, our office manager. I somehow worked out how to make a computer network – I do not remember any instructions asking me to do this.'

Shoshana did so unbidden within three weeks of arrival. She became Rory's assistant, ensuring that his bright ideas were actually followed up. She had, he recalls, 'a memory like a steel trap, had a checklist on a sheet of A4 paper with 50 things on it, standing at my shoulder checking that everything I had said was followed up'. After three years as his deputy, Shoshana became TMF's chief executive.

In 2006, the 'Pied Piper' effect was astonishingly powerful. By 2007, a system began to appear. A finance director by background, Richard Dwerryhouse found himself recruited for a post and a place he did not want. It was a year into the project, February 2007. His arrival was seen as a landmark in TM's evolution – and probably in Rory's too: 'Everyone was laughing because when I arrived, they said, "You're the twentieth person to arrive but the very first that we've actually recruited properly." I got out of private sector finance and started a career in the development sector. I was interviewed by someone from TM in London – I didn't want to go to Afghanistan. I thought development work was going to be tropical islands, palm trees, doing something worthwhile, but in a lovely climate. But not Afghanistan. Then I was completely seduced by them, by the spirit of the organization and what they were trying to do.'

Rory did not accept just anyone who arrived expressing wide-eyed devotion to a cause and a project that barely existed. Nor was every volunteer a success. A former army officer with whom he had served in Basra found he could not work in an organization without rules and support structures. This was not a project for the faint-hearted. Young architects, seconded from the Royal Institute of British Architects (RIBA) in London, used to designing loft conversions, imploded when faced with a building site, 50 Afghan workers to organize and the urgent need to prevent a mud building from collapse. The greatest failures were the occasional secondees from the UK's Department for International Development (DfID). It was perhaps hardly surprising that civil servants trained on long assessment processes and detailed procurement systems should quail when told, as Rory put it: 'If you take such a person and suddenly say, "You're now in charge of managing 300 Afghan staff and builders and a bomb is going off and the roof is falling down and we've run out of money and we need to get something done!" They simply couldn't.'

The DfID attachées both couldn't and wouldn't try to adapt. What is unpardonable is the refusal of DfID at any level to acknowledge that while TMF activity was about as different from, even alien to the way the Ministry worked, there might still be something to be learned about development from TMF's extreme focus, energy and momentum. Instead there was only bureaucratic hostility, disapproval and disparagement. Jealousy perhaps too. As a former ACE (Arts Council England) officer herself, Jemima Montagu knew about bureaucratic language and the great cultural divide it represented. Of this Rory seemed blithely, perhaps necessarily ignorant. Jemima's was a more measured perspective: 'The people who'd had a long experience in Afghanistan, knew the country really well, knew the cultural development sector, they were snooty, thinking, "Who are these young cowboys? What do they think they know?" Rory always carries a certain arrogance with him that rubs some people up the wrong way. Those who were doing things by the book were very ruffled by the Turquoise Mountain approach. Rory's line was quite mocking of the language of international development. I shared it, we all did. We laughed about phrases like "capacity building" and this unbelievable jargon associated with the funding. All of us were fairly gung-ho and thought, "Well, we'll use this language if we have to use it to get the funding." Rory's independent mind and creative thinking was prepared to push aside lots of received ideas and try and think of a new model.'

The development 'professionals' never accepted Rory, never acknowledged the success of TM, never dreamed of adopting some of TM's approach, manner or values. It was their failure, the nation's loss.

They were not the only group strongly opposed to the whole restoration project. Whatever the Afghan government or President might say, the Kabul Municipality had their own views and interests and not without reason. The entire area had long been acquired by the government in 1976 for an East German master plan involving a six-lane highway and concrete tower blocks. Murad Khane would have been bulldozed away. A dramatic showdown occurred within two to three weeks of the mammoth clear-up process started by 'Engineer' and his spade and wheelbarrow army. It was a nasty shock for Rory: 'The Municipality turned up and asked us to stop clearing the garbage. There was this fantastic standoff. Our people were there with their spades. One of the community elders stepped forward and said to the deputy mayor, "How dare you do this. I remember when you last cleared the garbage, I was ten years old and it was 1957." And the deputy mayor then retreated.'

The Kabul Municipality were however right: they owned the land, they had a master plan for redeveloping it. This strange Englishman and the local community of wheelbarrow pushers had no rights, no standing, no authority over Murad Khane whatever. Any lawyer would have said as much and Rory knew it. What they did have was the ear of the Afghan President. This support at the highest level proved decisive in keeping local bureaucrats at bay. The site was designated a site of cultural protection and the Afghan cabinet declared its preservation as a 'public good'.

What this episode did was to reveal Rory as a risk-taker of the highest order (some might say gambler). A prudent, cautious person would have pulled out and kept his memories of a marvellous dream that circumstances destroyed. Rory demonstrated prudence in another way by keeping his supporters and funders fully informed about the high level of risk involved in the project. The naysayers continued to gather and to voice discouragement. Like the prestigious, well-funded and hugely experienced Aga Khan Trust for

Culture (AKTC). If anyone knew about successful historic conservation in Afghanistan, it was AKTC with a string of successful projects to their credit. They had surveyed Murad Khane as a possible restoration project of their own but decided none of the buildings was worth conserving. Yet when they had first met Rory they dangled out a false hope and possibly a challenge to the vanity of this brash incomer: 'When I said, "Are there areas of the city I should look at?", they rather cheekily said, "If you think you have real political weight, you could try Murad Khane, but if I were you, I wouldn't touch it because we've concluded that it can't be done."'

This was advice from real historical conservation professionals. That it made Rory even more determined to take it on shone another light on his character. On one occasion, he and his team almost came to blows with local community leaders, some of whom remained highly suspicious of these British incomers. Why should any Afghan trust British intruders? What good had they ever done to the country over the centuries? As Will Beharrell recalls: 'We had this initial meeting on the rooftop of the prominent Shia shrine in the middle of Murad Khane on the riverfront. And Pahlawan Aziz, this main, unelected representative of that part of District Two, he and Rory started talking. We were joined by a dozen members of the Shrine Council. Rory started talking and Pahlawan Aziz was quite dismissive and began to look at "Engineer", who took over that meeting. It was then in Dari [the most widely spoken language in Afghanistan] only. It got very physical, which was a really early lesson in how to communicate there. Pahlawan Aziz grabbed Engineer's beard and made three points. He said: "There are three reasons why this project will fail" and he shook his head for emphasis at the end of each point. One was that we were coming to uncover treasure buried there by the British at the end of the

Anglo-Afghan War. Engineer was undeterred and grabbed Pahlawan's beard and made three counterpoints. We all kind of laughed at the end of it. There was agreement but there was also a bit of relationship building. We felt at least that we could come back and we did come back almost daily and began building a relationship with that community.'

By June 2006, Rory realized that his life was deeply tied in with the delivery of the Kabul project – a revived Afghan Traditional Crafts School located in a restored historic quarter of the city. What's more, he decided that if it was to succeed, it must be done quickly; results had to show on the ground. Momentum was key. Within the first six weeks, a calligraphy school was set up, comparatively easy to organize because it didn't need complicated equipment. A month later, the first woodworkers arrived. News travelled fast; the *ustads*, the traditional craft masters, appeared seemingly out of nowhere, sometimes out of Pakistani refugee camps. A jewellery school was started. Tommy Wide was despatched into the foothills of the neighbouring Hindu Kush to revive centuries-old pottery at the village of Istalif. Will Beharrell, a future doctor, urged Rory to set up a clinic in the future Murad Khane complex. A key strategic tussle took place between Rory and Will, one from which both learned lessons:

'Will Beharrell said he wanted to set up a clinic and I said, "Absolutely not, that's not in our strategic plan, we don't do clinics, we'd probably kill the patients." So he said, "Please let me just give it a go." And I said, "I really don't have any money for a clinic." Will said, "How much could you spare?" I said, "I could spare 50,000 dollars but that's all you're getting." So Will took it away, managed to convince the Japanese government to give him some more money. By the end of the year it was the most successful part of our entire project, seeing 27,000 patients a year. It made the community love what we were doing because we were producing good maternal healthcare, we were affecting infant mortality. All in the teeth of my opposition.'

From this, Rory drew an important lesson, one that became a characteristic of the entire TM project: other people had good ideas too, sometimes much better than his own. For Will, the flexibility in the way Rory responded was crucial. It was also a source of strength. For Rory was, or certainly became, a listener. A leader was not a dictator, as Beharrell observed: 'He's very impulsive, really. The better way of saying that was that he relied more on a sense of intuition and instinct, rather than any sort of plan. When people came along, he thought, let's just do it. Decisions were taken very quickly, which was all part of this tempo and the sense of urgency. Although Rory talked increasingly about detail, at this moment in the project I think it was more about tempo and energy and finding people that could do this for him.'

Most of TMF's 'early joiners' spent a good deal of time following Rory around the project. The much-lauded official business school maxim of 'MBWA' – management by walking around – summed him up perfectly, as Shoshana Clark had to observe closely. No one taught him to do it, he just did it: 'He's pure energy, vision, tangible, and people gravitate to him. He tramped around all day, generating ideas, making sure something got done, checking to make sure it was high quality. He iterates constantly. You've got to be willing to change direction and recognize there's a high error rate – you must be totally happy with [that]. He just loves difficult information being thrown at him. Synthesize, synthesize. The project was so complex and unwieldy, that was quite helpful.'

For Rory himself, the expression of momentum that TM needed if it was to succeed came from intense physical activity. He was a constant presence in, around and on top of the activity swarming all around him: 'The way I tried to reassure myself about the project was essentially by being endlessly on foot, walking through the project all the time. I stayed on top of it by being in the jewellery school every day, in the clinic every day, in the woodworking school every day. I was on foot six to seven hours a day. Quite a lot of what I was doing is an odd combination of extreme delegation and then diving down into very specific details. What I'm doing there is to set a standard, an idea of who we are. I'm not trying to micromanage the project. I'm more like a sergeant major walking around a parade ground. I'm trying to convey the spirit of the standard I want.'

I witnessed Rory at work on the ground when I visited the Murad Khane building site with him in my early days as a TMF trustee. I wrote in my journal at the time: 'What is important is that Rory is recognized by all, welcomed by all, greets them in Farsi, has little conversations, sometimes more substantial, with an easy grace which gives him an extraordinary quiet authority. More important, he has acceptance. In his Western two-piece suit and shirt he ought to stick out like a sore thumb. He does in a sense but he is also so accepted that he is almost inconspicuous.'

Lyse Doucet, the BBC's long-standing correspondent in Afghanistan, weighed up Rory's appearance and his manner. They were a calculated part of his style: 'Quintessentially British, very witty, with his royal connections, sartorial flair, he could have been an old British explorer. But he picked up local customs and every part of him was carefully calculated.'

Not just local customs. Rory's linguistic abilities are an interesting case. Certainly, he was adept, sounded fluent and flaunted his linguistic skills. Every leader has to have certain personal myths, to use those myths for broader purposes. How fluent linguistically was he? Natural linguist Tommy Wide was in a position to judge: 'At the beginning, I was struck by how bad his Dari was, because the myth was of this kind of incredible polyglot, but that's not true. He is a talented linguist, but he actually can't be bothered to put in the hard work. He understands Dari incredibly well for someone who speaks it incredibly badly. He often captures nuances that I wouldn't capture, even though I'd studied a lot more than he had. There was a certain amount of blagging going on with him. He's not good at disabusing people of the myths they have about him. Every newspaper article would say he spoke eight to twelve languages and he absolutely didn't.'

Tommy's observation about Rory's capacity to take in information, regardless of the exact precision of his linguistic understanding, struck Will Beharrell acutely: 'His listening skills were exceptional. If we had a dozen community elders all sat down on the floor, cross-legged, talking about something quite impassioned about the rental cost of their building or something, he seemed to be able to follow those discussions in a way that I couldn't although I probably knew more vocabulary. It was partly because he could read the room, he could read body language and intonation, had a real sense of the context. He was very quick to infer meaning and then very confident to assert whatever he'd inferred as the true dynamic of that room. This gave him a very effective way of chairing meetings.'

If Rory chose not to disabuse outsiders about the true extent of his linguistic skills, that was only a minor aspect of a leadership style that Tommy increasingly found attractive, persuasive and effective: 'Rory is this almost unique mix of imagination and eye for detail. [His] ability to connect the visionary to the intensely practical is what really sets him apart. Part of that is the hard driving, sceptical eye that he brings to everything. It's also then the ability to hire right. If you are a great visionary, you know that things only happen through excellent execution. Rory hired really wisely and could spot practical execution orientated people and got them in early.'

All of Rory's 'early joiners', a kind of Praetorian Guard, all enthusiasts to be sure, had their doubts and reservations about the project. The reality was that most of the Murad Khane site, despite the daily efforts of Engineer's 150-strong wheelbarrow battalion, looked and was a rubbish dump of collapsed mud walls, tottering buildings and occasional fragments of appealing decorated woodwork. It wasn't much to go on. Lots of people said so. Despite this, Richard Dwerryhouse, a down-to-earth finance person, saw why most decided to remain on board. Rory never accepted any negativity: 'Rory just wouldn't pay attention to that kind of stuff. Restore the Old City of Kabul, totally impossible. Goodness knows how we pulled it off. But one of the big parts of how it [happened] was having a leader who conveyed that he believed it was possible and was unwavering. There were so many hundred reasons why it shouldn't have happened and so few why it should. You needed the certainty and conviction that Rory would have about it. Couple that with the freedom people had in their roles in terms of expression. This visionary goal of a near-impossible task was a huge influence on me.'

Lyse Doucet suggests that Rory did not approach the task from the standpoint of 'its impossibility'. Rather the reverse: 'He turned it all upside down. Rory emphasized the possible in the context of what others might regard as the impossible.'

By mid-2006, TMF had momentum for sure, a determined, visionary leader and an extraordinary team of clever, adaptable, practical, youthful idealists for whom this was a kind of up-to-date 'Great Game' of their dreams. No one had involved them in such a challenge or given them such responsibility before. If it was to become much more than this, a pleasant diversion for the brilliant young, TM now needed three things: a definition of its purposes, more systematic organization and considerably more space.

Why was a definition of purpose needed at all? After all, hadn't Rory charted it in five pages six months ago for would-be supporters? Wasn't it clear from everything he said, everything he did, what TM's sense of purpose was? By his own description, he was 'still bouncing around at a million miles an hour setting all these things up'. Wasn't he demonstrating the 'sense of purpose' every minute of the day? Shoshana Clark clearly recalls that he insisted in those early days that 'we do not write a strategic plan', doubtless driven in part by his rooted aversion for bureaucratic 'development' cant.

Yet by July 2006, Turquoise Mountain had produced a detailed, glossily presented, lavishly illustrated report of what it was, what it intended to do and how it would do it. Given the prevailing and intentional atmosphere of inspired chaos that characterized TM in those first months, it is a remarkable document. Here is the commitment to restoration of 'a traditional building' in the old medieval city to house a centre for training in traditional crafts; the commitment to develop and revive Afghanistan's treasured traditional crafts. Also, the commitment to revive the community in Murad Khane and to put in paving and drainage. Not only were these comparatively limited aims overachieved, they laid the foundations for the much more ambitious programmes for every activity that followed in the next decade. The July 2006 brochure may not be a strategic plan in form, perhaps not in spirit, but it expressed TM's strategic purposes and direction in a way that no one could fail to understand. It also proclaimed the support at the highest levels that it enjoyed in Afghan and British society.

Perhaps the document is also a reflection of an internal process of evolution. Rory led, he inspired, he held the vision. He also devolved, empowered and distributed responsibility. The TM team knew that momentum, urgency, speed, focus and flexibility were not enough. Sooner or later, inspired improvisation would

27

collapse into uncontrolled amateurism. Some system was needed, some formal organization of how TM worked. Though the early days were, according to Jemima Montagu, exhilarating: 'It was a classic startup when I arrived, everyone crouching round tables, working till all hours of the night: "we've got to make it happen"; "we've got to do that presentation at the ministry"; "oh, there's an opportunity for some American funding quick". Everyone was mobilized. And then there was: "how can we repair such or such a house before it collapses?"; "we've heard about such and such an *ustad* and we must track them down". It was a completely committed startup type of phase.'

It wasn't just Jemima with her background in Arts Council England systems and organization who knew that something had to change. Professionalization was needed. Richard Dwerryhouse brought order and methodology to the finances which was not part of the founding ethos of Turquoise Mountain. Yet he also became intrinsically a part of it. TMF had this ability to absorb different styles.

Rory too understood what was going on, a quiet internal revolution which initially may have seemed alien to him and his instincts but ultimately, he too adapted. After all, he had attracted a group of generally young, non-specialist volunteers, all keen to wrap some degree of system or process around their part of the business. Whatever his reservations, Rory had to be part of this: 'They were very aware that what they were doing was often unwelcome to me. They would come in and say, "We have to sort this out" and I would take very little interest in what they were doing. And they would keep pushing ahead, coming to me with documents, saying, "Really, Rory, we must sign off on this and get this in place." Essentially they would wear me down, negotiate and convince me of things that initially I'd been a bit sceptical of. An example would be job descriptions and objectives – they bullied me into it. But I decided it wasn't such a bad idea to sit down with someone once a year and talk through what they'd achieved in the year before and what they were proposing to achieve in the next.'

Such changes of approach were milestones in the necessary professionalizing of TM. Could it be achieved without destroying its essential, founding atmosphere? Could it avoid turning momentum into inertia, risk and daring into playing safe? TM was special, possibly unique. What if it slipped into being just another NGO? No one wanted this to happen – that would represent betrayal, total failure.

For the moment, another pressing problem had to be faced. TMF needed a proper head office, a place large enough to house its growing numbers, its itinerant volunteers and its burgeoning craft schools. Kabuli word of mouth came into play. Rory heard of a mud-walled fort on the hill at Kart-e Parwan. On visiting the owner, he found far more than he hoped or possibly bargained for: 'There were all these sprawling gardens and outbuildings and I thought maybe I could rent the outbuildings to put the woodworkers in. Because we had this very generous, flexible money, I could get going very quickly – buy machinery, hire people and pay their salaries. By hiring the mud fort, I was able to provide free dormitory accommodation, where people could stay three to four in a room. I would get this extraordinary sequence of young architects coming out, then the VSO [Voluntary Service Overseas] sent me retired carpenters and ceramicists to come out and teach. I ended up with a curious collection of up to 20–25 volunteers ranging from a 70-year-old Dutch woodworker, a 60-year-old American potter and a lot of architects in their early twenties.'

Kart-e Parwan, always known as 'The Fort', became the expression of TMF culture. One of the last remaining such forts in Kabul, it had several courtyards and three acres of gardens that showed signs of being an old Moghul design. It was consistent with TMF principles, practice and values that the Fort was rapidly and immaculately restored. I observed it for myself on an early visit and described it in my journal: 'Immaculately replastered in mud, wonderfully conserved doors with fretted carving; newly carved window and door frames. Harmonious layout of windows and doors, with doors leading off the main courtyard. This is a nicely planted garden with fruit trees. The restoration of the Fort is itself an extraordinary achievement. Two peacocks, two dogs, an idyll.'

This mattered because restoration was a good in itself. Far more than an aesthete's whim, a dilettante's delight, it also provided a centre for the business activity that was characteristic of TMF. I observed this too in my journal: 'A constant stream of staff wandering around all day and doing business around a series of tables – the table in the kitchen, the table in the courtyard, the office table, carrying the informal into the business-like to new levels. They are young, dedicated, hardworking, professionally motivated and a model of how an NGO dedicated to results – by which I mean "doing things", I nearly wrote "achieving outcomes" – can work.'

Crucially, the restoration of the Fort carried a slightly different but even more intense message for Afghans. BBC correspondent David Loyn took a friend there on a visit. David's own reaction to the Fort was coloured by a fundamental set of his own prior reservations about the entire TMF project: 'Was it a bit of a dilettante effort? Prince Charles' involvement didn't help. What Afghanistan needed was concrete and roads and houses and streets and better sanitation – it didn't need to learn marquetry and basket weaving. But I moved much more towards thinking that at the heart of this, there was something really quite important that Rory was doing. The moment that I really saw it was when I went up to the Fort with a very close Afghan friend of mine. He burst into tears when we walked into the courtyard and said: "My family own a property like this, but we haven't done it up like this." It was a very powerful reaction from somebody I know quite well. What he said was that Rory and TM successfully achieved a recovery of lost Afghan skills. That sense of something lost that was regained was important – it became an important place for modern Afghanistan.'

It might never have become that, might never have been anything more than a brilliant transitory endeavour, a comet in the development sky that burned brightly only to vanish as quickly as it appeared. Few would have noticed its failure; fewer still would have lamented it except Engineer's devoted wheelbarrow army still labouring among the impacted plastic mounds of Murad Khane. The development community would have sniggered at the failure of a supposed alternative model to their time-honoured ways of working, counting and measuring. The Kabul Municipality would have dusted off the East German plans to bulldoze the whole place and run a six-lane highway through it. All this might have happened because by September 2006, Rory could see no way of getting the sustained, regular funding needed to keep the project going. As a last resort, he considered putting in some of his own money but that would never have been sufficient. Major public donors were sitting on their hands. For him, it was the darkest moment: 'I suddenly think, "Good God, it's all failed. I can't sustain this financially. I can't pay these people. I can't keep this going." The whole thing could have collapsed at the end of 2006 with a couple of buildings half-completed, some classrooms that had been decked out, some students who had done a few months' worth of training, no crafts sold anywhere and bulldozers coming in for the mayor to conclude his project, with my having spent $2 million on achieving exactly nothing.'

The outlook could not have looked bleaker, more desperate. Rory's father Brian Stewart, a former diplomat, happened to be visiting Kabul at that time: 'I went in to see him at about 3 a.m. and I said, "I just don't think I can keep this going. We're running out of money, it's awful, and I'm going to have to start laying everyone off." And he said to me, "Darling, don't worry, it's not your fault if people won't give you money for this. You've done your best, you've set up a wonderful project. But if all these rich people can't bring in money behind you, you can't bankrupt yourself trying to run it off your own money." And I remember feeling an immense sense of relief at this single phrase: "It's not your fault ..." It took the pressure off me and I got straight on a plane to California.'

As he flew halfway round the world on a mission of survival, Rory now had one thing firmly on his side in his moment of extremity. He had a real story to tell: 'It was wonderfully liberating to be able to go to California and say, "I'm not taking a salary. All these people are working for free in Afghanistan. We're running out of money. Give me some money to keep this thing going." It's a very different pitch. I raised a million dollars and got the project going again.'

Raising more money was one thing, but how fast do you spend it? How 'hot' should they be run? What Rory and his team realized was that by doing a lot in the first two years, the big donor grants from the Canadian and American governments would follow. Finance Director Richard Dwerryhouse believes that Rory probably did not fully understand the consequences and implications: 'Rory took a big risk, and it came off, to say: "We need to do something big here. We're going to have to burn through this money, show massive progress and that's going to bring new donors along with us". It might not have worked. In which case, he would have been lambasted in the press for having taken this approach. We could all have looked like absolute amateurs.'

Other financial crises would occur in the future, it was in the nature of the project. But from 2007, while it was never plain sailing, TM could forge ahead with clearing up and restoring Murad Khane, strengthening the craft schools and the technical institute, becoming more business-like and organized while never losing its hallmark energetic brio. It also became part of the Kabul scene for international visitors. Rory had a certain glamour to him which he exploited consciously. He knew that his team sometimes found the sight of him guiding yet another glamorous or wealthy individual over the project a distraction. But if momentum was one watchword, profile was another. Without it, funding would wither – it almost had. It helped that the senior military commander in the country told him: 'Yours is the only goddam project in Afghanistan that is doing anything.' As I noted in my journal: 'Everything else is mired in bureaucracy, mission, objectives, outcomes, deliverables, etc., etc.' I might have added: 'And what are they actually achieving?'

But a deeper, perhaps more uncomfortable, matter lurked behind the TMF rollercoaster. Who were the people driving it? One answer might have been: 'A self-selected group of white, British 25-year-olds, intoxicated by a dream of romantic "do-gooding" in a country ravished by war and ideological governmental impoverishment. Did they think Afghans needed what the white young guns believed they were doing?'

My impression is that the dangers noted above were implicitly understood and were part of an almost unspoken set of attitudes towards Afghans and Afghan culture. The tone was certainly set by Rory himself: 'One of the strongest things I wanted to convey to my staff was the importance of politeness to Afghans, being elaborately polite, how incredibly important it was that we were always on show. Nobody should ever feel, on a building site or even in our accommodation, that this was their private space. They had to be a champion of the project, they had to be able to sell it to a donor, sell it to a trustee. We had moral obligations too. We would keep employing the 86-year-old Ustad Abdul

Hadi because he was the greatest woodworker in Afghanistan and although he was basically deaf and couldn't do anything, he was our last link to the 1950s tradition. If we wanted to show the young apprentices that we valued the traditional crafts then we had to venerate this man and continue employing him. Given that we were dealing with a very traditional Afghan community, that also involved things that were very odd, literally giving bread to people. Or if I was negotiating with Kaka Azeem about his house and he admired my rosary beads, I gave him my rosary beads.'

No doubt the very open modus operandi that struck Tommy Wide on his very first day in August 2007 was also vital in keeping live connections with the Afghan community, as Director Jemima Montagu noted: 'If you're in DfID you're living in bunkers, behind closed walls. They don't see what's happening, they're not talking to Afghans, they're perpetuating a kind of them and us sort of scenario, a more patronizing attitude towards who you're working with. There's just not enough contact on an everyday level. We did have loads more of that. If we went to dinner at people's houses with colleagues, the women were still behind a curtain. I would go behind the curtain to say hello and to chat. We didn't drive around in armoured vehicles and we were just much closer to what was happening around us. That alone had a huge impact.'

But there was more to it than that. There was, in Deputy CEO Will Beharrell's experience, a real understanding of the tone expressed and the atmosphere TM created about themselves. Two words in particular mattered: creativity and honour: 'Honour's a word very much in currency in Afghan culture, perhaps more so than our own now. Showing honour to the people that we were working on behalf of, to the sort of traditions that we were trying to recover. And creative too because ultimately, we were trying to do something whose value was as intangible as it was tangible. Much of that lay in the imaginations of a small group of people. So alongside the sort of humility which comes with the honour point, it was the self-confidence which said, "we're going to do this". That confidence took us a long way. It wouldn't have happened without Rory.'

But it wasn't only Rory who set an example of how to behave to Afghans in Afghanistan. The BBC's David Loyn saw Tommy Wide as an exemplar of how to act, integrate even, in this very different environment: 'Tommy operated like an Afghan. He used to go to quail fights and he kept pigeons on the roof of Turquoise Mountain. I went up there one day with him and there were his pigeons. Walking with him, the blacksmiths outside in that extraordinary street outside Murad Khane, Tommy knew them all and talked to them.'

When he got his PhD in 2014, Tommy's Afghan friends observed that of course, this called for a proper celebration. In the community. With the community. And Tommy did not hesitate, he knew what to do: 'I bought and slaughtered a sheep in celebration. It's just about bringing an open mindset to the place you're in and a constant conversation. When I talked to my Afghan colleagues, I'd said I'd got my PhD and they'd say, "I hope you're going to have a party." And I hadn't necessarily thought of that. Just talking to people gave me the sense that that was the right thing to do. It wasn't particularly complicated. If you wanted to get on with the community, it just meant showing that you have the time for them.'

I was lucky enough to attend that party on September 28, 2014. My photos of the time show scores of the Murad Khane community sitting on carpets in the courtyard of the wonderfully restored Great Serai and tucking in to roasted sheep. His honour was their honour, his achievement their achievement. The sense of togetherness was palpable yet combined with such sensitivity and awareness. Tommy had a very realistic understanding of the limitations of his understanding of the Afghans. This modesty was the start of considerable wisdom. It was vital to know what you did not know: 'The nitty-gritty experience of community work is constant fighting, negotiation, trade-offs being made, and that's pretty true everywhere. Another thing for me was I spent something like seven years in total in Afghanistan, got my PhD in Afghan history, fluent Dari and Pashto speaker. I didn't know more than 3 per cent of what was going on in this one place, Murad Khane where I'd worked for many years. That made me realize, if that's the case, how the hell do we think we can understand a country like Afghanistan? I spent seven years basically in one street. And after all this study, I've no clue.'

Though he set the example of total respect for Afghan people and customs, it was no accident that those closest to Rory needed little instruction in adapting their behaviours and actions to the society they were working in. Will Beharrell recalls an occasion of such a spirit. TM had just found a great traditional woodworking master craftsman, *ustad*: 'The first *ustad* who came was Ustad Abdul Hadi, a master in *jali* work, the greatest woodworker in Afghanistan. We were told there were few if any other people in the country who knew about *jali* screens, these interlocking wooden panels that mediated traditionally between inside and outside space. He was gold dust really and venerable and respected and embodied what Turquoise Mountain was aspiring to do. I remember a delegation of *nuristani* carpenters arrived and they played on their *tablas* and brought musicians with them. We had this wonderful impromptu dinner with *nuristani* music and at the end they showed us what they'd made – they brought loads of their own products with them, carved chests, and bowls and chairs. And we thought, let's add a *nuristani* section to the project, so we did.'

It doesn't follow that merely because Rory and his closest colleagues relished exploring Afghan culture and preserving and reviving it, they might not still have been seen and dismissed as cultural tourist outsiders. Wasn't it just another instance of the time-honoured and occasionally derided Western interest in the exotic? One person possessed of a certain objectivity was Tamim Samee, Afghan by birth, Western educated in computer science, who had returned to Afghanistan. Tamim was close to TM and later became a board member. What did his cultural antennae tell him about the fundamental atmosphere of TM vis-à-vis Afghans?

'I straddle the two cultures, so much that I don't really see from one singular perspective. I didn't see Rory as, for lack of any other way of saying, a kind of colonial white person coming in to save an indigenous culture. What he wanted to do was worthwhile. Certainly, the institutions in Afghanistan that were supposed to be doing this, they were not doing it. The Ministry of Culture had no interest because everything that was connected to the government was very political and very divisive. And nobody, even in any governmental capacity, or any of the other NGOs that existed in Afghanistan, were talking about woodcarving, were talking about illumination, talking about calligraphy. That kind of a school did not exist in Afghanistan either. So I welcomed it from that perspective. I did think that there must be something more to this for Rory than just saving Afghanistan culture and that's always been true. In the end, I think Afghanistan got something out of it as well.'

It might be easy to underestimate the awareness of key TM staff of the extraordinary position they found themselves in, the responsibility they brought to it and their devotion to it. Tommy Wide found himself in the middle of an almost high table debate: 'Every night, the dinner table was an ongoing conversation about the limits of what foreigners could do in a country like Afghanistan. We were intensely aware of it and worried about it: were we doing more harm than good? Were we projecting some kind of fantasy view of Afghanistan onto a country that was actually quite different from our imaginings? Yes, there was a bunch of middle-class white guys working at Turquoise Mountain but it was also overwhelmingly an Afghan organization. One of the benefits of the kind of amateurism that TM engendered was that there was a humility and an openness to our Afghan colleagues and an essentially Afghan way of doing things. Being all amateur "twentysomethings", we didn't think we knew what the answer was. We weren't battle-hardened development professionals who moved from conflict to conflict with their playbook. We were always trying to align ourselves, to understand the Afghan way of doing anything. That probably saved us from some of the more egregious mistakes that we could have made and other aid players did make.'

Underlying it all, as Rory shared some of his deepest thoughts about the Western aid effort with Lyse Doucet, cross-legged on an Afghan carpet: 'We should never have said we would transform the country. We should have worked towards making it a "better version of Pakistan". There was a joke that Western officials spoke of making Afghanistan "like Switzerland"! The Afghans said, "We don't want to be like Switzerland, we're not Swiss."'

Lyse Doucet caught the deep pragmatism at the heart of Rory's own intense practical efforts: 'He said, "Let's be more modest. Let's do what we can do as best we can." And he railed against "all or nothing policies. Either we do everything in Afghanistan or we take it all away".'

By May 2008, Rory decided that he had more than achieved what Prince Charles had asked him to achieve three years previously. My wife Annie and I visited him again in Kabul in May 2008, out of love and friendship and also as a trustee of the Foundation. I recorded in my journal the 'incredible progress' at the Fort with a flourishing calligraphy school and a sizeable woodworking workshop. The presence of the craft masters, the *ustads*, was strong – a reminder that without their accumulated knowledge of centuries-old crafts, these skills and traditions would die out. Murad Khane I described as a 'building site, the highest compliment I could find, with 150 Afghan labourers on site, each with a hard hat, an ID card and hi-vis jacket, but none with hard boots. All wore Afghan sandals'.

At the heart was the fully restored Peacock House – named after its woodcarvings. I found it 'a joy, with lovely shutters, fine plasterwork and a naturalness to the restoration that is beguiling. It now sits in a clearly expressed urban environment with paved alleys, open spaces planted with trees or a well or a water pump. It has the beginnings of a true urban flavour'. I might have added that it was lived in by families, cheerful with children. Less than three years previously it had been a pile of wrecked mud buildings, shattered wooden shutters and six feet of impacted urban rubbish, peopled with wild dogs and scavenging goats. The Kabul Municipality wanted to bulldoze it; development professionals turned away with distaste. The scale of what can only be called 'Rory's transformation' remained largely unacknowledged in many professional circles. In May 2008, I found myself writing in my journal in anger: 'Murad Khane is both a dream and something hard-headed, a combination of a vision, reconstruction, urban re-generation, craft re-generation, economic revival. It has been delivered to this point of actuality in two years! Is anyone listening, anyone thinking?'

What were the elements in Rory's leadership style and approach? Naturally vision and practicality, a rare enough combination. But far more was needed as TM evolved over time. 'Permissive' leadership might be one way of describing it, a style that encouraged his team, enabled them, but also demanded they exercise personal responsibility. There was no time for a learning curve at TM said one, you were 'in at the deep end from the start'.

'Extreme delegation' was another description, involving a very flat management structure with eight team leaders reporting to Rory directly. This might have allowed him to micromanage. Here, he seems to have oscillated, offering what one called an 'incredible amount of space' to start a project but then wanting to know 'absolutely everything about apparently quite random parts'. This apparent contradiction may be explained by another comment which suggested that Rory 'set the tone but didn't want to micromanage'. Or another view: 'Huge vision and obsession with detail'. Few can manage both and know when each is relevant to the situation. Did Rory himself always know when he was leading or when he was micromanaging? Probably not. Did it matter? Probably not.

Perhaps at the heart of his leadership was an approach to risk. The team saw – how could they not? – that he was not scared of challenge. But he was always very calm. Above all, he always took the risks upon himself: 'What I said to them at the time was "Don't worry, I'm responsible financially. I'm very happy to write a sheet of paper saying you are hereby authorized to proceed, to spend this money and if anything goes wrong then it's me." And if they say, "But Rory, the police are turning up and the community are saying we can't work in this area and the mayor's coming after it," then I say, "Go ahead, tell them to come and talk to me."'

Rory never passed the buck. It began as his project, developed as his project, he enlisted scores of people to deliver but never shirked from facing up to the consequences. On his last night in Kabul as chief executive, May 28, 2008, my wife and I ate with him at the international community's favourite restaurant, L'Atmosphere. I concluded in my journal: 'Rory's last night as MD leaving the child he has conceived, brought up, shaped, inspired and made his own. He is not sentimental, but suddenly realizes how much he loves these traditional peoples, with their graceful ways of behaving, their courtesy, their gentleness, their endurance, this is what he leaves. He feels part of them, is part of them. And he will miss it'.

Perhaps that is why he managed to lead what Trustee Tamim Samee called the 'passion project' in the way he did. More importantly, TM continued after Rory stepped down in July 2008. He immediately took over as chairman of the trustees to maintain continuity and the confidence of international supporters.

Three years later, in May 2011, the project now directed by Shoshana Clark, Murad Khane was officially declared fully restored. It became an Afghan-managed charity with a supervisory and fundraising board in the UK. An improbable, six-year-long journey was over. Few really believed that the total restoration of the Old City district of Murad Khane was possible, still less that it was likely. It had started as a 'jolly good idea'. After three years, the judgement was 'aren't they doing well!' After six years, the only honest reaction was: 'we had no right to think it could be done'.

Much of the credit for the fact that TMF did not wilt once Rory was not closely involved must go, he insists, to Shoshana Clark, who morphed from a 26-year-old middle grade teacher into a manager, a negotiator, fundraiser and leader. She was by no means the least important of those who responded to Rory's long-distance attraction: he could lead and also move on.

The full restoration of Murad Khane was marked by a ceremony which my wife Annie and I were lucky enough to attend. I hope my journal entry at the time caught some sense of the atmosphere, the overwhelming feelings of achievement that filled the air: 'The speeches are made, the tears flow, the sense of completion really starts to kick in. What must they feel like? In "jargo-speak" – yes, I do hate it – the project has been delivered; the "outcomes" are as promised; "capacity" is being built; "national identity" through indigenous craft traditions is being created. Even in the miserable reductive language of the "jargonauts", TMF has been a roaring success. Some are undoubtedly jealous; few NGOs or government departments can point to such true completion'.

The outstanding question is why the development community took such an ungenerous view of Turquoise Mountain, its culture, its working methods. Was there nothing to be learned from its effectiveness, its closeness to the Afghan people, its belief in culture as an essential ingredient in development? The BBC's David Loyn measures the sheer gap in philosophy and practice between the UK's DfID and TM. DfID has its systems and, observes Loyn, something else: certainty.

'The development world are very sure that the way they do things is right. The bandwidth for creative thinking, in development, in government, is very narrow. They tend to like doing things in scale, which tends to mean deputing the work effectively to UN agencies or to big implementers. They are very obsessed with outcomes. Rory's work does not fit. The kind of metrics the development world operates don't really lend themselves to immeasurable and intangible things that Turquoise Mountain did. Like my friend who walked into the Fort and burst into tears. You can't put that into a plan. I think the lack of willingness in the development world to think very creatively will tend to work against the Rorys of this world in the future so it will feel like an aberration.'

Probably, the official approach to metrics and especially those related to sheer quantity and cheapness amount to a major barrier. It was reinforced by the fact that TM operated in a field called culture, which traditional development hardly knew how to recognize, still less to measure. It believed in what it called integrated development that chose to be involved with multiple issues rather than a single one. Ultimately, the unbridgeable gap between the TM practice and methodology and DfID came down to the most basic difference and sense of difference: it was about people. That's what Country Manager Tommy Wide believes: 'We were a maverick organization that the development community thought was doing it all wrong, that development work was technocratic and was about the application of best practices, institution building. We came in with exactly the opposite approach, which was: "We don't really know what we're doing but we think Afghan culture is extraordinary and valuable, and we want to support it to tell us what we can do". That worked for us. We were amateurish, we made a million mistakes, but we just had a staying power that meant that by 2014/15, we were seen as a major established and respected player. Which is extraordinary to me when I think of how we were mocked and ridiculed in 2007.'

None of this makes the personal, physical and philosophical obscurantism of the development community attractive or defensible. It is not. The conclusive criticism of those attitudes is that even within their chosen criteria of physical, practical effectiveness, 'outcomes', they got Turquoise Mountain wrong. Rory Stewart sets the record straight: 'Within the space of four years, we'd restored over a hundred buildings in the centre of the Old City of Kabul. We'd created a crafts institute that was the leading institute in Afghanistan. We'd had exhibitions. We'd sold millions of dollars' worth of crafts. You don't need to spend two years writing a strategic plan and doing risk assessments, you can just get going and start clearing garbage. You can do an enormous amount with volunteers. You can have a very light structure initially and you can build the structure around you. Part of it is that you need an entrepreneur for whom this is their absolute 24-hour-a-day, seven-day-a-week commitment and that they're prepared to put their own money, time and reputation on the line.'

Which of course was Rory Stewart. How remote was the Turquoise Mountain practice from the everyday routines of the development professionals, how shocking that they refused to consider adopting a single element in the TM (non-existent) playbook.

This is not a story of other people's lack of imagination but of the realization of Rory Stewart's vision. It involved flair, imagination, daring, risk, cheek, determination, stubbornness, generosity, humility, respect and decency. These ingredients enabled an unlikely vision to be realized through intense pragmatism. Not the least important part was that Turquoise Mountain continued after he ceased everyday involvement. The Foundation steadily applied its practices and principles in Myanmar, Saudi and Jordan. It had all started in the winter rain of Kabul, gazing at piles of mud and rubble. Everyone else turned away, Rory Stewart didn't.

Today, Lyse Doucet can judge it over time: 'Other aid projects have all vanished. Turquoise Mountain is still there. It is about the past, the present and the future. It is an extraordinary achievement.'

Observations

+ Turquoise Mountain started without the benefit of extensive prior research. Almost certainly, any consultancy would have advised against it.
+ The original TM team largely self-selected itself. Enthusiasm and adventure were their criteria, as were youth and local knowledge and language expertise.
+ From the start, Stewart resisted setting a strategic plan. As TM became more organized, it did so but often against his instincts.

+ Visionary leadership and strategic direction were combined with deep delegation and insistence on personal responsibility.
+ Turquoise Mountain people never thought they knew better, or were better, than Afghans and their culture.
+ Conventional development metrics decided that TM's works were not susceptible to formal measurement. Those applying such metrics were looking in the wrong places.
+ Turquoise Mountain Foundation adopted a strong supervisory governance model from the earliest days. Good governance was required to supervise the urgency of the TM style of management.
+ The TM Crafts Institute preserved national craft traditions on the verge of obliteration and nurtured the next generation of crafts artisans.
+ The TM approach of restoring the physical environment and nourishing craft skills and those who possess them is holistic, effective and unique.
+ The fact that some find assessment of TM's work and achievements difficult reflects on them rather than on TM's work.

References

Rory Stewart, *The Places in Between* (Picador, 2004).

Turquoise Mountain Brochure: July 2006.

Turquoise Mountain Foundation Annual Report and Financial Statements: 2008, 2011, 2014.

John Tusa, unpublished Afghanistan Journals: 2007, 2008, 2011.

2

'The Show Woman and Her Three Thousand Children': The European Union Youth Orchestra, 1978–2018

Featuring interviews with:

Robert Albert, former Chair, European Union Youth Orchestra (EUYO) board

Jeanne Davis, sister of Joy Bryer (Secretary-General of EUYO)

Patricia Haitink, lawyer, married to Sir Bernard Haitink

Huw Humphreys, General Manager, EUYO, 2002–06; Head of Music, Barbican Centre, 2014–present

Lesley King-Lewis, board member, International Youth Foundation (IYF)

Marshall Marcus, Secretary-General, EUYO, 2013–present

Martijn Sanders, Chief Executive, Concertgebouw, Amsterdam, 1982–2006; Co-chair EUYO 2020–present

Nicola Wallis, General Manager, ECYO, 1977–78; Director, Aberdeen International Youth Festival, 1983–2003, latterly Board Member, IYF

Colin Window, EUYO Tour Manager, 2000–present

It was a special occasion. On 28 March 1978, the platform of the great Concertgebouw Hall in Amsterdam was crammed with an orchestra of 140 young musicians. It was the first public concert of an entirely new ensemble, the 'European Community Youth Orchestra' (ECYO), consisting of some of the most talented young musicians from the EC's then nine member states. Carefully selected through live auditions, rigorously trained in the taxing repertoire they would play, they faced an expectant audience, the challenge of mastering Gustav Mahler's huge Sixth Symphony and under the baton of one of the world's most brilliant conductors, Italian maestro Claudio Abbado.

Most importantly, the concert was not about showing parents and families how well their offspring could play, demonstrating the value of early musical education. It would deliver performance at the highest level, aspiring to professional standards, and would do so in the cause of the promotion of European values and ideals through arts and culture. Musical excellence was the vehicle, European unity the inspiration; the driving vision was that of just two people, the secretary-general of the fledgling orchestra, Joy Bryer, and her husband, Lionel.

It should not have happened at all. It was too unlikely, too ambitious, too improbable. After all, who were the Bryers to muscle in on the European musical world at such a level or any level, come to that? He was a rugby-playing South African dentist who once played the violin in the Johannesburg Philharmonic. She was an American PR executive with no background in classical music. Yet they were invoking a European vision to pioneer something new: a youth orchestra so good that audiences would forget their youth and admire only their playing. Here were the Bryers on 28 March 1978 to have their presumptuous dream tested in the most demanding environment.

There was, though, nothing amateur about the preparation for the first concert and subsequent ambitious tour of a further six European capitals. The Orchestra's *Yearbook for 1978*, its first ever, proclaims the scale of the Bryers' ambition and the thoroughness of their approach. A black and white, grainy-imaged volume of no fewer than 68 pages, it spoke of a huge amount of political and bureaucratic planning over and above the musical preparation. Former British Prime Minister, Europhile and keen amateur musician, Edward Heath, advised Joy Bryer on how to approach the EEC's political institutions for support. He and his close colleague, Baroness Elles, knew that merely sticking the European Community's name on an organization would impress nobody. More than labelling was needed. In 1974, steered by Elles, the European Parliament's Cultural and Youth Committee had officially endorsed the creation of such a youth orchestra. On 22 April 1976, the European Commission confirmed its official patronage. Neither of these declarations alone meant assured funding but they were essential building blocks in the ECYO's institutional existence. As Joy always acknowledged, 'Ted Heath taught me everything about dealing with Europe.'

The 1978 Yearbook, a founding document, demonstrated this systematic, calculated approach in detail. Its pages carry messages of congratulation from the Queens of England, the Netherlands and Denmark; the King of Belgium, the Grand Duke of Luxemburg, the Presidents of West Germany, Ireland and France. More than one colleague recalls Joy's famous cry: 'We have to meet Queen Beatrice [of the Netherlands]. Beatrice is quite my favourite crowned head of Europe' (she did know many of them). Clusters of prime ministers, musicians, sponsors and donors follow, covering many pages. All advertisers had been instructed: 'This is the First Youth Orchestra of the European Community'. They got and spread the message.

Each of the nine constituent nations had an honorary committee, each an administrative committee, all loaded with people of influence and listed in their honorific glory. The members of the orchestra are listed and named rather late. This apparent order of precedence revealed important parts of Joy Bryer's priorities and sense of how influence must be courted and success sought. There was a triangle of power. Claudio Abbado guaranteed the orchestra's excellence. Ted Heath facilitated the political and bureaucratic positioning. Joy created, protected and projected the image. Truth is, she loved the schmoozing of the great and good, negotiating with culture ministers, and was brilliant at it. Few could have ridden the horse of musical excellence and the beast of bureaucracy as well as she did. But she was only an American PR woman. How did it come about at all? Her daughter, Lesley King-Lewis, is convinced that Joy's passion for Europe goes back to her grandfather, Thomas Levine, who emigrated from Ukraine: 'He left Ukraine because of the pogroms. A pioneer, very successful businessman, he arrived in Boston speaking no English in the 1900s. He was in construction; he built the first ever shopping centre in New England. His daughter, Molly – his younger daughter – was known as the "Mighty Atom". He had huge faith in her, she became a pioneer and started the first modelling agency in Boston in 1944. So Mum was just one in a long line of pioneers.'

Rebellious and unconventional, Joy opted for university in Mexico City, then moved to the Sorbonne in 1948. Accompanied by her sister, Jeanne, aged 18, they got on their bicycles and rode from Paris to Brussels. Lesley recalls the impact that ride made: 'They bicycled through war-torn Europe. From Paris, she went to Northern France, where there were people still living in caves, she saw the disruption in Rotterdam, Amsterdam. These early experiences influenced her two passions, Europe and the peace of the world.'

Jeanne recalls how Joy was appalled by the destruction, the complete wreckage of Rotterdam, the sight of heavily bombed

London, the 'depredations of war everywhere, people living off dried and condensed milk'. Normal as such 'deprivation' was for anyone living in post-war Europe, it still came as a shock to a young woman from sheltered Boston, Mass. The memory of this destruction lingered as an almost subconscious motivation for Joy later – there had to be a better way.

It might have remained a distant memory but for a chance conversation many years later, which her husband Lionel Bryer had with a musician. Blyth Major was one of his dental patients and also managing director of the Midland Youth Orchestra in England. Together, they cooked up the idea of a festival of international youth orchestras to be held in St Moritz in the summer when winter sports resorts and their hotels were notoriously empty. Lionel was professionally active in high-end dentistry, Joy had a well-established PR business in London. Something, someone, had to give. According to a long-time colleague, Nicola Wallis, Lionel made Joy a suggestion that he knew she would not refuse: 'They looked at it not as just an event for youth orchestras, but a bringing together of young people with a common interest, get them to mix with each other, form friendships. A festival of international understanding through orchestral music grew in their minds. Joy was so full of those ideals, the energy that woman could create was amazing. Lionel was smart enough to realize that once his wife got her teeth into something, there would be no holding her back.'

It was still crazily ambitious. St Moritz had no concert hall so they would put up a tent instead. But they went one step further, says Wallis: 'They decided it would be quite interesting if, rather than just having individual concerts, they would form a special orchestra to be drawn from the best of all the orchestras attending the festival. That started the very first year in St Moritz, the idea of an international orchestra being created, more or less, during a summer course.'

Happenstance was playing its part. Joy gave up her PR work to take on full-time management of the festival. The division of labour with Lionel suited them both and their particular skills. The 1969 St Moritz International Festival of Youth Orchestras was the milestone. Happily, a full-length 50-minute film was made about the event. Directed by the distinguished documentary filmmaker, Revel Guest, *Last Summer We Played in the Alps* was broadcast on BBC Television. It is a vital document to this day in understanding how the Bryer machine worked and how the EUYO idea developed.

Supported by the Swiss Tourist Board, the festival would involve 11 youth orchestras from eight countries attending for a fortnight, bringing in a total of 1,000 students. Each orchestra would give one concert. Rehearsals would take up seven hours a day. During the first week or so, the best players would be chosen to play in an end-of-festival orchestra to be conducted by the legendary 80-year-old maestro, Leopold Stokowski. Getting him was a coup, no question. How did they do it? As Nicola Wallis remembers, it was 'pure Joy', a mixture of daring, insouciance, innocence and risk: 'Joy, being the person that she was, said, "Right, well, we need a really, really top star named conductor." They drew up a gold star list and came up with Leopold Stokowski. How do you get hold of Stokowski? In those days, you could look him up in *Who's Who*. Joy just wrote a letter to him. Stokowski replied, saying, "Yeah, I would be interested", which, the Bryers being complete amateurs in this scene, thought, "Okay, that's good", not realizing this was quite extraordinary. What "Stokey" did though, because he had no idea who these people were and what it was, decided, "I'll just have a holiday at the same time." He arrived early, after a summer snowstorm. This elderly gentleman was seen creeping about the main street of St Moritz, obviously looking for the concert hall. It only came to light later on that he had been out there earlier just to suss it all out. Anyway, he decided to live dangerously and go for it and stayed.'

If this was a huge piece of luck, the Bryers hardly noticed. They had invited a great conductor to conduct, he had agreed. Wasn't it that simple? Yet most of the youth orchestras only came because of the promised Stokowski participation. In truth, according to her lawyer brother Robert Albert, Joy was on very flimsy ground. There was no contract with Stokowski, she just hoped an exchange of letters was good enough. On arrival, 'Stokey', as they always called him, refused to sign a contract unless he had the right to approve the documentary film – he got it.

Judging by the documentary, the silver-haired, softly spoken Stokowski was gentle and approachable with young musicians a quarter of his age. They may have warmed to him because of his famous film appearance with Mickey Mouse in Disney's *Fantasia*. It was given to few actually to shake the 'Great Mouse's' hand! Stokowski's observations sound routine in conversation though reminding his young listeners that music was made up of three elements, 'duration, intensity and frequency', may have brought them back to fundamentals.

On the podium, however, faced with a selected orchestra who had never performed together and represented several different national traditions, 'Stokey' proved a firm taskmaster, master of detail. The film is an essential reminder of how far the youth orchestra movement had to come in the next 50 years. In 1969, such orchestras were something of which the players' families would have been proud. But the strings sound sour, the winds only just blending, much of the phrasing tentative. Stokowski insisted on ensemble, on volume, on being in time – 'Put your bow on the string'; or 'Play piano, you play forte, I hear you too much'; 'Look at the conductor, I don't know what to do with you. We cannot give a bad concert but if you play like that, it will be a bad concert'. One American student observed that it was 'good for you to be bossed around by the maestro'. They failed to understand that this was an essential part of reaching standards of performance excellence that must become the norm if the youth orchestra movement was to be anything but a pleasant diversion.

It would have been easy for the Bryers to be discouraged by the mediocrity of the St Moritz experience. More likely, certain fundamental ingredients of the future model at least suggested themselves: musical excellence based on thorough selection, followed by intense musical preparation, culminating in public performance under world-class maestros. None were givens at the time. It needed one of the St Moritz festival conductors, the Czechoslovak, Walter Susskind, to answer the frequently put question of why youth orchestras needed to perform at all when their main purpose was surely to learn by rehearsing. As Susskind observed drily: 'To play only at rehearsals is like trying to ski on the kitchen floor.' And he vividly summed up the ideal the Bryers were seeking but probably had not then put into words: 'The blend of youthful enthusiasm and disciplined playing, their utter devotion to the noble art and the results of assiduous practice, their spirited attitude and affectionate understanding create an atmosphere of pure and dedicated music making and music enjoyment such as even the most sophisticated audiences rarely experience at concerts of professional orchestras.' This would prove as eloquent a description of the aims of the fully realized EUYO 40 years later as it was in 1978.

Within four years, the Bryers had the opportunity to take their ideas and example further when the City of Aberdeen, struck by the tourism potential of a festival of youth orchestras, invited them to make Aberdeen their home. Besides, it was a cultural poke in the eye for rival, snooty Edinburgh. As the principal administrator, Nicola Wallis remembers the spirited but unfocused nature of some of the events. It was international, it was about all the arts, it was about getting the young together and letting them have fun: 'When they reached Aberdeen, it had extended into ballet, contemporary dance, folk dance with dance groups from Africa and South America, truly global in terms of representation. What Lionel did on the final night was to put together a huge variety show, which used to go on for hours. The Aberdonians loved it because it was worth their money, very good value for that ticket for over three hours.'

Aberdeen over, the entire festival was transported to London. It was being noticed; it was having an unexpected influence. It spawned youth orchestras in Germany, Italy and South America, but one further stage had to click intellectually. Typically, it came from Lionel, insists Nicola Wallis: 'When we joined Europe in 1973, Lionel being Lionel just thought, "hmm, Europe." He's not somebody who just sits on his laurels and does nothing else. The idea of thinking of Europe, not only as an economic community, but to look at a cultural side planted itself in his head. Because orchestral playing was his thing more than everything else, he thought: "There are nine countries here. Let's go around those nine countries, audition the best players and form a big orchestra with a star named conductor and then tour – that will give a whole new dimension to our joining Europe.' When you think of his vision, it's extraordinary. He was far ahead of his time.'

Joy in the meantime was making the annual youth orchestra festival work. Casting her net internationally, in 1976 she had invited to Aberdeen a Venezuelan orchestra, the fruit of an innovative radical programme of youth music education, *El Sistema*. By an extraordinary coincidence, Marshall Marcus, later secretary-general of EUYO, was only three years on working for José Antonio Abreu, charismatic founder and organizer of *El Sistema*. In later years, Abreu regularly asked Marshall if he would find him this '*joybria*'. The clipped Venezuelan accent made the name impossible for Marshall to understand. He soon found out: 'In Venezuela, there's a kind of myth about this whole Aberdeen experience. For them, it was their first great international triumph. The story I used to hear in Caracas was that the Venezuelans had gone to this festival in Aberdeen and they'd won. Abreu was so impressed with Joy and what she was doing, he invited her out to Venezuela. And Joy actually told me, I could reconstruct the exact hotel on the coast by the airport along this beach, where he put her up. And she said that he wanted to know how she did things.'

The fact that Abreu with a global, radical reputation for music education looked to learn from Joy even before she was in her prime is extraordinary. Marshall Marcus even uses the word 'mentor': 'They both were people who had this vision of the positive energy that comes from getting young people to play together in orchestras at a high level of excellence, young people from different circumstances, from different countries. They were very similar thinkers in some respects and they shared this quality of being people of vision and action. It's incredibly rare. You find people who are great managers, who are great doers, who are implementers. But they very rarely seem, in my experience, to be necessarily the vision person in the organization as well.'

Few have worked closely with the two most effective and influential musical educators of their time. Marshall Marcus is in a position of knowing how strikingly different they were as people, different in their complexities: 'I used to say that Abreu was like a cross between Mother Teresa and a Renaissance Pope. First of all, the power of the vehicle that he was driving was staggering. Like Joy, he never accepted "No". That only led to a different way around the problem. I think Abreu was one of the great strategist chess players – his mind was often years ahead of the situation. There was the strategic mind and the driving, implementing person. And there was the vision, the fire at the centre of it. Joy may have been less the chess player and more intuitive but just like Abreu, there was this incredible impulse driving her. And just like him, she lived the job 25 hours a day, every day, every day of the week.'

In Aberdeen and London as in St Moritz, Joy knew that a star conductor was needed to take the festival forward. Her tactics didn't change; after all, they had landed 'Stokey'. Having identified the brilliant, youthful, Claudio Abbado as the 'chosen one', she found his address in Milan and just wrote to him. The apocryphal version of the 'Persuasion of Claudio' is worth re-telling. Joy parked herself in the lobby of Abbado's hotel in Milan and just waited for him to come down from his room. Her irresistible presence made the irresistible offer, as Nicola Wallis understands it, but the timing was perfection: 'It was a real carrot for Claudio, who was that much younger and wanting to promote his own career. He liked the concept, he liked the idea of the international gathering and cultural mixing, and so he agreed and said, "Under one condition, that somebody comes up and trains the orchestra for me." In other words, he didn't want to do the drudge work. This is when James Judd, already part of our music department team, got a huge lift in his career. James did the most brilliant job and was able to hand over a readymade product to Claudio and then Claudio just dropped his magic onto it.'

Judd's role was recognized by music critics, one of whom wrote: 'Judd coaxed a precision and brilliance from the orchestra that would have done credit to many professional ensembles.' Intense musical preparation never vanished from the EUYO's core principles and practices.

EUYO General Manager Huw Humphreys saw a video of conductor and orchestra at play in off moments in Aberdeen. He too observed Abbado's single-minded side: 'You can't over-estimate how important Claudio was in those early days. Claudio fed off the youth aspect of it. There's a video of him playing table tennis with the players, having water pistol fights with them. It brought out his childlike element. It was said later that Claudio Abbado would learn pieces of music with the European Union Youth Orchestra so he could perform them later with the London Symphony Orchestra and then record them with the Vienna Philharmonic Orchestra. He embedded them in his own stellar career, which also led to remarkable offshoots like the Chamber Orchestra of Europe.'

Abbado was also a practical joker, sometimes at Joy's expense. He once hid Joy's handbag in the Green Room — she barely existed without it. According to Nicola Wallis, she became hysterical. 'Claudio, you're being wicked,' said Nicola. Abbado shrugged and winked. On another occasion, as Joy was preparing to give her introductory speech before a concert, Abbado just went onto the platform and began playing. Despite this, Nicola insists he was, 'sort of fond of her.'

A certain ambiguity in their relationship revealed itself in the vital next stage of the ECYO's actual formation. With the nine-nation orchestra an emerging reality, who would be the first permanent conductor? Who else but Abbado. But someone had to 'make the ask'. Revealingly, it was not Joy herself, recalls Nicola, a rare occasion when she seemed to show an apparent lack of confidence. Or was this a last-minute canny decision to avoid possible rejection: 'We were in Washington when Claudio was rehearsing at The Kennedy Center. Joy said we wouldn't be let in. I said, "Let's try." Then she said: "You talk to him, you know him much better than me from Aberdeen." I made the offer, he thought for only a few minutes then said: "On one condition. I don't get paid." And we went out for pasta.'

Months later, the brand-new European Community Youth Orchestra made their debut appearance at the Concertgebouw, Amsterdam, under Claudio Abbado. For the next 35 years, until Joy Bryer stepped down at the end of 2012, she led, personified, represented, spoke up for, raised money for and embodied the values of the orchestra, which grew from the 'First Chamber Orchestra of the European Community' to one of the most notable and effective EU cultural ambassadors and its values of unity, co-operation and understanding. It had been a long decade of experiment, learning, opportunism and the final evolution of the developed vision – an orchestra for the young musicians of political Europe. They would drag culture and identity centre stage and Joy would be there waving the banner of idealism from the front.

The balance of work and responsibility had to evolve. Up to this point Lionel had often been the initiator, the creative thinker. Now while being an essential partner, he was most significant for being the personal guarantor of the orchestra's finances. EU institutional support was important. Lionel's financial guarantees to the banks and the auditors were vital. The whole European youth orchestra venture was in an important sense a private family enterprise. Only such a bizarre set-up would have allowed Joy to seize the opportunity and situation and achieve what she did over 35 years. Secretary-General Marshall Marcus recalls first meeting Joy informally at her penthouse flat in Sloane Street, London, in reality to confirm his appointment as chief executive. He could do the job, but was he the right kind of person? Was he Joy's person?

'I go up in this rather rickety lift, with Verdi going full belt in the background and come out into the apartment. That's Joy, she's always at the top. The apartment's very much her, bright colours, she hated dark colours, kind of lemon yellow, and all these knick-knacks and pictures and beautiful stuff around. Joy was impeccably coiffed, what I call "Philharmonia" hair. They wanted to see how I handled myself in the formality of that situation. It was the "how to handle a knife and fork and was I good at smoked salmon" kind of thing. That was when I felt I was beginning to get to know her. The phrase "huge personality" could have been invented for Joy. I'm not sure I've ever met any bigger personality.'

Many would find that daunting, even off-putting. And could it exist without having a huge ego? And might that not get in the way of the essential cause? Joy's daughter, Lesley King-Lewis, makes an important distinction: 'She had a huge ego but she put the orchestra first. She was using her ego to achieve something that was so important to her. I think that's a really good distinction, because it was that authenticity that comes across. That makes it even more powerful to combine authenticity, passion and charisma. And the biggest quality we haven't discussed, *chutzpah*. She had unbelievable *chutzpah*.'

After working with her for several years, Marshall Marcus is well placed to make a fine distinction. Of course Joy's sense of personal ego was well, perhaps overdeveloped, but it was largely put in the service of the orchestra: 'I know many people who have larger egos but have achieved a lot less and maybe the point is this, that some people are larger than life and they have large egos. But in order to be successful, they have learned effectively when to curb the ego in order to achieve things for the organization. In the end it always has to be about the organization.'

But there was much more to her than this. Joy was almost impossible to put off, virtually impossible to resist, because she couldn't be put off. Nicola Wallis observed this ability at close quarters: 'She was a determined lady, she didn't understand the word "no". If anybody said "no" to her, she just talked straight through it and came out the other side. By which time the person she was talking to was either lying down, de-fanged, or just weakly agreeing. She had that ability to create a storm but at the end of it, everybody sort of loved her. Because she was so passionate and she could talk the hind legs off a donkey. What she said was not complicated; it was very clear. She just had the power to floor any awkward meeting. Some people did emerge shaking and thought, "no, never ever again". What is so extraordinary is that she developed her relationships with all these prime ministers and heads of the EU Commission. As they all moved on to other jobs if she ever came across them at some function, they would spot her, cross the room and "Joy, darling!" and hugs and kisses. But for Joy, it was: "You're my friend, I'm going to hug you, and then get what I want out of you. You're going to love it while I'm doing it".'

In other words, Joy never heard the word 'no'. For her it signalled the start of the negotiation. Her reaction to two other words reveals important parts of her character: 'cost' and 'risk'. For many, these words are fearful, signals of danger, best avoided. Joy faced them. Huw Humphreys recalls: 'I would say that she worked from the philosophy that where there was a will, there was a way. She never thought that the cost was the problem – [it] was a challenge to be surmounted.'

Joy's attitude to risk was, if possible, even more robust in the experience of Lesley King-Lewis: 'Mum didn't really assess risk.

Nothing was ever too risky for her. It was not so much how she assessed risk, more how she dealt with a failure. She would dust herself off and take on the next thing. The risk was she failed. Failure wasn't in her DNA. When you look back at her mother and her grandfather, it wasn't in their DNA either.'

These indomitable characteristics are important for a leader, great for outlasting politicians or bureaucrats, persuading donors and sponsors, or personifying a vision in the most defiant and glamorous way. These were the qualities the figurehead of any and every organization needed. Yet Joy also bewitched the players, the young, the 'kids'. Figurehead she might be, mother figure she was too in an essential and enduring relationship with her 'children'. After all, inspiring the young, bringing them together was the whole point of the EUYO. It was almost a ritual, certainly part of the schedule, as Huw Humphreys remembers: 'What was also really extraordinary was at the start of every tour, she would always give her speech to the orchestra. That speech was all about those original ideas and she must have given that speech countless times. She had the orchestra members, some of whose English was not the strongest, eating out of the palm of her hand. They knew this speech was coming because they'd all heard Mrs Bryer was coming: "Mrs Bryer's coming to this rehearsal". It was like feeding from the original source that was the inspiration of the orchestra.'

Nicola Wallis heard several of these speeches. Never about music, they had a kind of innocence to them which perhaps made them even more effective: 'Young people are quite smart. They loved the fact that she would come out with some ridiculous expression. Of course, not all of them would understand English that well so there were instant translations spreading throughout the orchestra. And because of all these wonderful musical errors, they just loved her all the more. But she loved them, there was this kind of warmth and enthusiasm. She made it quite clear, they were preparing to be serious young musicians and express their art. And she would explain what they were all sitting in this room to do. It was not just about making music, it was something which was actually far more important and was going to influence their future lives, their future thinking about others.'

Colin Window managed the tours for the orchestra for more than 20 years. He saw the effect Joy Bryer – always 'Mrs B' to the players – had on them. It was quite simply inspirational. Every head turned when she entered the room, a diminutive figure, immaculately coiffed, magnificently overdressed, never to be ignored: 'She told them they were ambassadors for the EU and their own countries. They had to show self-regulation, good behaviour and pride. They were involved in a great act of togetherness. They took it from this person from another generation because of her warmth. They saw her longevity, her endurance. They saw history in front of them and she was a powerful image.'

What did Joy give them? According to her brother, EUYO Chairman, Robert Albert, she transmitted 'enthusiasm, energy, belief in themselves and being part of a wonderful organization.' Fundamentally, she knew she had a 'duty of care' to the musicians, a duty she fulfilled to the day and to the letter. As to her message to them, her beliefs and thoughts changed little in almost 40 years and were regularly expressed in the orchestra's annual yearbook. But there was evolution too. In 1967, she called for 'one united voice on the manifold international problems that beset the world to have a profound impact on mankind'. By 2006, the goal was to 'encourage harmony and creativity' because Europe was about 'more than economic activity'. By 2009, a distinct position was emerging: 'We stand outside the moneyed world although we rely on it for our existence'. The challenge to the young was also more demanding. Young musicians should 'achieve more goals, more integration, more cultural diversity and open borders and indeed more democracy'.

By 2010, with personal, physical frailty now an issue, a more elegiac tone emerges. Heroism is needed more than ever, she wrote, involving 'willingness to take risks, to protect those who are weaker than oneself and to defend freedom'. One sentence of that message reads as a personal *cri de coeur*: she writes of 'devoting one's life to a cause that is greater than one's own narrow self-interest or happiness'. By 2013, after stepping down as executive leader, her words are explicitly valedictory: 'Celebrate what we have, great cultural diversity, the potential for long-term economic growth, democracy for all our citizens and above all, peace.' It was, of course, far too much to ask for.

If there is a certain naiveté and a disarming lack of political sophistication in Joy's beliefs and writings, they matched the passion and lack of guile of her famous speeches to the young. Listening to them year after year, Colin Window saw her as 'fearless, classless and not a snob'. And as the players stamped their feet like a football crowd, chanting 'Mrs B!, Mrs B!, Mrs B!' there was no doubt that Joy had communicated the basic message behind the EUYO. And the young, her 'family', bought into the message and the ideals and values behind it. Perhaps too there was an understood sadness felt by the young musicians, as Huw Humphreys observed: 'It was like working in a sweetshop in a way. Because unlike any professional musical experience that you will have in your career, these players are there solely to make music. They are not going home to worry about putting the kids to bed, they're not worried about doing the shopping. If a rehearsal ends early, they're cross. They want to get everything out of these tours that they can. The problem with the EUYO is that you go through your whole professional career and life is never that good again.'

Joy Bryer's role, responsibility and challenge was to keep many people happy, stimulated, motivated. This had to be done at different levels, in varying ways with a complex range of tricks, methods and stratagems. She had to be a skilled manipulator as well as everything else. Of the several constituencies that she managed, not the least complex was that of principal conductor. From Stokowski in St Moritz to Abbado in Aberdeen and thereafter, she knew as a PR person that the EUYO needed star quality at the very top. Keeping it there proved complex, troublesome and finally upsetting.

Certainly, Claudio Abbado as founding music director gave the fledgling, innovatory organization everything hoped for and few would have dared to predict. Abbado had demanded a properly prepared and trained orchestra. He got it and that commitment to musical excellence was, says Lesley King-Lewis, built into her mother's professional approach: 'You needed to be able to demonstrate you could create the best. At that time no one really took the youth orchestra movement very seriously despite the example of the National Youth Orchestra of Great Britain. But overall, the standard was pretty mediocre. So this was the first orchestra. That was phenomenal, both the quality and the ideal. How do you achieve that quality, where you have to build the infrastructure? So in every single country, you find the most talented instructors, musicians in order to audition these kids, the best kids from their country. Once they got to the orchestra, the training happened. The infrastructure had to be built, put in place, and at all levels, maintain that level of quality of the individual, as well as the quality of the experience.'

And if Abbado thought the orchestra good enough, the musical world followed: Karajan in Salzburg, Bernstein, Barenboim,

Mehta, Giulini, with soloists such as Jessye Norman to match. Playing with this stellar orchestra was also invigorating for conductors no matter how famous. The legendary director of the BBC Proms, Sir John Drummond, where the EUYO frequently performed, regarded Joy Bryer as 'indefatigable', a person who gathered a 'roster of conductors the world's greatest orchestras would find it hard to top'. Vladimir Ashkenazy, Drummond noted in his memoir, *Tainted by Experience*, 'seemed as young as the players bouncing onto the platform and grinning with delight at what they did'. At the other end of the seniority scale, Drummond wrote admiringly of the actions of Carlo Maria Giulini after his EUYO concert: 'Giulini never came to after-concert parties but he came to one after his concert and sat for over an hour surrounded by intense young people plying him with questions, which he answered with characteristic gentleness and calm.'

For Drummond, who saw all the world's leading maestros on the platform of London's Royal Albert Hall, Abbado was just a 'genius with young people'. The whole musical world, it seemed, wanted to hear them playing with him. The orchestra's schedule of countries visited during Abbado's leadership is exhausting to read, ranging from Mexico to China, New York, St Petersburg and most other cities in between. Abbado also taught Joy how vital it was to treat the young musicians well: 'Give them good accommodation, good food and good concert halls'.

Huw Humphreys sums up Abbado's founding principles: 'We ask these people to play as professionals. We ask them to share rooms, we don't pay them, but we treat them like top professionals. They could play any orchestra in the world off the stage when they turned it on. It was extraordinary.'

It was a reflection of Joy Bryer's loyalty that she humoured Edward Heath in his wish to conduct the orchestra. Hadn't he after all secured its position in the EU's institutions? Wasn't a small reward reasonable? Heath's colossal, personal vanity and insensitivity led him to a grossly exaggerated estimate of his musical abilities. Despite pressure from Heath's colleague, Baroness Elles, Drummond refused to let him conduct at the Edinburgh Festival. He received an abusive phone call from the Baroness, who called him a 'disgrace'. This was followed by a threat from a festival sponsor to withdraw funding unless Heath conducted. Drummond offered Heath the shortest piece he could think of, Mozart's 'Marriage of Figaro' overture. He left the Usher Hall to go for a walk with Abbado during the actual performance. On their return, Drummond found that Heath had in fact conducted the far-longer 'Magic Flute' overture, then harangued the audience about Europe for a further fifteen minutes.

Later, it took the authority of Berlin Philharmonic's legendary Herbert von Karajan to defuse the situation. Faced with the suggestion that Heath wanted to conduct at the Salzburg Festival, wrote John Drummond, Karajan told Heath: 'You must conduct Mozart's "Jupiter" symphony. What's more, I will come and listen.' Karajan's ruthless guile did what Joy's loyalty could not do: overcome her misplaced loyalty to Ted Heath the politician by treating him as a musician. By all accounts when they had to endure his presence on the podium, the young players of the orchestra just ignored him. They immediately spotted, recalls Nicola Wallis, that it was safer to follow the orchestra leader instead. Others judged Heath more bluntly: 'He didn't have a clue.'

It was in Salzburg too, that most elite of festivals, that Abbado played one of his little jokes on Joy. 'We must have some workers in the audience,' he insisted. Joy returned the next day disconsolate and empty-handed: 'Claudio, my darling, I've looked everywhere. There aren't any workers.'

Joy's relationship with Abbado was one of wary mutual self-interest. She and her succession of able managers had created an instrument of wonderful quality. Abbado played it superbly and it suited him to do so. In the music profession, it was a byword that 'If Claudio asks you for something, you never say "no". If you do, you are finished with him'. He wanted the orchestra to expand into eastern Europe, where there were scores of brilliant young musicians. For Joy, expansion would always be in line with the ideals of the European Union. As it enlarged, so too would the orchestra. As a fully paid-up member of Italy's champagne socialists, Abbado regarded the entire Brussels-based European project as a basically capitalist ramp towards which he felt little sympathy and probably some antipathy. If he did not actually fall out with Joy, he certainly did with Lionel Bryer.

Highly intelligent as he was, formidably driven, charming, essential as the EUYO's financial backer of first and last resort, even family members recall Lionel as being 'thick-skinned', 'too full of himself' and with little sense of the effect he had on other people in a room. He was, said one friend, 'tough' with everyone. He rowed with the BBC management at the Proms. Worse still, he tried, it is said by some, to tell Abbado what repertoire to perform with the orchestra. At all events, Nicola Wallis recalls that by the end of the relationship, Abbado simply refused to negotiate with Lionel in person or to visit the Bryer house in Cadogan Square. Instead, she conducted negotiations at Abbado's King's Road home. It was a sad end to a magnificent relationship lasting 16 years, which had brought glory to both conductor and players. Now Joy had to find another music director of equivalent renown. She found it in the austere, undemonstrative Dutchman, Bernard Haitink.

On the face of it, he and Joy could not have been further apart as people. The gap, according to Haitink's wife, Patricia, was almost too big: 'Joy was an absolute force of nature. She was not a big person, but she was larger than life. She was brimming with enthusiasm. I think Bernard was slightly alarmed by her in a way because she was almost over the top. But he was extremely fond of her and he had a lot of affection for her and they got on pretty well on an annual basis for a number of years.'

What Haitink always found difficult, certainly antipathetic to him as a good republican Dutchman, was the social razzmatazz with which Joy surrounded every concert. Patricia Haitink remembers it well: 'The thing that upset Bernard about Joy was her desire to have as many ambassadors and high commissioners at a concert as possible. That was her measure of a successful concert. This did lead up to a little dust-up between Bernard and Joy, because she was talking about the high commissioners and he said, "You and your high commissioners!" And she said, "Bernard, darling, there's only one tonight!" And she actually got very upset. And he had to go the next day, I think, and put his arm around her and say, "Come on, Joy, it's alright." He realized he'd upset her and actually that's the last thing he wanted to do.'

Unfortunately, neither Bernard nor Patricia could stand the 'EU-branded' blue dresses and bow ties that Joy insisted the orchestra should wear: 'It was wonderful for Joy to sit in the Albert Hall and see the orchestra dressed in their blue dresses – which Bernard hated, by the way. She always called them "my babies". And Bernard railed against this. He said, "They're young musicians, you shouldn't treat them like children. You should treat them like grown musicians and not make them wear these blue Laura Ashley dresses with the starry scarves and so on. And the bow tie, the starry bow ties." All this sort of thing he didn't like at all but I understand why she did it.'

Given these quite significant cultural differences, why did Haitink stay? According to his wife, Patricia, because of sheer musical quality: 'That was always fantastic. We saw so many of those young players later in Berlin Philharmonic, Vienna Philharmonic, LSO since those years and they all come up and say, "Oh, we remember this concert. And we remember Bruckner's Seventh". These concerts were a huge thing for them. The quality, first of all – the orchestra was fantastically well prepared by the time Bernard got there. He wasn't going into the first rehearsal. They would already have had sectional rehearsals with very good-quality tutors doing *tutti* rehearsals. By the time Bernard got to them, they were note perfect – he only had the fun bit.'

CEO Martijn Sanders witnessed one occasion when they just couldn't stop playing together, just for their mutual enjoyment. Haitink and the orchestra had four days scheduled for rehearsals for the next concert. After two days, he was on the phone to Sanders at the Concertgebouw: 'Bernard calls me and he said, "We're finished, the rehearsal. We know how to do it. Now we have two or three days on our hands and we decided that we would play the Brahms Four." I said, "Bernard, but there is no public performance of that." He said, "No, just for fun, the orchestra and I will do Brahms Four. Do you have the scores of that in your library?" The answer was yes. We put them in a taxi and that was the Brahms Four that nobody ever heard.'

Like Claudio Abbado before him, Bernard Haitink loved the players and treated them as fellow professionals. There was something profoundly moving about the relationship between the 87-year-old Haitink and the more or less 18-year-old EUYO players. He was, of course, offering a lifetime of experience to them. This made Haitink's last concert with the EUYO so intensely moving. It was on 29 August 2016 at the

Concertgebouw, Haitink's 'home' concert hall, to perform a piece deeply identified with him, Bruckner's 'Seventh Symphony'. Already frail, he came onto the platform for the final rehearsal quietly, slightly assisted by his wife, Patricia. I recall it vividly. A few words with the orchestra, the baton raised, a gentle down beat and then the intense lyrical flow from the lower strings, a breath of sound, more than a whisper, a line emerged, clear, limpid, moving but propelling the whole symphony from this simple spring of sound. Did Haitink stop them there? Some more quiet words; the calm re-set, the simple down beat and the opening bars sang anew. All on a single down beat. All that flowed seemed inevitable from that opening gesture. So small, so big.

Afterwards, my wife and I asked the Concertgebouw Orchestra's principal cello, Gregor Horsch, if he could explain how Haitink did it. He paused before saying, 'I have been playing for him for more than 20 years and I still don't know.' That evening, Haitink conjured greatness from the players; they took in wisdom. Such exchanges varying in intensity were the stuff of the EUYO experience.

Bernard Haitink's appointment as music director ended in 2000 after a six-year spell. Musically distinguished throughout, the EUYO had in fact suffered a near-death experience sparked by the orchestra's success during this time. It came, sadly, not from outside the organization but from within the family and sprang, say some, from the depths of Lionel's character. By the mid-1990s, with the orchestra's success beyond question, Lionel was looking for something new. The orchestra presented no conceptual challenge or opportunity for innovation. After all, his business ability and acumen kept the EUYO solvent; his financial guarantees kept bankers and auditors happy; his management had built up healthy reserves. It was time for a new venture – move the whole youth performers' concept into European Youth Opera and Ballet. It would be a huge step, but it was his dream and he felt that he had built up the reserves to fund it. Joy tried to resist, sensing this was a step too far. Despite her and other objections, Lionel ran a youth opera season in Baden-Baden in 1997, then mounted an entire production of *Eugene Onegin* in Paris, in 1998. These two years wiped out almost all of the EUYO's reserves. According to the opera professionals who found themselves involved, he was a 'total amateur, wholly out of his depth'.

The situation was, according to one eyewitness, 'horrendous and very scary'. Powerless against Lionel's determination, Joy became increasingly concerned and was often in floods of tears at the prospect of losing almost two decades of devoted commitment with the EUYO. Somehow, with huge damage done to its financial reserves, the EUYO itself continued seemingly untarnished. Haitink himself hardly noticed. It cannot have been easy for the Bryers personally and may have taken a heavy toll on their health. But the show went on.

Bernard Haitink was succeeded as music director in 2000 by Vladimir Ashkenazy for a 15-year period during which the EUYO continued to spread its wings and earn a global reputation from Brazil, Japan, China, Korea to the United States, Abu Dhabi, as well as all the European capitals. Every musician, it seemed, wanted to play with them. It seems fair to say that Ashkenazy, 'Vova', was Joy's favourite music director of them all. Her sister, Jeanne, says that Vova's departure in 2015 when the board decided that change was needed hurt Joy deeply but by then change was in the air, physical health fragile. Lionel had died in 2006 after some years of dementia. In 2013, aged 83, after a punishing 35 years of travelling, negotiating, cajoling, charming, inspiring, begging, representing and fighting for the EUYO, Joy knew that change was essential.

She herself had done everything that she could, far more than most would have attempted. Some might have called time on a glorious project which had done what it had set out to do, far more than anyone would have dared to imagine. Her brother, Robert Albert, says the possibility of 'calling it a day' never crossed her mind. The idea was very much in the musical world atmosphere, as Marshall Marcus discovered when he was deciding whether or not to take the job of chief executive: 'It's one of the first great youth orchestras clearly, the first ever proper international youth orchestra. For a while it was way out ahead in the field, it was the only international game in town. But then gradually more international youth orchestra started. Somebody I talked to about whether I should take the job or not said: "Be careful, it's a crowded market!" My view was that if this was going to move on, then change had to be allowed to come in.'

It is easy to underestimate the actions of the founder of an organization when they decide to move on themselves. It is highly unlikely that Joy Bryer knew how antiquated the EUYO's organization had become. For this international organization with a worldwide reputation had the organizational structures of a cottage industry, certainly a family one. Lesley King-Lewis remembers the 'working' atmosphere vividly: 'Mum's offices were always in the home so costs were kept down and provided the working capital. Our house was always full. Mum had our offices at the top. We lived in the middle bit and Dad had his surgeries below. And whenever we came home, you know, we would be meeting great musicians. I always remember Leopold Stokowski when I was very young coming for Sunday lunch. It was always noisy, busy.'

Little changed. When Huw Humphreys arrived as the orchestra manager in 2002, he was startled by the offices he found at 65 Sloane Street: 'I can remember everything about it from my interview. Her old office on Sloane Street was unlike anything I had seen in my career. I started working at Harold Holt in '94, where there were still telex machines and the fax machine was relatively new. But Mrs Bryer's office was the only office whose sole piece of technology was a battered typewriter. It was there the whole time I was there.'

It was a full decade later when Marshall Marcus caught the full impact of this on his first working day in the EUYO office in January 2013: 'I walked into the room which was to be my office and there was a desk. On the desk, there were pictures of the family and a typewriter. I remember thinking, where is everything? Next door, papers all around the place and books and things. Next door, the general manager's office with piles and piles of paper with tiny pencil handwriting on. I thought I'd walked into the wedding table scene in Dickens' *Great Expectations*. Next door, I found a Dickensian figure doing all the notes.'

One unanswered question was how had the EUYO succeeded, let alone survived for so long? Another was how had it carried out its complex business with such primitive tools? Perhaps the most urgent question was since Joy Bryer knew that change was needed, could she come to terms with it? She had taken the more honorific position of president of the orchestra, Marshall was the new, executive secretary-general with full authority yet their early approaches had to be wary: 'We were a bit like boxers walking around each other, trying to work out what the space was which we'd both occupy in this new situation. People had said that the orchestra needed to change. Whether she had accepted that is a different matter. What I saw was an organization in which everything seemed to be being done in the same way that it had been done for many years.'

Marshall's approach was shaped by a seminal musical experience from a few years back. He was well aware that the orchestra he was taking on was, almost literally, 'Joy's baby'. After all, she often spoke of the players as 'her children' and increasingly, as her 'grandchildren': 'I realized there would be no point in my coming into work and saying, "Okay, I'm now in charge. This is what's going to happen". I remember hearing Mariss Jansons talking about rehearsing the Concertgebouw Orchestra as its new music director. In a radio interview, he was asked, "When you came to the Concertgebouw, what changes did you make?" And Jansons replied, "You don't go to the orchestra and make changes! You go to them and you watch, you play and you listen. And maybe if you're lucky after a while you make changes." My first thing was to listen and work out what was going on.'

This proved a constructive way of approaching change and transition in a deeply entrenched, personally run organization. Marshall was having to adapt an organization which for no less than 35 years had been run by one extraordinary person. If Joy Bryer knew that time was no longer on her side, she didn't necessarily find the culture change and the transformation of ways of doing business any easier to understand or to accept. She deserved respect for the realism involved in stepping aside to allow the EUYO to move on. Marshall was very aware of the scale and nature of the task: 'These were people who operated in a different geological time period. Joy had grown up through that. She did know Europe's crowned heads of state, she knew prime ministers and the presidents of the European Commission. But the world had, was and is changing a lot. I wanted to find a new way of doing business. The second big change was the extraordinary discipline and technique and ability that these players had. But I felt that the players were a bit infantilized, like a "youth orchestra". I brought some of the work I got out of *El Sistema*, which was this incredible joy and openness in playing. The big artistic thing I wanted was to change, to open the players more, to fear failure less, to risk more.'

Throughout, he was particularly tactful when it came to suggesting to Joy that things had to be done differently: 'If you begin to feel the power ebbing a bit, that must be a difficult thing. First of all, I tried to be extremely respectful. Of course you had to be because she was the vision, the heart, the DNA, the mother of the organization. But you need to do business in a different way. She respected that I was trying to keep *her* institution going. I was always careful to put it that way. It was easy for me to say it because it was true. I was trying to keep her flame burning and I still do.'

Joy had one last characteristic coup to carry out. Although she would never put it like this and might not even have fully understood why it mattered, the EUYO's governance needed not just renewal but root and branch reform. Put bluntly, the controlling board was a family affair; it had no external, objective supervisory members on it. For the entire period of her leadership, her brother, Robert Albert, was chair; her daughter, Lesley King-Lewis, was one trustee; the other two in a board of just four were Lionel's business associates. There was nothing illegal in this. Lionel Bryer guaranteed any possible deficit; accounts were audited, the board never traded insolvently or anything like it. It was just not governance as generally known and almost universally practised. If Joy was not strong on the contemporary principles and practice of good governance, she could recognize anno domini. The board needed a new chair. The rest was the pure Joy of old.

One evening at the Barbican, she waylaid me coming into a drinks reception. I knew her from the past through many musical and family connections. 'That's the one,' she announced to her daughter, Lesley. 'Will you become chairman of the orchestra?' I suddenly felt like all those countless European politicians, diplomats, musicians and supporters faced with the royal command. Resistance was useless; besides, I was keen to work with the EUYO. It suited me. In short order, we invited Ian Stoutzker, musician, philanthropist and longstanding chair of the London Symphony Orchestra's Development Council, to become co-chair. Together, we expanded the trustee board, including major figures in European music such as Martijn Sanders, former director of the Amsterdam Concertgebouw. It became a proper instrument of governance and its membership reflected its European base rather than a family concern.

Martijn, as a newcomer to the board, caught some sense of how hard it was for Joy to hand over: 'She was still running the orchestra in her mind even after she stepped down from her throne. When I was joining the board, she invited me for a glass of champagne. That resulted in an hour-long speech about how the orchestra should have been run. For people it's very difficult to say goodbye. And that must have been hard for her.'

In a sense, Joy's permissive reconstruction of the EUYO trustees was her final gift to the organization she had created and loved. I doubt she fully understood why it mattered or what it involved. It proved a crucial step in the EUYO's evolution when facing a truly existential financial crisis in 2016. The EU proposed changing the basis on which it funded all cultural organizations. In future this would be done on a project-by-project basis involving bids for each and every project. But the EUYO was an organization, not a sequence of discreet bids. If this was to be the new funding regime, they simply could not survive. This was not an idle threat. Trustees and executive knew we were facing closure after almost 40 years of endeavour and success. We would not risk trading insolvently; we could close the organization down because we could not keep it going.

Marshall Marcus recalls what happened next: 'Three of us sat down and we said, "OK, we need to go public on this." It was as if you've got to put your finger up to the wind and see whether there was enough support for the orchestra to make a campaign. It was one of the most staggering experiences of my life to discover quite how much support for the idea of the orchestra there was. That made me think it's got to be worth putting together a real campaign. And one of the most interesting few weeks of my life was that campaign. It would have been impossible without the previous decades of what Joy had built up.'

The response from the musical world was incredible, starting with a round robin message from members of the Berliner Philharmoniker calling on the German culture minister, Monika Grutters, to intervene to save the EUYO. She was strongly supported by Italy's Culture Minister, Dario Franceschini. In just a few weeks, the EU changed its mind and found a way to amend its cultural funding policy, allowing the EUYO to continue. Marshall witnessed the scale of this unprecedented climbdown and the reason behind it: 'What really astounded me is how unbelievably powerful the EUYO brand was. I remember a couple of organizations coming to me afterwards and saying, "That was amazing what the orchestra achieved, how did you do that?" They thought you could just unload the formula. But the fact was, as I told them, that without the hinterland, forget it. Not only were there thousands of alumni that thought the orchestra was a great idea, not only the politicians and musicians, it's the only time I could have called up any musician in the world and said: "Will you support this campaign?" No musician ever said no. When you recognize something with such extraordinary value and worth, that never changes. Its value will always be there.'

Its value was the fruit of the extraordinary person who was 'Mrs B!' So what example of leadership, of innovation, does her daughter, Lesley King-Lewis, take from her? 'Be courageous, fearless, take risks. But underlying all that is knowing what's your purpose. And always, what's my legacy? What do I want to be known for? How am I going to leave this world and leave it a better place than the one I was born into? Many people don't have that purpose and that's okay. But if you want to make a change, those who are going to be successful, have that confidence that you can do it no matter if people laugh at you, no matter if they don't believe in you, no matter if you get those days where you think it'll never work, we could go bankrupt. It's that belief that you can do it.'

Doesn't every organization need its Joy? Shouldn't they insist on seeking and harnessing the qualities, the manner, the commitment to success that she brought? As long-serving chief executive of a leadership foundation, Lesley King-Lewis knows the realities of corporate existence: 'A lot of big companies, they're all buying incubators because they realize that innovation is not coming from within. The minute you buy an incubator, many companies start imposing control and bureaucracy. You cannot innovate without taking risks. You want the entrepreneurs and you want their innovation, but you need a culture where failure is tolerated. Once you start imposing controls, you lose it. They find it very difficult to let people free to innovate.'

There are no places for the Joy Bryers of this world in such environments. To the end, her sense of timing, of drama, was impeccable. On Armistice Day 2018, members of the EUYO played at the ceremony at the Arc de Triomphe in Paris marking the centenary of the end of the First World War, with 70 heads of state present. Joy would have loved that, she deserved it. She died in hospital that same afternoon aged 88.

Observations

+ Unbridled egoism is about the individual; it is a poor counsellor and a fallible instrument. But controlled egoism in the service of a cause is a powerful tool.
+ Nobody realized their dream project by taking it easy and assuming it will happen. A dream project involves a thousand failures.
+ An innovator combines strategic farsightedness and intuitive vision.
+ Cost and risk are not obstacles in themselves. They are warnings, challenges, but they are not a signal to stop.
+ Ignoring warnings about practicality is not the same as stupidity. Daring to reach for the impossible is the only way of making it happen.
+ Stepping down from full control of a project to a more supervisory role is difficult and deserves sympathetic reactions from others.
+ There is no substitute for well-organized, systematic governance as a basis for a successful organization.
+ Established organizations struggle to harness the power of innovation and originality. They should try harder to adapt to the inconvenient demands of those who can provide both.
+ Where are the rules which say that 'rules are made to be broken'?
+ No opponent of a good idea ever says they were wrong. Nay-sayers will be nay-sayers, that will always be their problem.
+ The individual judged to be 'impossible' is often the one person to make the impossible happen.

References

European Union Youth Orchestra Annual Yearbooks: 1978, 2005, 2007, 2008, 2009, 2010, 2013, 2015.

John Drummond, *Tainted by Experience – A Life in the Arts* (Faber & Faber, 2001).

Revel Guest, director, *Last Summer we Played in the Alps*, BBC Television 1970.

3

'Two Impresarios': The Hare and the Tortoise

Featuring interviews with:

Nic Beeby, Technical Director, Edinburgh Festival 1980–85

Sheila Colvin, General Manager, Aldeburgh Foundation (now Britten-Pears Arts), 1989–97

Chris Denton, Chief Executive, St Martin-in-the-Fields Arts 2021–present

Richard Jarman, Chief Executive, Scottish Opera 1991–97

Joe Melillo, Chief Executive, Brooklyn Academy of Arts, 1983–2018

Alex Poots, Chief Executive, The Shed, Manhattan, New York 2014–present

Graham Sheffield, Arts Director, Barbican Centre, 1995–2010

Peter Vergo, Emeritus Professor of Art History and Theory, University of Essex

Claire Whitaker, Director, 'Serious' 2006–2020

Johann Zietsman, President and CEO, Adrienne Arsht Center for the Performing Arts of Miami-Dade County 2008–present

The two people could not have been more different: in physique, looks, character, background, personality, style, manner and outlook. One, John Drummond, created a radical approach to arts festival programming with the Edinburgh Festival of 1983, 'Vienna 1900'. The other, Graham Sheffield, pioneered new ways of integrating arts programming over extended periods, first with 'Meltdown' at the South Bank Centre between 1993 and 1995, then 'Only Connect' and 'Inventing America' at the Barbican between 1997 and 2010. Each was an innovator of a distinct kind; Drummond with a single, intense cultural explosion, occasionally imitated, never equalled, whose creative aftershocks continue to this day. Sheffield with an approach to making cultural and artistic programming connections over extended periods often followed in theory, seldom bettered in practice.

Side by side, they would also have made a strongly contrasted pair. Drummond, six foot four inches tall; Sheffield, a (comparatively) modest five feet 10 inches. Each proved highly effective in their own way and for their own needs and purposes, which were as different as were their physiques. Yet they had much in common. Each was a solitary child from a supportive, perhaps even doting family, with an attentive and admired mother. Each was an unapologetic, almost sensual lover of and relisher of the physical things of life. Each was an enjoyer of the arts and each wanted to share their love and experience of the arts with others. Both were brought up professionally in the BBC, an organization adept at raising broad-spectrum generalists. Each had a degree of self-knowledge, though some would say somewhat limited, about their own character.

It was hard and painfully won knowledge in Drummond's case, in the recollection of his close friend and colleague, Richard Jarman: 'When John came out of Cambridge, he wanted to be an academic, but he hadn't got the necessary level of degree and he'd been told that he was not capable of doing it. This left a scar on him for years. Then he encountered the legendary arts impresario Huw Weldon at the BBC. Huw was his huge mentor, but a tough old cookie, and would tell John in no uncertain terms what his failings were. Huw Weldon both led him, but enforced his feelings of intellectual inferiority. John himself would often say: "I have got an extraordinary mind, the photographic memory which enables me to tell you what was behind the tomb of the third chapel down on the right in an Italian cathedral. I have no capability, no capacity for abstract thought at all. I just have a certain sort of memory and facility, a quickness.'"

Whatever these correctly acknowledged shortcomings, Drummond always played to his strengths. If this was an admirable example of his self-awareness, something he was not always given credit for, it sometimes became still more direct and probably painful, in Jarman's experience: 'He was a contradictory man. Underneath all of the bravado I think it was fuelled by a sense of inferiority. He felt he went to the wrong school, came from not a grand background. All the name-dropping was ludicrous, this was all part of a kind of cover-up.'

It became though a key part of Drummond's public persona, his very demonstrative showman-like act that served him well for years, if at considerable personal cost. It is also undoubtedly the case that the 'Drummond manner' lost him support, as his best friends, like Britten-Pears Arts General Manager Sheila Colvin, never conceal: 'He's a Marmite person. There were definitely people who disliked him intensely, and resented him. Resented him because he could be patronizing. He believed in what he believed in. He could be dismissive – people don't like to be dismissed.'

Drummond's fuse of patience was a short one and cost him dear over the years. If there were equivalent internal angsts in Sheffield's mind, they never showed themselves. Or at least in more manageable ways: 'Am I an introvert? Sometimes I'm a solitary person and I do value my occasionally solitary grumpiness, which I channel through my piano playing, which is intensely solitary and demands enormous mental discipline. But when it comes to programming and running venues, I'm not alone. I derived a lot of energy and inspiration from the colleagues with whom I worked. To that extent, I'm gregarious. I've always worked as a soloist but in a large organization, which is different from working as a soloist freelance.'

And there was never any doubt about Sheffield's sense of responsibility to audiences: 'You have to be ahead of your audience, but two steps not ten steps. If you're behind the audience, you're always just giving them what they know and therefore you're never expanding your taste or their taste. If you're a couple of steps ahead, you can lead. If you're too far ahead, they can't see you. I was always trying to say, "Look, these are my enthusiasms, come with me and share them". That's what I mean about a voyage of learning about myself. I always treated my job as a privilege to have, but there was something I wanted to learn myself. Perhaps that's more selfish than arrogant. But I tried to communicate my enthusiasms, I don't think that's arrogant.'

Sheffield and Drummond: two contrasting characters, each devoted to the arts, who applied their skills and passion in their particular ways, destined to innovate but to do so differently. In Drummond's case, the key word was 'threads', a way of breaking down existing art form barriers and conventions where a series of unconnected concerts, dramas and exhibitions were judged to be all that was called for, what was needed. He was always looking for 'threads' as a way of building coherence into the usually random, if excellent, collection of events that made up most festivals.

The threads, recalls Richard Jarman, came from a vast knowledge of the arts he was planning: 'He wasn't the least bit up in the clouds, he had a breadth of interests. And this memory was able to pick up and harvest all this knowledge on a huge wide spectrum, which is what you want in a festival director. He could synthesize. His press conferences were legendary because he had that capacity to pull threads together. He did it more or less on the hoof. He wasn't reading off a script. There was a checklist of names he had to remember, so he'd be able to pull people out and make connections. Making connections was his major philosophy about the Festival. The most memorable occasion was at one of his famous parties after a performance in his first festival. On the floor of the main room there were Witold Lutosławski, Merce Cunningham and Alexander Gibson, all having an animated conversation. Composer, choreographer, conductor. And John turned to me and said, "That's what festivals should be about."'

Sheffield's emphasis and instincts were perhaps more ordered, more systematic, but never lapsed into rigidity or the formulaic. Johann Zietsman watched him at close quarters at the International Society of Performing Arts (ISPA): 'His knowledge of new artists and new ways of expressing artistic endeavours was second to none. He always seemed to know about almost any genre you can think about. He would know what the latest movers and shakers were doing. He was very often the catalyst to help new artists succeed and gave them chances and believed in them. Not only did he know about new art, he often helped to create new art.'

There was another dimension to Sheffield's approach beyond encouraging the young and promising: he understood the necessity of creation and creativity even in, or especially in, what might seem the routines of arts programme planning. The Shed CEO Alex Poots saw this evolve in practice in Sheffield's mind and hands: 'Divine idea-making rarely happens like that. It's normally a few steps and then you realize you're somewhere else. What Graham brilliantly did was: "Well, how do we keep doing that but introduce the future?" I think "Meltdown" showed him that there was greatness in other areas than just purely classical music. He was someone who could be trusted with the Crown Jewels. I think he was transformational. Was he revolutionary? He was the man who could usher in change. And that's a different skill base, potentially, to the kind of revolutionary figure who might have had the first idea.'

As a well-established producer for 12 years of BBC Radio 3 cultural and music documentaries, Sheffield bristles at the suggestion that he was a 'safe' producer cushioned by and in a 'safe' organization. Revealingly, his two best-remembered programmes were about wine and skiing, two life-long passions. Even he concedes that after 12 years of some inevitably routine work within the BBC, however admirable, he needed a change. There was something in him struggling to get out.

Becoming director of music projects at the South Bank Centre, Sheffield was given as his remit to stop, as he recalls it, emptying the Royal Festival Hall, which a heavy diet of modernists such as Harrison Birtwistle and Pierre Boulez was doing. There was nothing in Sheffield's BBC background and programme making record to suggest that his approach would be as radical as it became. Perhaps even he did not know in advance. Either way, that makes his appointment either far-sighted or plain lucky.

Drummond's appointment to be director of the Edinburgh Festival was even less likely. Especially as one of Drummond's referees, the peppery Huw Weldon, wrote a staggeringly ambiguous letter supposedly in his support: 'Many find him difficult and he was not always good with people. I have never met an artist who did not respect and admire him.' Fortunately, the second sentence carried more weight with Edinburgh City Council than the first. Some came to regret it. Richard Jarman recalls being quizzed about Drummond by an existing member of the Festival staff: 'He didn't know that I knew John. "John Drummond's been appointed as director. Who is this person? Does anyone know him?" I just kept schtum. One forgets now but he was scraped out of the BBC, he wasn't a name that people knew, completely eclipsed by directors like Humphrey Burton. He was considered a very young appointee to the Festival directorship. Actually, he said, "Strangely enough, I'm one of the oldest".'

Comparatively unknown, comparatively old, with no experience of running a festival or any kind of complex artistic venture, it was in many ways a risky appointment and so it proved. At this narrow point in their careers, the fortunes of Sheffield and Drummond come together. Each was an unlikely appointment to an undefined role. The fact that each proved to be innovative and memorable was as unpredictable as it was unintended. No one could imagine Drummond's 'Vienna 1900' festival just five years after taking over, nor predict Sheffield's 1993–95 'Meltdown' programming.

What they did have in common was picking excellent support teams and colleagues, though they did so in very different ways. Drummond's approach was entirely personal. This is how he 'found' Sheila Colvin: 'A friend in Edinburgh, an internationally influential gallery owner, Richard Demarco, contacted me and said: "You've absolutely got to meet this man John Drummond, he's amazing." He'd also obviously contacted John and said, "You've got to meet Sheila Colvin, she's amazing." John took me to a restaurant in Beauchamp Place in London and we discovered that we shared a birthday. We just got on. He asked me about what I'd done with my life and I said to him, "Nothing very structured – I went from one thing to another but they were all interesting." And John said, "That's really what I want – somebody with a varied, more general background." I think he spotted an openness to new ideas. Bob Lockyer, Drummond's partner, said to me, "Drummond wasn't sure you had a sense of humour." And I said to him, "Yes, she does."'

In his autobiography, *Tainted by Experience*, Drummond described Colvin's recruitment as 'the best thing that happened to me in the Edinburgh Festival years. She is one of the most capable and gifted women I have ever met'. Richard Jarman's involvement was equally personal. The two used to meet at the Arts Council's dance panel.

'I started talking to him after we'd had our committee meetings. His first line to me was, "Of course I'm different from my friends. I don't like opera. I like ballet." We developed a friendship and we'd spend evenings together and he'd take me back to his flat and we'd play records and he was quizzing me. He'd put records on blind and say, "Who is this, what is this?" And I had a good record of guessing sometimes that it was actually Julius Katchen playing a Brahms piano sonata. He was impressed by that.'

Once appointed as festival director, Drummond invited Jarman to join him. His later description of Jarman as 'the best gundog in the world. Whatever I shot, he retrieved', while undoubtedly accurate, reads rather patronizingly as a record of a longstanding and close personal and professional relationship. More important is Drummond's summary of this crucial trio of colleagues: 'We were all new to festivals but we all had enthusiasm and commitment.' Still, to have a major international festival run by not just one but three people without experience of such activity was a risk of the highest order. There is no sign, no record that the Edinburgh City Fathers had the remotest inkling of who or what they had let themselves in for.

Sheffield's approach was to recruit skills and specialisms. He had time but the way he did it spoke volumes about his approach and understanding of needs. Recruiting an arts marketer such as Chris Denton might seem obvious but Sheffield saw that marketing had become something more demanding. Denton was the beneficiary: 'The evolution of art marketing is one of moving from "tell and sell" to audience engagement and diversification. Graham got that early on, that marketing was important. I loved the fact that I was part of the arts team. That was revolutionary. Marketing would be around the table on an equal footing with the programmers. And the issue of who are we doing this for was always on the table as well. Who are the audience? At the end of the day, to be an artistic leader, you've got to be able to listen, but you've also got to be able to lead and have a vision. That's what he did.'

Claire Whitaker and her company, Serious, specializing in jazz and contemporary music, was another recruit, providing an added specialist skill which Sheffield knew he lacked: 'One of the things that's been a thread through Graham's career is surrounding himself with good people. He stays working with them for a long time. Graham's very good at letting people be brave. People could try things and felt supported and enabled to be bold. And that boldness paid off. It worked in terms of profile, in terms of artistic recognition and audiences. That's been a thread through Graham's career, he's very good at working with ambitious people and facilitating that work.'

Sheffield was also aware that he needed strength in the sometimes contentious area of programming across the art forms, breaking out of the formal silos in which so much arts programming existed. Alex Poots was one of his earliest appointments: 'One of Graham's great gifts was his lack of conceit and power control. He was smart enough to bring people around him, to realize there's excellence in all forms of music. You needed people who could see what the excellent aspects are and not focus too much on those areas that were not so good. He didn't have the kind of ego that would want to be top dog, to be seen as the only person and to be doing it all himself. I would not be here were it not for the opportunities that Graham bestowed on me.'

The Sheffield approach to creating and running a team looked and was more systematic than Drummond's. That did not mean that the very unbureaucratic, intensely personal method Drummond developed was not effective. It was right for him, it was right for Jarman and Sheila Colvin. As Colvin recalls, if the style was personal, it was effective: 'John didn't sit in an office with the door closed or anything. We did socialize, socialize all the time but we didn't down tools at half past five or anything like that. He wanted some threads through it, certainly. John liked his threads.'

Drummond knew how weak he was personally on the technical side of what was a huge logistical task, creating and running a concentrated three-week festival where any mishap would become a very public failure. Nic Beeby, technical director of one of the Edinburgh theatres, recalls how he was recruited: 'One of the first things he said to me was, "What do you do when you have to say 'no' to somebody, they can't have something?" And I said, "I would try and sort out what they could have." And he just said to me, "Right answer." And that is the way it continued. He said, "I can't think of anybody better to do this." John was somebody who handed you the baton and expected you to run with it.'

Throughout their years together, Beeby found that Drummond, supposedly a remote arts lover distant from the realities of arts activity, was very practical in his response to technical difficulties: 'He gave me the ability to make mistakes and learn from them. I don't mean that he was sympathetic to mistakes, it was just that if something was very difficult, he didn't stand over you to try and tell you what should be done. He allowed you to work it out for yourself and then apply that solution. He would understand there was a problem. Then he would ask you, "What do you think the best solution was?" He wasn't someone who just expected the Universe, the Earth and the Heavens and everything else, regardless of the cost. He was quite pragmatic about how the best solution could be achieved. He realized that if you try to achieve something that is not achievable, you end up with a disaster.'

At this point, a major divergence appears in the Drummond/ Sheffield experience, one that was to have a big impact. During his career, Sheffield worked in and for large organizations: the BBC, the South Bank Centre, the Barbican in the City of London Corporation. Whatever he thought of their rules and practices, he was at least part of an organized machine. They provided an administrative structure within which he could work. He did not see it as a creative straitjacket. Rather, he was freed to do what he wanted to do: programme the arts as well as he could. This proved an incalculably precious freedom, which he seized without hesitation.

By contrast, Drummond found the Edinburgh City Council a local authority that was lumbering and backward even by the standards of its peers. Astonishingly, it was reluctant to acknowledge that in the annual International Festival, it had a precious resource and economic opportunity for the city, for the region and indeed for Scotland. When Drummond observed that the Festival budget was similar in size to the District Council's graveyard budget, one councillor roundly replied: 'We have a statutory duty to bury the dead, there is no statutory duty regarding the Festival.' The celebrated journalist and polemicist, Bernard Levin, described Edinburgh City Council's annual debate about Festival funding as the solemn civic ceremony of 'The Grudging of the Money'. But it was not only the City Council whose approach left everything to be desired. It was, recalls Sheila Colvin, as if the citizens of Edinburgh did not value it either.

'Some people in Edinburgh made an absolute conscious decision to leave Edinburgh during the Festival. People said things to John like, "I'd like to come to your festival but I can't, my cousin's coming from Spain." Those kind of attitudes just floored him. That's when he would lose his cool occasionally, unfortunately. He was impatient with lack of interest, lack of engagement, wilful ignorance, lack of being open to a new experience. Then they disliked him even more.'

Drummond had a vision for the Festival's place in Edinburgh's life. As he wrote in his memoir: 'I wanted to get the arts and the city to talk to each other and to generate a really festive atmosphere. At Festival time, I was determined to break through Edinburgh's "snobbery and exclusivity" to show its citizens a warmer and more companionable world'. His intentions were not reciprocated. Drummond felt that Edinburgh regarded 'those of us who worked in the arts as the lower orders'. He recalled being told by a local businessman 'I don't suppose a long-haired weirdo like you has ever seen a balance sheet.'

Feelings boiled over in a wholly unhelpful way recalls Richard Jarman: 'I remember one council meeting where Drummond launched into a monologue about their lack of understanding and so on. And he ended up, of course: "Trouble with all of you lot, you're just in trade" – not the best thing to say to a bunch of people. In a way he was right, of course. John worked his arse off for the Festival and so did we all. He thought the Edinburgh Festival was completely unique, special and good for Edinburgh. Behind the trade barb was the knowledge that trade did bloody well out of the Edinburgh Festival. At his final board meeting, the Lord Provost, a slightly timid sort of man, came to the end and said, "Well, John, the time has come for us to say goodbye. Some of us have enjoyed working with you some of the time."'

It is undoubtedly true that Drummond was not an easy or biddable council employee, indeed a very unlikely one. Even his close colleague Richard Jarman says, 'My idea of a nightmare would be to be John Drummond's line manager.' But there were faults on both sides. Such destructive and demoralizing exchanges could go down in the all-too-familiar canon of 'arty remoteness' and 'bureaucratic philistinism'. How they are interpreted and judged will vary. The Council was crass; Drummond probably overreacted. It all took a huge amount of his time, sapped his energy and diminished his effectiveness. Looking back, the cards were stacked against him from the start.

Sheffield for his part could concentrate on the job in hand benefiting from an organizational 'quiet life'. It must have helped that he was never a 'public figure' as Drummond increasingly was. Always a more discreet figure, Sheffield could operate almost under the radar of intense public scrutiny. Such were the strikingly contrasting practical and psychological foundations on which both were to be major innovators in arts programming. For innovators they proved to be.

For Drummond, the opportunity came in time for his first Festival in 1979. He noticed that the opening day was the fiftieth anniversary of the death of the greatest twentieth-century impresario, Serge Diaghilev. It was also the twenty-fifth anniversary of the legendary London exhibition about Diaghilev by the master ballet critic, Richard Buckle. Drummond was a huge admirer of the Russian impresario who spoke both to his love of ballet, his imperious showmanship and to speaking Russian, which Drummond had learned during his National Service. He had made two television programmes about Diaghilev and later wrote a book, *Speaking of Diaghilev*. Here was his thread for his very first festival, an artistic calling card if ever there was one.

Then the work began. It was, recalls Jarman, quite a shock: 'I find myself thinking overwhelmingly of the process of planning this festival rather than the event itself. It was a tremendously exciting process, not least because John, Sheila and I were all to various degrees new to this game and were on a voyage of discovery. When I look back on it, I was always amazed at how much we achieved through sheer ignorance – if we had been more experienced, we might have been more cautious! But we were all swept along by John's vision, his strategic (yet practical) thinking and his ambition.'

Much was inspired by opportunism and by the creative alchemy at the heart of the Drummond way of working. Richard Jarman saw how it worked, especially with performers: 'Drummond saw himself as a multi-polymath and Diaghilev was his role model. The fiftieth anniversary to the day on which Diaghilev had died in Venice gave him the perfect platform. I remember long conversations in the office programming with the conductor Gennadi Rozhdestvensky what would be the ideal opening programme. Conversation with him was wonderful because Gennadi – or "Noddy" as we all called him – had that sort of mind as well. He'd pull a piece out of the ether that people hadn't thought about for years and would draw the connections and that fitted in exactly with what John wanted.'

Drummond insisted on dealing directly with major artists face to face rather than through agents. A communicator, he had charm and musicians such as Claudio Abbado responded to it and to him: 'Abbado was key to his whole time at Edinburgh, as the LSO under Claudio played at every festival. John got quite close to him and I remember him coming back from a lunch with Claudio and saying that he had really opened up to John about the trauma of passing his fiftieth birthday and getting old!!! Likewise, with Jessye Norman and Janet Baker, who both relished his company. John managed to make them laugh! The day the first brochures arrived from the printers in 1979, he opened one up, then said of the Usher Hall programme: "It's not half bad – Abbado, Muti, Tennstedt, Ozawa – quite a good line up, don't you think?".'

The result was an opening concert of Prokofiev's somewhat unfamiliar 'Chout' and Stravinsky's 'Rite of Spring'. With Diaghilev sprinkled steadily and effectively throughout the three weeks, the most daring enterprise was an exhibition of ballet costumes, 'Parade'. Moving and bewitching in its design, with mood changes of lighting both to create drama and to protect the textiles, the costumes almost seemed to come alive, to be inhabited by bodies that floated in and out as the lighting changed. I saw it and it was a mesmerizing experience.

Drummond was enough of a pragmatist and an opportunist not to enslave the entire festival to one idea. As he observed later: 'Themes are poor masters but good servants.' When he had the chance of presenting a production of Shakespeare's *Richard III* by the Georgian Rustaveli Company, a lightning trip to Tbilisi convinced him that Edinburgh must see it. In Georgian. Jarman is convinced that only Drummond's deep personal commitment to the values of the company brought the project to the Festival: 'We spent 48 hours in Tbilisi to meet and see the Rustaveli Company. It was an intoxicating time as we were plunged heart and soul into the life of this extraordinary body of men and women. Starting with a dinner in the home of the company's director, Robert Sturua, I looked up from the groaning dining table to see a portrait of Stalin on the wall facing me. Food, wine, jokes, reminiscences, opinions and toasts flowed abundantly and with huge warmth.

'The meal ended with a group of the actors singing Georgian plain chant, which was devastating. But through all of this a true spirit of friendship was established, way beyond the reach of the Moscow "Goskoncert" government minders. We were able to have direct, frank and intelligent discussions with Sturua about programming and how to deal with the question of a very strange language. This was not a booking of a theatre company from some agency list, but a deeply personal commitment by John.'

Was Shakespeare's *Richard III* connected with Diaghilev? Of course not. Was it Festival material? Of course. It was a sign of Drummond's 'go anywhere, see anything' approach to gathering material. For an audience member like me, it was a landmark experience in the theatre.

It would never have been possible to find a unifying thread for each successive festival though there were attempts to do so that amounted to little more than labelling. It took Drummond a further three years to find one that was more than a mere thread but created an overarching intellectual and cultural theme. But 'Diaghilev' in 1979 was more than a dry run, a forerunner, excellent in its own terms. It had threads, it had glamour, it took risks. It showed what three clever, inexperienced but knowledgeable people could do at a festival starting from scratch. Did Drummond, super pragmatist and opportunist, sense that this trusted core trio could do it again, do it better and that a great idea would emerge, given time?

Sheffield's first innovation at the South Bank Centre could not have been more different. He had to restore the organization's general appeal to classical music audiences but needed to woo the jazz and popular music promoters who thought the Festival Hall too 'stuffy'. He also took a radical look at the entire nature of a vast rambling and uncoordinated art centre, lacking creative coherence, with only its buildings to provide an identity. Significantly, Sheffield did so without resort to consultants. He could draw conclusions about the South Bank's arts programming from the actual box office numbers. Besides, as he added: 'If you have a job like that, it's your responsibility to come up with ideas.' And Sheffield did with a strikingly clear analysis: 'You're in a multi-artform institution and you see the artforms not working together. You also see a lack of personality behind the venue. The venue itself has to have some kind of artistic vision itself and not just a one-night stand, where you see a concert and go away. I thought also that the resources of the Southbank were not being used holistically, to create something which embraced the totality of what the Southbank had to offer.

'It so happened that all attempts to offer a programme during the summer months had not added up to much. "Meltdown" seemed like an opportunity to bring things together in a festive sense but not in a saccharine sense. You actually had to have something worthwhile in the summer period that would be out of the ordinary, not just a series of events. It was literature, music, dance, cinema and the art gallery. And we said, in the first instance, to the composer, George Benjamin: "If we gave you carte blanche, what would you be able to do with this, using the resident orchestra, using the ensembles, whatever it was you want?" We set aside a budget and commissioned pieces and allowed him really the run of the toy shop. That's essentially what it was – his expression of his own personality through the resources of the Southbank. That doesn't seem very radical now, but it was quite radical at the time.'

It was beyond merely radical. Look at the offering: a multi-art form festival, running in the unfashionable summer months, curated by a leading modernist composer. Ambitious for sure, foolhardy perhaps, a formula for failure possibly. It was 1993. 'Serious' Director Claire Whitaker puts it into the perspectives of her own experience: 'What "Meltdown" started and became looks so familiar now. But in the nineties, it was really pioneering. "Meltdown" started from a contemporary classical point of view and then moved into a whole range of genres, which gave a different perspective. It was that that was so interesting, allowing a focus on that perspective, which feels part of our lexicon of programming now. Then it was very new, fresh. "Meltdown" was an amazing project, it got riskier by the year. The riskier it became, the more successful it was. It influenced thinking around arts programming a lot.'

If it was to mean anything, 'Meltdown' had to be more than a one-season wonder. It needed to continue and Alex Poots witnessed its progression into still more adventurous artistic territory the following year, 1994: 'When I joined, the series curator was Louis Andriessen. That was a very smart choice because Louis is in a way the European – he doesn't like to be called the European minimalist – whose new music was influenced not just by classical but also by jazz and certain rock instrumentation. By choosing Louis, you inevitably had to embrace a wider range of musical disciplines but it was still within the canon of classical music. It wasn't until the third season when the curator was Elvis Costello, who was a pop person, but reached over the aisle into the classical world. I thought the sequencing was very thoughtful, because it went from pure classical to classical reaching out, and then on to a brilliant songwriter who also had shown interest in classical arrangements and music.'

All the signs are that cautious radical Sheffield knew where he wanted to take 'Meltdown'. Here were classical music and pop and rock side by side in the same sequence of programming. By 1995, he could feel that he had achieved something distinctive: 'The making of "Meltdown" was when Elvis Costello agreed to do the third year in '95. People said, "My goodness, when did Elvis Costello curate a festival at a main public sector venue?" But he alongside a lot of other musicians of his type were deep thinkers, not just pop/rock artists but had deep connections to world music, rock music, jazz music. We were able to broaden the palette in a radical way in those three years, from George Benjamin to Louis Andriessen to Elvis Costello.'

This should not be surprising. Behind the immediate demands for a radical new type of programming for keeping an innovation fresh, Sheffield had a broader philosophical perspective. He would not have been able to develop or even express it within the BBC. It involved a view of the entire modern classical scene and where it might go: '"Funky modernism" of the school of Steve Martland and the Dutch minimalists brought a more radical edge to the programming and appealed to a different audience. I was trying to show that you could have different aspects of contemporary music. It wasn't just monolithic, post-Stockhausen, post-Schoenberg serialism, Darmstadt school and so on, it was much broader than that. "Meltdown" didn't just exist in isolation, it was also trying to portray the Southbank as a kind of place that was much more catholic, not just espousing one school of artistic activity.'

Not for the last time Sheffield's outlook included awareness of the place where he was programming it. There was also a disarmingly personal motivation involved: 'It was partly, from my personal perspective, a voyage of learning for me. Which sounds selfish, but I'd been brought up as a classical musician, with exposure to some of the pop music of the '60s, but quite narrowly focused at university and through home life. I needed to broaden my own outlook in order to do the job properly. I still felt quite narrowly focused in music. So part of me was saying, "I wouldn't mind learning about this as well." And taking the audiences with me.'

Such a total commitment to the audience existed in a very different way in Drummond's instincts too. Neither looked to impose tastes on listeners, both wanted to share their knowledge and enthusiasms; both knew audiences couldn't – and shouldn't – be bullied. With 'Diaghilev' and 'Meltdown', each had taken their own first step towards the innovation that would make their reputation. The first risk had been taken, bigger ones would follow. Each would rise to them in their own particular way.

Drummond's festival programming in 1980, '81 and '82, the mid-years of his directorship, was lively, inventive and often brilliantly entertaining. It was though recognizable as typical festival programming, with dashes of random wonder surrounded by, but unconnected with, others of a similar kind. Excellence, yes, discovery, perhaps, connection, slight, intellectual cohesion, never. Plenty of threads for sure but never the persuasive, unarguable coherence of a unifying intellectual, cultural perspective. When one did emerge, there was an appealing innocence to the way that it did.

Turn-of-the-century Vienna had always had a strong appeal for Drummond. In a short space of years, the city had seen major developments in art, music, theatre, design and words. To call it merely cross-pollination would have been wholly inadequate. It was far, far more, he wrote: 'The great figures of turn-of-the-century Vienna wrote as well as painted, painted as well as composed, described as well as designed, thought as well as did, and argued endlessly with each other. Our century has been dominated intellectually by ideas that first found expression in Vienna.'

Mulling this rich proposition over, aware that 1983 saw the centenary of Wagner's death and of Anton Webern's birth, Drummond was told of an ambitious Hamburg State Opera double bill of works by Zemlinsky. Common sense interposed itself. Faced with his torrent of enthusiasm, Sheila Colvin enquired: 'Who is Zemlinsky and if he is so good, why don't I know his work?' In one sense, recorded Drummond, the 1983 Festival was an attempt at an answer to this question.

Drummond also had a mission of intellectual correction to undertake. While Sigmund Freud, Gustav Klimt and Egon Schiele were known and broadly accepted, the writers of the time were less obviously influential and the composers – Schoenberg, Berg, Webern – 'have become the C20s least favourite bogeymen – the Second Viennese School'. All part of 'Vienna 1900', they needed to be seen and understood through all their myriad personal and creative connections.

On this occasion, as Drummond pitched his ideas far and wide, he found others keen to join in. Richard Jarman remembers the atmosphere of near-exhilaration: 'Vienna was different in that it was planned from the word go and a very large part of that festival was grounded in that. He would have different conversations with different people. Talks with Hamburg opera about the Zemlinsky operas. "Look, we are doing this Vienna theme. Please don't bring your Magic Flute, no, we don't want Lucia di Lammermoor, we want Zemlinsky." It was one of those ideas which just felt right. One could see the possibilities, because that Vienna movement covered so many different art forms in itself. Right from the start, John was wanting to make a big theme. One had never really fallen into place until this idea of Vienna came across. Suddenly people were offering things that fell into it or could be persuaded to think about it. And people didn't need much persuasion.'

To capture the interrelated complexity of the time, the work, the people, the relationships is almost impossible. It was all driven by a sense of intellectual purpose and, in Drummond's mind, of intellectual clarity. One masterstroke was needed. A unifying exhibition capturing the people, the painters, the paintings, the very physical look of 'Vienna 1900'. Drummond first met Peter Vergo, an academic at Essex University, at a Kandinsky exhibition at the Scottish Arts Council's gallery in Edinburgh in 1979. He knew Vergo was a major authority on all things visual in Vienna.

Sheila Colvin was present when they got together: 'John wanted to ask Peter if he could organize an exhibition that could match his vision and he outlined his ideas. Peter said, "By an extraordinary coincidence I'm just about to take a year's sabbatical and I would love to do this." Then Andrew Patrick, Director of the Fine Arts Society, put us in touch with the London-based CEO of Q8 Oil, Bruce Dawson. He contacted Creditanstalt in Vienna. They came on board with substantial support. It was all coming together, it absolutely came to its apogee in '83.'

Vergo and Drummond rapidly agreed on the shape and purpose of the exhibition. Neither was interested in 'just another exhibition!'. They saw it as including sculpture, politics, architecture, drama, music, all the arts of the time. Most daringly, when would they do it? That very same year, 1983, not just a tight timetable surely a well-nigh impossible one for a major exhibition starting from scratch? Vergo said, 'I'll draw up a list of objects. If we get 70 per cent of them, it will be worthwhile and a knockout exhibition too.'

Its philosophy was at the heart of the Festival. You would see an object, a manuscript, a painting, a portrait and see a performance related to one of them that evening in a theatre, or concert hall. The intellectual ambition cannot be overestimated. As Vergo wrote, the exhibition would show 'how the work of Mahler, Freud, Kokoschka, Berg, Kraus, Zemlinsky and architects like Kolo Moser and Josef Hoffmann interconnected'. Because that was what the entire Festival would do as well. I can confirm personally as a festival visitor that making connections in such a way was not only unheard of elsewhere but added immeasurably to the audience's experience of 'Vienna 1900', as displayed in Edinburgh in 1983.

It was typical of Drummond to join Vergo in Vienna for the treasure hunt of exhibition objects, perhaps the kind of activity he loved above all. It was revealing for an outsider like Vergo to see Drummond at work. They spoke the same language, they trusted one another. Drummond, he said, worked like 'a demon' as the reality of his vision took shape before his eyes. It was a bravura performance, recalls Vergo: 'The Viennese were knocked sideways by his ambition. "1983?" they said. "You're doing it THIS year?" It would be impossible today, but 1983 was a different world.'

Together, there seemed no limit to their daring, sometimes with Vergo in the lead: 'We went to the Historical Museum of the City of Vienna, a major city cultural institution. One of its star exhibits, prominently displayed, was Arnold Schoenberg's portrait of Alban Berg. A composer who was an artist painting a portrait of a fellow composer, Alban Berg. Drummond said, "You'll never get it!" I said, "Let's try." Drummond bet me a bottle of champagne that I wouldn't. I got the painting and the champagne.'

The object was the purest expression of the interconnections 'Vienna 1900' was seeking to capture. At festival time the atmosphere was intense, almost intoxicated. I shared and felt it as a visitor. It seemed almost everyone understood they were taking part in something special. Sheila Colvin in the Festival office certainly did: 'You just felt that something extraordinary was happening. The exhibition was so interesting. And heavens above, we had all of Schoenberg's family here. Once you're in the middle of it, you're so busy being in the middle of it. Afterwards, it became even clearer what an extraordinary festival it was.'

Drummond himself was on a permanent high. Perhaps one of the reasons for its success was the combination of intellectual confidence, presentational showmanship, repertory innovation and unashamed didacticism. Vergo ended his essay about his 'Vienna 1900' exhibition like this: 'The inter-relations between the arts, the changes that occurred in society, in intellectual and political life are important threads running through the exhibition, whose purpose is to evoke a sense of time and place, to paint a picture of a period so similar in many ways to our own and yet so far removed from us'.

Drummond was in still more reflective mood in his own Festival Yearbook essay: 'Change does not just happen; it is instigated; while the pace and acceptance of change depends on the existence of a cultural climate in which artists of different disciplines know and can learn from each other even if often by rejection'.

That was not the cultural world that he saw all about him. And there was an almost stoic recognition that his audiences might not be ready to look as closely at themselves in the intellectual mirror of the past as he would want: 'It is a tidy and convenient thing to package the past. Order in history is often nothing more than the outrageous invention of the historian. But there was a *Zeitgeist*, a Viennese spirit of the age, and it still matters. Whether we like it or not, we are the children of those ideas.'

Stoic certainly, valedictory too. That was Drummond's last Festival – physically exhausted, demoralized by Council bureaucracy, worn out by fighting for his artistic beliefs. Undermined too perhaps by his own reluctance to occasionally fight a tactical battle, his elevation of disagreements to matters of high principle. Some would say that he was his own worst enemy. True or not, he was without question the creator of the most coherent, intellectually ambitious annual festival that anyone has ever seen. Whatever his failings, that remains some monument to his many complex and manifold abilities and virtues.

Drummond was to have an outwardly successful and long career back in the BBC, first as controller of BBC Radio 3, then as a long-serving director of BBC Proms. No one could presume to call that any kind of failure yet for his close friend and colleague, Richard Jarman, even the years at the BBC Proms could not compare with the dazzling star that was 'Vienna 1900' in Edinburgh, 1983: 'His Proms were full of good things but you can't point to something in the Proms, or indeed Radio 3, and say, "Well, that was absolutely John's achievement." "Vienna 1900" was the summit. It's the thing he would be remembered for most. Something that happened for three weeks, which was utterly extraordinary and distinctive, and you could say it displayed John's abilities in a nutshell.'

The trajectory of Drummond's career: explosive achievement followed by admirable predictability. Hardly a failure though perhaps even to Drummond personally something of a disappointment. Yet it should not have been a surprise. Drummond was a polymath, an artistic jackdaw with a daring flair for picking up the brilliant, the unexpected, the diverting. The BBC Proms were about music alone, he didn't even enjoy opera. A large part of his artistic personality, his impresario's genius, lay unused on the shelf. It might have been frustrating but if it was, he never spoke of it in those terms.

Drummond's was an extreme example of one possibility of an artistic career. Graham Sheffield's could hardly be more different. He was appointed arts director at the Barbican Centre in 1995; I became managing director just a few months later. Neither of us had illusions about the weakness of the 12-year-old Centre's artistic reputation with critics despite some notable annual festivals such as Humphrey Burton's 'Tender is the North'.

This was how Sheffield took stock of his new responsibility; I did not disagree with the analysis: 'The Barbican was a very formal institution. Chaotic in its layout but still formal in a kind of Soviet way. It didn't brook for any kind of flexibility or audience movement. Coming to terms with the aesthetics of the architecture and the building took me a while, to understand how to make the building work, because the building was such a strong statement in its own right. The programming ethos of the Barbican was so conservative that it was hard to know where to start. Contemporary promoters wouldn't look at it; younger audiences wouldn't come. The LSO was doing sterling work of a certain kind and the RSC was churning out Shakespeare by the yard. Almost every space in the Barbican was unfit for what it was doing. It was the case of the architecture leading the thinking in the sense that we had to do radical things with the spaces in order to do more radical things with the programme. There was little or none of the international approach that you saw in the two templates that were in my mind at the time – the Edinburgh Festival, then run by Brian McMaster, and Brooklyn Academy, run by Joe Melillo. I was always looking at those programmes and thinking, "Why do we not see this in London?"'

Concealed in that overview is an important clue to Sheffield's approach to humanizing what was sometimes felt to be a scaly dragon of a building clad in a protective, even defensive, carapace of concrete. Chris Denton, his marketing and audience development manager, spotted the problem and the opportunity: 'The problem here is defining something by its buildings. If you define it by its buildings, you're missing the point. It's what goes on in and around and outside the buildings, which is what matters. With the Barbican Centre, whether you like it or loathe it, whether you got lost in its labyrinth, it was defined by its buildings. More so than any other arts centre, the Barbican needed to put art at the top of the mountain to change that story.'

To do so, Sheffield looked abroad to New York, where the Brooklyn Academy of Music (BAM) with its arts director Joe Melillo was opening windows on an entire new generation of composers and performers. It was not, Melillo insists, experimental art, but mature artistic work from artists ignored by the Manhattan arts establishment: 'There was no contemporary non-traditional performing arts festival in New York City in 1983. This was to be the first time that a cultural institution, an artistic enterprise of the city of New York, was throwing the gauntlet down to create a performing arts festival with that unique focus. They were New York City based artists who were being denied opportunities to do work in their own city. Philip Glass, Laurie Anderson, Steve Reich could not get their work done at the recognized citadels of performing arts culture for New York City in 1983. Carnegie Hall, Lincoln Center for the Performing Arts, they blocked out these New Yorkers who were creating large-scale complicated works. But these New Yorkers among many others had to go to either the British Isles or the continental European communities to get their large-scale work done.'

Graham Sheffield was one who responded to the revelation of the BAM artistic scene. This was not without risk. Why should the still-conservative London audience respond to the most innovative work coming out of the United States, usually by almost unknown or at least unfamiliar composers and performers?

Chris Denton saw the scale of the challenge Sheffield faced: 'At that point you had an environment where classical concerts were very formulaic. The context of that time would have been a model that was tried and tested and stuck in the mud. He was a revolutionary at that point because of what he was kicking against. The history of the Barbican was it had never really found its way. It had no identity. You needed to do something bold, some "10,000 volts shock treatment", because you were playing catch-up with the Southbank Centre, which was doing it perfectly adequately. The Barbican had to be made "cool". Barbican became known as a cool, genre-blurring sort of venue, which was cutting edge. The work we did on the identity and the brand and all that was bold. I think his programming reflected that.'

Of all the 'cross-art form' programmes Sheffield developed, 'BITE', the Barbican International Theatre Event, was a first pioneering project and utterly different from anything available elsewhere in the United Kingdom: 'I felt that BITE was the absolute epitome that I wanted to express through a cross-arts lens in the fact that it was beginning to include technology in a way that hadn't been imagined before. You think of the work we did with Merce Cunningham and the digital dance work. Also, the visual arts were involved in the programme, and dance, and opera, none of which had been seen ever on that stage. It was also risky because I remember you put aside £250,000 in the first year as a contingency, which we had to use. It took a year for people to know what the bloody hell had hit them because we were pumping in big shows, probably too fast for the audience to catch up.'

If 'BITE' was the start of the 10,000 volts treatment to put life into the Barbican's Frankenstein-like arts reputation, Sheffield then took what was perhaps a similar risk. A single festival devoted entirely to new American arts in 1998. No one could fault Sheffield for lack of ambition: 'The "Inventing America" idea was even larger than "Meltdown" at the South Bank because this was taking the venues and doing something for a whole year in all the spaces and essentially painting the venue with one colour. That's something you'd never do nowadays. It obliged the artform and the resident ensembles to work together in a way that nobody could ever have foreseen. I remember the John Cage day, when we had stuff all over the place and people were discovering corners of the Barbican that probably had never been touched since it had been opened.'

Alex Poots is under no illusions about the scale of the unfashionable risk Sheffield took with this keystone project: 'He pointed in the right direction. "Inventing America" is still one of the great ideas. I'll never forget the *Daily Telegraph*, I think it was, which said, "A year of American culture! We could get through that in one weekend." It was such an ignorant thing to say. And I thought, right, let's prove them wrong.'

Here, Sheffield, in some respects a cautious or at least a prudent person, was taking risks on a Drummond-esque scale. He put his judgement on the line, based on decades of experience in the arts: 'If I'm being self-analytical, yes, I have some wacky ideas; yes, I trust my instincts, more than maybe I should sometimes. No, I don't like reading long consultants' reports. Yes, I'm sometimes opportunistic in that I see potential where others may not see [it] and having the guts to go for it and convince others to support me in that change. It's just seeing the potential and going for it.'

Sheffield certainly recognized potential in the work Joe Melillo was presenting at BAM. But for Melillo, the relationship was a two-way street: 'When you cast your eyes over the world, it's the Barbican that comes up as being: "Oh, they're interested in theatre, they're interested in dance, they're interested in opera and every innovation and progressive idea that relates to that". Graham was supervising a group of curators in dance theatre and music. Meeting his people and talking about artists, talking about projects was a very important resource for my work in Brooklyn. My job was to find the most mature artistic work coming from these contemporary communities that would have resonance in New York City. That meant the production values had to be perfect. The content had to have gravitas to it. It had to be something that we'd never seen before. He got it. It's the aesthetic quality that maintains throughout my experience with Graham. I learned from him. I was learning about his perception of art, his perception and understanding, of his own art, music, and his governance of the curators who were part of the Barbican structure and his interaction with them.'

Sheffield's real creative trajectory of more than a decade at the Barbican was as lengthy as Drummond's was brief. If little could match, still less outdo the astonishing energy and daring of the early years of 'BITE', 'Inventing America' and their successors, his approach to arts planning was established as a kind of norm to be assumed, aspired to: working with all the arts, encouraging their interaction and co-operation, helping them to feed off and with one another. He hated the silos in which too many of the arts existed most of the time; he wanted to wean audiences off their resort to silo-visiting. His ideals remain, his approach too as valid today, perhaps as urgently needed, as it was a generation ago in 'Meltdown'.

The two impresarios remain separated in the way they exerted their influence. The difference should not be surprising. Drummond's method was public, upfront, daring and fearless. Few were left unimpressed.

This real ability to perform and persuade in public came with occasional unexpected terrors attached. On their way to Tbilisi in Georgia to see the Rustaveli Company, Drummond knew he would need the best of his National Service-acquired Russian language on such an occasion. Credibility, authority were involved. Richard Jarman witnessed those too: 'John was terrified about his Russian because he was supremely confident on the outside, but a bag of nerves inside. We were transiting planes in Frankfurt and I had studied Russian, not A-level Russian but that kind of level. So, I spoke Russian a bit. We were sitting in Frankfurt airport and he said, "You're going to have to test me on my Russian." We spoke Russian a bit or I tested him on verbs. Of course, he didn't need it at all when he got there.'

When the BBC Symphony Orchestra visited Moscow in 1986, I was present when Drummond delivered an entire press conference in what seemed like fluent Russian. It was a *tour de force*. Yet anxiety lurked behind the bravura. Jarman recalls his linguistic uncertainty involving Italian: 'We were putting the '82 festival together, which was all about things Italian. We were going to meet the minister of culture in the Senate Building in Rome. And he said, "My Italian's far too rusty, I don't know what I'll do." So he spoke a bit of Italian over lunch together. Then he met the minister, the switch turned on and he conducted a monologue with this poor minister in fluent and idiomatic Italian for half an hour.'

Drummond's ability to mobilize support in the most public ways was his way of persuading and exerting influence. Sheffield's, as his character suggested, was more private, more personal, more collegiate, more practical and in Claire Whitaker's experience no less effective: 'He was very good at that melting pot of ideas, of choosing the ones that were going to be taken forward, or listening to the people that work for him about the ones they wanted to take forward. It was relatively nimble to work at the Barbican. There was a shorter chain of command, an ability to get Graham in a room if there was a problem.

There were a couple of big opportunities that we had, things that were strategically potentially quite tricky that we had to get sorted. We were able to do that on the day.'

The two impresarios had subtly different estimates of their own nature and character. These too are revealing. In *Tainted by Experience*, Drummond sounds a perhaps uncharacteristically modest note: 'I am not a specialist but a generalist with more than a superficial knowledge of several different areas.' To which even his critics might add approvingly, 'Some generalist!'

Sheffield digs somewhat deeper in an important part of his character which brings him closer in approach to Drummond: 'I absolutely hate indecision. I've always been more of an impulsive person, which squares with what I say about going with my gut feeling ahead of research and retrofitting research to my ideas. I'm impatient so, using the vernacular, I've never been great at "fannying" around. The frustrations that have come have been from the slow nature of decision-making in big organizations, certainly at the BBC. If I see somewhere, I really want to get there.'

Both got to their strikingly different destinations using different methods, deploying their strikingly different personalities in whatever ways seemed appropriate. One left behind a model of how to shape a festival that remains unbettered to this day. The other created a blueprint for planning long seasons of the arts in a way few have matched. At once loners and intensely gregarious, both were passionate in their beliefs about the precious value of the arts.

Sheffield managed to be both innovative and original in his thinking and to carry it out within the confines of large organizations. Perhaps his sometimes-understated manner disarmed concern at the nature of what he was really doing. It wasn't so much that the organizations he worked for wisely accommodated his inventiveness, rather that he adapted his overt manner to innovate in a bureaucratically unthreatening way.

Drummond in his Edinburgh Festival incarnation was an unbiddable genius incapable of managing his instincts for the slightest accommodation with paymasters whom he regarded as fools. In his later BBC career, he played the role of artistic court jester for the BBC governors with easy, persuasive, practised charm and humour. But it was no good: his genius for the imaginative, the daring, the thrilling had gone. It was a hollow act. Even the BBC in all its tolerance would have found the Edinburgh Drummond impossible to handle. If that was their loss, given that it was not on offer, it was far more Drummond's personal tragedy.

Contrasted as they are, yards apart in manner, personality and outlook, what if each had been able to learn from the other? What if Drummond had a fraction of Sheffield's systematic, intellectual approach to programming? And if Sheffield had several doses of Drummond's showmanship and capacity to persuade and entertain? What if Drummond had been more cautious and Sheffield had taken more risks? What an arts impresario we might have had. But don't overlook what the two, with all their differences, or all their acknowledged shortcomings, actually achieved. Perhaps they had to be as they had to be. Audiences benefited.

Observations

- ✦ Arts impresarios are not taught, they may emerge.
- ✦ A major arts leadership role depends on knowledge, not power and authority. Knowledge is the basis of personal authority and comes from personal curiosity.
- ✦ Possessing knowledge about the arts does not make you a better person than those who may lack it or just know less.
- ✦ Love of the arts is not a selfish activity; knowing about the arts is a personal and professional responsibility.
- ✦ Understanding the arts cannot be delegated to outside consultants as valuing the arts cannot be guided by or reduced to mere numbers.
- ✦ Personal expertise allows the arts leader to take audiences where they did not know they might enjoy going. Personal knowledge should not leave audiences so far behind that they do not wish to follow.
- ✦ Understanding the physical nature of an arts venue is essential for working in it successfully.
- ✦ The arts must be imagined before they can be presented.
- ✦ The arts are led but must also be managed. If the two activities are in tension or in conflict, the arts will not flourish.
- ✦ Arts creativity can be explosive or linear. It depends on who is detonating the explosion, who is developing the line.
- ✦ There is nothing to be said for the safe or routine in the arts. Practised caution turns out to be boring and without a future.
- ✦ Creativity cannot be achieved by careful calculation.

References

John Drummond (director) BBC Television 'Omnibus' 1968 *Diaghilev: The Years Abroad; Diaghilev: The Years in Exile.*

John Drummond, *Speaking of Diaghilev* (Faber & Faber, 1997).

John Drummond, *Tainted by Experience: A Life in the Arts* (Faber & Faber, 2001).

Edinburgh International Festival Guide 1983: 'Vienna 1900'.

John Tusa, *Making a Noise: Getting it Right, Getting it Wrong in Life, the Arts and Broadcasting* (Weidenfeld and Nicolson 2018).

4

'Spanning the Globe': World Service Television News

Featuring interviews with:

Rachel Attwell, Editor, BBC World Service Television, 1995–2000

Sir Michael Checkland, BBC Director-General, 1987–92

Christopher Irwin, Chief Executive, BBC World Service Television, 1990–94

Sharon Purtill, Office Manager, BBC WSTV, 1987–95

Ian Richardson, News Development Editor, 1991–97

Richard Sambrook, former Director, BBC Global News

Jack Thompson, WSTV News Reporter

'Every journey begins with a single step,' says the old Chinese proverb. So it was with the start of what was to become the BBC's most-watched TV channel. Like all first steps, the first live transmission of BBC World Service Television News at 7 p.m. on 11 March 1991 was partly routine: a half-hour news programme to be sure, but one with a wholly international reporting agenda. A pleasantly, electronically modified version of the time-honoured BBC World Service radio identification tune, 'Lilliburlero', a modern-ish twirling globe, led briskly to a personable, white, male journalist presenter at a desk. He and it seemed to inhabit a very small space indeed. There was no sign of a studio of any kind, just a desk and a hand-painted backdrop. It might have existed in a broom cupboard (it did).

Without frills, the presenter led viewers watching on European cable networks, hopefully, through a steady sequence of international news stories. Opposition in the streets of Belgrade was growing to Yugoslavia's President Milošević: was he more interested in holding Yugoslavia together, or just devoted to Serbia? US Secretary of State James Baker arrived in Israel as six Arab gunmen were shot trying to infiltrate Israel. The question on every lip: could a land for peace deal break the cycle of violence in the Middle East for a generation? Organization of the Petroleum Exporting Countries (OPEC) ministers gathering for the first time since the Gulf War to talk about cutting oil production quotas. It is at once a remote yet a distressingly familiar world.

The TV journalistic format though was perhaps surprisingly, new: a wholly global news agenda made by a BBC radio division, BBC World Service, that had never broadcast in television before. Many in the BBC thought it shouldn't do so now in part because it did not know how to. Of domestic news from Britain, there was none. That was the point. It was a news service for the world, not a single nation. Those taking part were aware of its potential and its true aims.

One of the first of the news presenters, Jack Thompson, had no doubts about the underlying ambition: 'We needed to challenge the American view of the world and the news output of pro-government organizations in China and Russia. There was a feeling that we should challenge Murdoch with coverage that was deeper and more extensive. We really knew our stuff and wanted to pass on our knowledge and expertise.'

This first single step would ultimately lead to the creation of one of the most influential television news networks in the world. It would have to overcome political opposition,

internal indifference and hostility within the BBC, regulatory
scrutiny, attempts to close it down, financial crises. It would
live with cultural clashes, constant uncertainty and continuous
questioning. That it did so was principally the work of just three
executives: BBC Director-General Michael Checkland, James
Arnold Baker, head of BBC Enterprises, and Chris Irwin, later
to become chief executive of WSTV. Each responded to a great
idea, a bold idea: 'to span the globe by 1995'. Each would own
it, nourish it, defend it, develop it, make it happen, turn it from
a dream into reality. It could never have been achieved by just
a single person, that would have been to ask too much. Oddly,
they never worked as a group, but each intervened and took
responsibility at critical moments with decisive action. Their
personal commitment proved to be its secret weapon.

Over the years, many individuals had indeed tried to 'own'
the big idea. It had taken almost a quarter of a century to take
the first step of that very ordinary-looking first news bulletin.
Before that, every attempt to start a World Service Television
network of any kind had failed sometimes ignominiously. The
path was strewn with casualties; the wonder is not that a first step
was finally taken, but that anyone had the stamina to persevere
beyond those initial disasters.

As far back as 1968, Charles Curran, the director of BBC
External Broadcasting, precursor of the later BBC World
Service, proposed an ambitious scheme. Bush House in
central London's Kingsway – home and seat of external radio
broadcasting – should launch an international television
service. In high visionary style, in some senses prophetic,
Curran dreamed of a service delivered to a global audience by
satellite, those satellites launched into orbit by rockets bought
by the BBC. This was so far ahead of anything in the realms of
broadcasting practicality at the time that it crashed and burned
before receiving serious scrutiny. A notional cost of £40 million

and the fact that Bush House worked with effectiveness and distinction in radio but had no expertise in or inclination for television hardly helped matters.

It was 16 years, in 1984, before another director of BBC External Services, Douglas Muggeridge, put his toes into the water of what would always be a contentious subject. The problem was less that Muggeridge's TV scheme, in contrast with Curran's earlier Space Age fantasies, disastrously lacked vision: for him, a television channel consisted of Bush House's radio-based journalism illustrated by still photographs and explanatory graphics. It would be cheap for sure but well short of the brave new world intended for the BBC's international arm. Muggeridge's major offence was a politico-bureaucratic one: he told no one within top BBC management that he was going public on the idea. The BBC Director-General, Alasdair Milne, his superior, was incandescent and publicly rebuked and humiliated Muggeridge. This was only the first occasion that BBC internal politics were to prove a determining factor in the wavering fortunes of something that might finally become World Service Television.

Faced with these hard lessons, the incoming MD of BBC External Broadcasting in September 1968 might have been pardoned for never letting world service television cross his lips. Indeed, he might have been advised so to do. That newcomer was myself. I was not indifferent to the ugly lessons of the past, prudence demanded that I should be. But I was aware that the world had changed, the environment in which any discussion of WSTV would take place was quite different, especially politically. For in April 1986, the United States bombed President Gaddafi's Libya. The comparatively new global news network, CNN, was there to cover it in detail, by the minute, every day.

A huge shockwave swept through the BBC, according to newsroom editors such as Ian Richardson: 'When the

Americans bombed Libya and CNN came into its own, there was the feeling of "my God, we the BBC are being taken to the cleaners by CNN". The awful feeling, as we sat in the newsroom, watching CNN on all the screens around the newsroom and thinking, "why aren't we there?". There was an awful lot of scepticism about television. "World Service radio is great. Why do you need television? It's terribly expensive at any rate". It didn't occur to most people that we should be involved in it. Except for those of us sitting watching CNN on TV screens thinking, "well, why aren't we there?".'

Chris Irwin, soon to be a foundation figure in the successful establishment of WSTV, also witnessed the CNN shockwaves sweeping through offices across the BBC – and something else too: 'Offices on the third floor in Broadcasting House were tuned into CNN television, watching what was happening there. They were not listening to World Service. We were watching Ted Turner. For me, it was a realization that it was just not credible to think about the BBC being represented worldwide without a strong television leg. The problem was that there was a great scepticism about the motives, the commitment, the reliability of World Service radio colleagues as allies. I remember very intelligent, very trustworthy, wise colleagues talking about the "Bush House loons". The perception was that Bush House "radio purism" was really too great to be accommodated in the real world of television.'

Great institutional and cultural clashes were to come, many of them arising around this deep philosophical fault-line. In the political, international and journalistic crisis of 1986, fresh understanding and a new clarity were required. Some, like BBC Director of Resources, BBC Television's Michael Checkland, soon to become director-general, had that understanding: 'I always wanted to be a competitor to CNN. When I'd been involved with the commercial side of the BBC, and before becoming DG, I visited CNN and met Ted Turner [CNN's owner]. When I went around hotels around Europe on international travel, I couldn't bear the fact that I saw CNN all the while. The BBC was not there. The more it came across my desk as a possibility, in a sense through experiencing CNN, I was thinking, "we've got to do something about this". The ideas entirely came via the World Service, never from News and Current Affairs, never from the domestic BBC. Because they saw "overseas" as Bush House's problem.'

This left the responsibility for finding a funding method on Checkland's desk and his personal agenda, a responsibility that he took upon himself. His search for funding for WSTV had to be flexible and adaptable and would certainly take him to some unlikely lunch tables: 'We had this bizarre evening with Robert Maxwell. He arrived an hour late and we had champagne and caviar. I took the opportunity to ask him for a couple of million pounds for WSTV. My colleagues were amazed that I did this but I was trying to think of any radical way we could find to get money into the BBC. It might not have gone down well if I'd been successful, but in fact, Maxwell didn't agree.'

Daring pieces of opportunism like that apart, the far larger problem holding up WSTV's faltering evolution was the faultlines opening up within the BBC at almost every stage. Bush House purists thought TV brash and unsuited to covering the dense, myriad complexities of global news. TV News and Current Affairs knew that domestic British viewers and listeners would be bored to incomprehension by what they judged to be the obscure news obsessions of their opposite numbers at Bush House.

Former Director, BBC Global News Richard Sambrook observed it at close quarters: 'As ever within the BBC, there's always territorial jockeying. The Television Service felt they knew about television and the World Service was about radio.

Therefore, if there was going to be a new television channel, it should be run by people who understood television. Which was a pretty short-sighted view because the crucial thing for a global channel was the global expertise and insight that it could offer. You had to have something which could tap into the journalistic expertise of the World Service, but use the TV production expertise of the rest of the BBC as well.'

Such entrenched attitudes apart, based on habit and prejudice as much as on reason, Sambrook points out that in 1986, BBC newsgathering itself was a frail thing, reluctant as the BBC itself might be to admit it: 'The BBC at that time prided itself on international news, of course, with the World Service. But the BBC's UK service had very little foreign coverage. It had no television bureau on the European mainland and very little resource elsewhere. It lived quite a lot off the news agencies – Reuters and WTN, as it then was. In terms of global coverage and scale, BBC news gathering was nothing like what we take for granted today.'

The BBC is often described, pejoratively, as a monolith. This is far from the case and was certainly not so in the 1980s and 1990s when WSTV was emerging. The BBC consisted of four strong, almost independent baronies: BBC Television, BBC Radio, BBC World Service and BBC News and Current Affairs. They were shortly to be joined by the BBC's new commercial arm, BBC Enterprises. Each was led by a powerful managing director dedicated to maintaining the interests of *their* barony. Some with a historical perspective likened it to 'bastard feudalism', not intended as a compliment. It proved almost too much to expect that the barons and their vassals might subsume local interests in the pursuit of an overriding BBC aim and project. Was BBC World Service Television to be such an overriding collective, central BBC priority? Only in the minds of a very few. Who was to make it one? The bombing of Libya and CNN's dominant response at least kept the notion of WSTV alive, but without central organization and a central sense of purpose it was a struggle. It was left to BBC World Service and to myself, its new and inexperienced managing director, to pursue. For me and my colleagues, we floundered and ended up in a series of institutional and financial dead ends. We had the idea, we could not deliver it.

Leaving aside the editorial and programme making challenges, the blunt reality was that there was no funding for WSTV in any shape or form. The only approach to funding that we could conceive of was a further tranche of the direct government grant in aid, which funded BBC World Service radio. Within weeks of my taking over as managing director of BBC World Service (BBCWS), in November 1986, we submitted a bid of £7.8m to the Foreign and Commonwealth Office (FCO). To reinforce the strength, purpose and ambition of our bid, Director-General Alasdair Milne hosted a small dinner at Broadcasting House for the permanent secretary at the FCO, Sir Patrick Wright. He made it quite clear that the government would not fund any such project. Many years later, Wright assured me that the FCO itself had not opposed the idea of WSTV. But the Foreign Secretary, Sir Geoffrey Howe, was so frightened of a row with then-Prime Minister Margaret Thatcher that he put the WSTV file at the bottom of his in-tray whenever it rose to the top.

The idea was, surely, officially dead. Somehow it would not quite lie down. Pilot programmes continued to be made at BBC Television Centre throughout 1987 under the most exiguous of conditions and a variety of shaky financial pretexts.

Office Manager Sharon Purtill was sent on a three-month attachment from Bush House newsroom. It turned into three years, working on the final pilot programmes while also running news trainees from both Bush House and television news. She worked and lived on scraps of unused BBC news resources and sheer goodwill: 'We did pilot programmes in the beginning, where we'd come into the newsroom after the TV One O' Clock news bulletin was over and take over the newsroom desks. Then we would beg, borrow and steal people who were interested and were prepared to give some of their time to help us make the programme. We would call on those that had been through the training programme already to help out in the evening. It's as if we used to get the newsroom "for free" afterwards. And when the TV Nine O'Clock News came off-air, we were able to use their studio to record the pilot.'

This extraordinary internal BBC pragmatism allowed pilot programme making activity to continue even though the project as such had no bureaucratic or financial existence. There was no formal authorization. These programmes existed at a low level of activity completely distant from the high-level politics being played out on a very different plane. If in Westminster political terms, WSTV was dead, we only came to know what actually happened much later. Mrs Thatcher would indeed have argued with Geoffrey Howe about a BBC proposal for WSTV, probably hand-bagged him. She had 'no inclination to do the BBC any favours'. She was under huge pressure from Chief Executive David Nicholas and Alastair Burnet, the authoritative main presenter at the far more politically simpatico Independent Television News (ITN) to fund their own planned international news network. The fact that theirs never got off the studio floor was less important than the fact that David Nicholas's guerrilla tactics in Downing Street quashed any slim chance of the government funding the WSTV project. By March 1988 it was finally, politically buried.

Negative as this seemed at the time, Chris Irwin now believes that it was the decision that set WSTV on a more productive path: 'I think the government may have been right. I don't think they were as obstructive as we sometimes painted them as being.

We funded WSTV in the end without government funds. All Thatcher was doing was following her own position vis-à-vis public finance and saying, "There must be another way, there must be a better way".'

Certainly, BBC minds now focused on more commercial directions for WSTV funding, woefully inexperienced as we were here too. If this approach required a business plan, we needed a leading merchant bank to draw one up for us. It was not a success. The City advisers adopted conventional ideas from within BBC TV and News to the effect that WSTV would make individual programmes to be sold as and when possible. Irwin, an increasingly influential figure, was already ahead in his thinking. Such ideas were inadequate. It was time, he argued, to think of an entire network, a connected sequence of integrated programme material within an overall network schedule.

This was a much bigger proposition and certainly needed, if any competition was to be offered to CNN: 'The merchant bankers' plans were too programme focused, not service focused. They conceived of World Service TV as a series of discrete news programmes which would be sold around the world. I've never believed in non-streamed broadcasting. You need to lever the perception of BBC in all its breadth, to wrap up the news element in other programming sweeteners in a total network, a linear service. You need to have the programmes that sustained the place for news in the overall schedule.'

Irwin alone was wrenching the entire concept into a new and ultimately the only possible viable form. In due course, he spelled it out: 'I don't think that that debate was ever really forced out into the open. Many people still conceived of BBC World Service television as the BBC World Service television "news programme". Undoubtedly, that was a jewel. Whereas my view was always you had to see it in the broader context. I created problems for my own back there, because the argument then became, "can you get decent programmes to surround it?" To me, the individual news programme in isolation was boring. That may have been part of my original scepticism about the project that this wasn't sufficient by itself.'

At least WSTV now had a concept and a conceptual head that shaped its future. No one was thinking with Irwin's radicalism or imagination. Without his vision, the whole project would never have flown. At least the City contribution to the faltering development of WSTV was to make us realize that we needed someone to run it as a venture in its own right. It could not just be an appendage of BBCWS or TV News. Another dead end followed. We engaged major headhunters to find this executive head of a new global TV news channel. This turned into near-farce. Headhunters' shortlists are notoriously unreliable, often padding out a very small cadre of possible candidates for a post with a bevy of the unlikely or the plain unsuitable. In this regard, the headhunters engaged by me at BBCWS excelled themselves. It was indeed a shortlist of just four intended to fill a demanding position in the undefined but potentially revolutionary field of international news television. For this, Irwin, myself and two other colleagues on the selection panel were faced by a bizarre group of candidates.

The occasion is burned into Irwin's memory: 'The headhunters let us down badly when they came up with some very odd people. One had run a specialist fast food chain of restaurants. Another was clearly a beached senior executive who had been working in the shipping industry. The interviews we did with these people were totally dispiriting. We had been seduced by these lovely headhunters to look at a list that was so unlikely from our perspective yet we were not confident enough of the real external world to think that we could make the judgements necessary to run a commercial operation. The BBC inferiority complex, if you like.'

In the aftermath of that disastrous afternoon, we took one decision that proved correct and shaped the future though it was not immediately clear that it would. The best person to be chief executive of the future WSTV was not just staring us in the face, he was sitting alongside us at the interviewing table: Chris Irwin. He had the knowledge, the TV satellite background, he knew the BBC, he was an entrepreneur by instinct. Most importantly, he had already formulated the vision for WSTV. Now he could try to realize it. The future WSTV was no longer just a great idea, now it had a leader.

It was time to take stock with my BBCWS colleagues, or at least those who believed in the desirability of a WSTV network. What did we have to show for what was in effect four years' work since I became BBCWS managing director in September 1986? It was a bleak look at a barren stock. The government was against us; most of the BBC was indifferent or actually obstructive; there was no funding; there were pilot programmes but none that made a decisive case for the potential of an international news network. Then history played its hand.

Saddam Hussein's invasion of Kuwait in the first Gulf War in August 1990 was covered in authoritative, microscopic detail by CNN. The BBC's international reputation as a supposedly global news broadcaster was shredded. It was a second institutional humiliation. At a board of management 'awayday' at Buxted Park in Surrey, Director-General Mike Checkland and I got together. He was emphatic: 'CNN is taking us to the cleaners, this can't happen again'. We had before us a detailed paper sent by Chris Irwin on 6 December 1990, setting out exactly how a WSTV channel would work.

For once the stars of good fortune were aligning in a previously unpredictable fashion. Armed with support from the BBC's board of management, Checkland decided that at the board of governors' meeting immediately following, he would propose a joint venture between BBCWS and the BBC's commercial arm, BBC Enterprises, 'to lay the foundations of a television version of the World Service'. This was typical Checkland strategic vision. He was fortified by the emergence of a possible solution to the funding question. It came from what some would have seen as an unlikely source, the head of the BBC's commercial arm, BBC Enterprises, James Arnold Baker. It was wholly unexpected. Baker ingeniously pointed out that the money earned from the BBC's European cable services belonged entirely to the BBC. It was not related to the licence fee that paid for domestic broadcasting, nor was it connected with the grant in aid, which funded BBCWS. It was money which the BBC was free to use, politically and constitutionally, as it thought fit. Checkland saw it as the key that opened the door to setting up actual broadcasting. How extraordinary that the proposal should have come from the person whose job it was to earn money for the BBC handing it over to be spent in this way?

Checkland knew how remarkable Baker's initiative was: 'It wasn't in BBC Enterprises' financial interest at all but James was a rounded man, he was a proper human being. He saw a wider picture than just the straight commercial. James's proposal absolutely turned the key on the project.'

Chris Irwin wholly endorses the Checkland judgement of Arnold Baker as one of the founding fathers of WSTV. In his role as head of BBC Enterprises, Baker could not have had any direct interest in furthering the possibility of WSTV. James was not 'editorial', he was not a 'programme man': he was a commercial operator. Finding funding for the putative WSTV was not remotely in his remit. Irwin accords the credit where it is due: 'It was typical of James's sort of maverick brilliance. It was both maverick brilliance and generosity of spirit. He came up with this very plausible way of dealing with it. Because it wasn't commercial. It wasn't advertising. It lubricated the whole thing. If you've got two or three million pounds, you can service quite a lot of capital with that money.'

That was generous and it was certainly daring. What followed was audacious. Checkland had to persuade the BBC board of governors to approve a historic project of which they knew a little in outline but very little of substance. There was no formal board policy paper before them on the basis of which they could take a decision. If ever there was an issue where the governing body of the BBC should take a major policy decision based on full information, it was surely this. In fact, the BBC board of governors saw no paper on the historic proposal for a World Service Television at all. The rest is history, Checkland in risk-taking mode, an executive using their power and authority at his disposal. It was a board coup: 'I timed it, knowing that as people get near lunch, and quite like lunch, I said, "We'll just slip it in at the very end." And we did. We said, "We've got this idea for funding World Service Television. It comes from our European cable income. It's very important we compete with CNN and others." And the BBC governors said, "That's a good idea" and then went off to lunch. Keith Oates, the "business" governor from Marks & Spencer, said, "That's the most important thing we've discussed today and we're just leaving it like that!" It was only he spotted that I'd slipped it in.'

My own memory of that meeting is that the Checkland coup was as direct, authoritative and effective as he recalls. Certainly, I reeled out of the BBC governors' meeting incredulous that four years of frustration, opposition and dead ends was at an end. Irwin provided the strategic framework; James Arnold Baker had the imagination to provide the financial means; Mike Checkland had the ruthlessness to drive a coach and horses through the bureaucracy. Asked years later what he was most proud of in his time as director-general, Checkland replied, 'Starting World Service Television.' His questioner sounded surprised. He should not have been. Without Checkland, it might not have happened at all. Now it was up to Chris Irwin to deliver the project.

Such was the long and stony road from the very first dreams of WSTV in 1968 to that first pilot programme on 11 March 1991. Important as it was, that programme itself was the smallest of small steps. If WSTV was to be taken seriously in the spectrum of international television journalism, still less a competitor of the well-established, professional and authoritative CNN, then it had first to become a 24-hour network – a tall order of the highest kind.

Ian Richardson witnessed its achievement under the first WSTV editor, Johan Ramsland: 'When you think that it was started in March 1991, with a half-hour programme, and then in October/November it went to the full 24-hour network. Johan Ramsland, his deputy, John Exelby and a handful of colleagues were given three months to put the channel on air. They did it because Johan didn't know it was impossible. It's an absolute triumph. It was absolutely crucial for WSTV.'

Credibility of the fledgling network apart, Chris Irwin, now chief executive, needed something to sell to raise money. The initial funding from BBC European cable networks was essentially seed corn. It was only enough to launch the channel and give it credibility, but far more was now needed to fund a 24-hour network for years ahead. Irwin became an international salesman: 'I was basically doing one continent a week. I was in Hong Kong for monthly meetings. When we got to the United States, trying to get the US interested, that again was highly intensive. Then a colleague said, "New Zealand are keen to get into things," and he had a contact in Australia so went down from Hong Kong to the Antipodes. And then he had a contact in Mnet in South Africa so went across to South Africa. It was just on the go all the time. I was going to territories I didn't know terribly well and trying to sell something that was of benefit to them but would also give greater benefit to us.'

It was not enough for Irwin to win contracts. Now that WSTV was a reality, he had to mind his back politically within the BBC. Far from enjoying unalloyed support for a huge venture from which the BBC would benefit, Irwin found that internal rivalry, even jealousy, were rife: 'The metaphor I had for what I was doing was that of a fighter pilot in the Second World War. I realized I was provoking many hostilities amongst my BBC colleagues, not least in the News and Current Affairs division. My view was that as long as I moved on to the next stage of the project fast enough, the very nature of the BBC wouldn't allow people to catch up with what I had just done.'

Given that I was in a sense Chris Irwin's line manager – it was, after all, 'World Service Television' – I am conscious now of failing to protect him from internal BBC bureaucratic attacks as I should have done. I should also have taken greater care of his personal and physical welfare. He insists to this day that he felt fully supported and protected, given free rein to 'buccaneer' but never to be inhibited or micromanaged by me and Checkland. But Irwin's travel schedule was extreme by any standards, driven – in his own words – by a 'latter-day imperial mission'. If that was what the job and the situation demanded, and he believed that it did, then so, apparently, it had to be. But it was Irwin who ended up paying a considerable personal price: 'I think it's probably why, in my late fifties, I began to get cardiovascular disease. I believed at the time I was working that one only needed to sleep four hours a night. That was the way I would justify it to myself. Get on a plane overnight. And if you really believe in four hours a night, you can do it. Catch up on sleep at weekends. It was mad, but it was very lovely. I enjoyed it very much.'

Irwin's sheer enthusiasm was infectious to his home-based colleagues. Safely ensconced in the mere challenge of making programmes, they were well aware that they needed him to bring home the contracts. Ian Richardson saw his approach: 'If there hadn't been Chris Irwin working on this project and determined to get it going, it wouldn't have got off the ground. He was very determined, very imaginative, very creative on the financial side. He was very good at getting people to understand that they could put money into it. But Chris was someone who specially loved flying. I was amazed at the amount of things he came up with. He was a guy who took the view that "well, why not? Why not?" Sometimes we used to look at him and say, "oh, blimey, how's he going to do this?" The knowledge of what he was doing was limited to a fairly small number of people.'

One of those who fully appreciated the scale and intensity of what Irwin was doing was Director-General Mike Checkland: 'Chris was a powerhouse. He just charged in every direction and was intellectually strong. Which is why we put him in your direction in the first place. I realized he was wasted writing speeches and working for me. He needed a proper job to do. He was a self-starter.'

Irwin would be the first to acknowledge the role played by colleagues as assiduous as himself in making contacts and travelling in their pursuit. Late in 1991, with the WSTV running on a 24-hour schedule, the team discovered that the powerful Li Ka-Shing family in Hong Kong was keen to start a continental-wide TV service. As part of it, they needed a news channel to complete their package. At first it seemed a natural fit for both the Ka-Shing TV and Irwin's WSTV. The Hong Kong negotiations, recalls Irwin, were hard, inevitably so. He had just bought one of those airport 'business theory' self-improvement books. It turned out to be surprisingly useful: 'One of the great things about *The Strategy of the Dolphin* was it said: "when you negotiate, negotiate just by listening to the other person, find out what they want. And then when they're feeling they need it, you give them what they want, you offer them the answer to their inner needs." The Li family told us what they needed. We explained what we could give them and then at a later stage said, "Our terms are such and such."'

It was not to prove quite so easy and led to one of the most dramatic turning points in WSTV's early history. Irwin and colleagues were playing for very high stakes with questionably strong cards. But still they played them: 'We had a very dramatic second negotiation, which had gone on for a week. At the last minute, we thought we'd got a price. At the very last minute, the Ka-Shing family let us know that wasn't what they were prepared to pay. I was staying in the Mandarin Hotel in Hong Kong with my colleagues. We had a midnight conversation and agreed to ring the Ka-Shings overnight to say: "Chris is incandescent with rage, he's walking out". We got on a plane back to London, which in those days had to stop at Delhi on the way. When we got to Delhi, we told the people at Delhi airport: "We're with the BBC. Could we have a room and a telephone because we need to ring Hong Kong?" And they had to patch us through from the BBC through the British Airways office in Delhi through to Hounslow, then back to Hong Kong, where we had this conversation. It resulted in the Chinese climbing down and sending the son, Richard Li, over to London for two weeks. He stayed at The Savoy and we negotiated in their company house in Mayfair and got our deal. But it was a most marvellous moment of tension. And it gave us £10 million a year, which was what we needed to run the service.'

Irwin was not only a super-motivated, possibly slightly manic salesman for the idea and the reality of WSTV, he was manager of a dedicated team. Most importantly, he was now the visionary leader, a position and a role he took seriously. He focused on three things in particular: 'One was to have a very simple mission statement. I always thought the best mission statement was Churchill's for Special Operations Executive (SOE): "Set

Europe ablaze". So my words for WSTV were to "Span the Globe by 1995". And that was a message I kept on spouting wherever I went. The other one was "Resource rich, cash poor". The second important thing was to inculcate these into my team. We used to have a deliberately collegiate atmosphere in World Service Television. I came to the view that you don't ever want to run an organization with much more than 40 people. You need to know everything you can about the people and you need to relate to them on a personal level so they've got a sense of personal commitment to you, and you to them. The third thing, and I feel shame to say this now, was a sense of "the other". The "other" in our case were the purists in BBC World Service radio, television news and current affairs – basically, anyone else in the BBC who looked like being obstructive.'

Admirable as Irwin's goals were, excellent as his defined objectives, correct as the leadership approach was, the seeds of his later fall can be seen in those remarks. He had evolved into the leadership of the WSTV project with remarkable and effective qualities yet he also had to operate in a large, manipulative organization composed of strong personalities, shifting alliances and a keen impulse towards opportunism. For that he required some of the characteristics of 'team player'. If he was somewhat lacking in this department, that denouement lay ahead. For a brief moment, though, WSTV looked almost stable; the channel was running, the funding was secure, it was getting noticed even by its deadly rivals, recalls Ian Richardson: 'We got a phone call one day from CNN, complaining that the signal had gone, the World Service Television signal had gone. Had we cut them off? We said, "No, we'll check – one of the satellites has got a bit of a glitch." Up to that point, we weren't aware that CNN were monitoring us all day long.'

On the other hand, cultural rivalries lived on. Bush House's own newsroom had to be challenged: why did they have CNN on the screens and not World Service television? Some of the more senior people still didn't rate World Service television, thinking CNN got all the good stories. Unfortunately, they had a point which needed addressing. Worse, internally, the whole BBC found it difficult to value a network which had huge potential but was still struggling to have it realized. Richard Sambrook ran into just this wall of incomprehension: 'I had to do a presentation to the BBC's commercial board. I started it by saying, "We're talking about the BBC's most accessible channel." And there were a few guffaws round the table until I pointed out the audience figures and the reach. I said, "By a long margin, this is the BBC's biggest channel and the one that projects the BBC's brand most powerfully around the world. And you were talking about cutting it further or closing it." That was an argument which had real force at the time because nobody had thought of it in those terms. It was seen as a poor relation and a bit of a problem.'

However reluctantly, recalls Sambrook, the BBC could not quite turn its back on the 'poor relation'. There was a further difficulty: WSTV itself had to admit that it was not good enough as a product, it looked amateurish. Sambrook analysed the complexity of the situation that needed putting right: 'In the early days, the television production values weren't great. CNN had more investment in production and was a bit glossier. There wasn't a lot of international competition in the early years. That coincided with a period in the rest of the BBC news services where they were merging radio and television. A lot of radio people were learning about television and television people learning about radio. In that period, production values deteriorated a bit. It was not as good as a BBC channel should have been. That was because the BBC wasn't really able to put its full weight behind it.'

Put accurately, too much of the BBC chose not to put its weight behind WSTV, notably News and Current Affairs and many in the commercial arm, BBC Enterprises. Domestic broadcasters saw their licence fee obligations as lying with the domestic viewers and listeners. Foreign news was by definition just that – foreign – and by extension remote and strange. Many even in BBCWS saw WSTV as an alien entity polluting the purities of the most accurate picture of global events. BBC Enterprises, locked in a loveless marriage with WSTV, saw it as a cost and irksome rather than a source of income. WSTV was a great idea bereft of a powerful and committed owner, supporter and advocate. Checkland spoke up for it as director-general, as did his senior colleagues in BBC Television and Engineering. I spoke up for it as managing director of BBCWS. Yet neither of us was in a full position of ownership. WSTV's complex funding structure made that impossible. Neither of us had the final authority to overrule the internal tensions and conflicts. In reality, the project was kept going by the editorial staff, who believed in its value and would not let go. It was time for them to take over and they did.

Within months of WSTV becoming a global 24-hour news channel, its programmatic weaknesses could no longer be ignored. There was no use pretending, Richard Sambrook recalls. For the BBC, WSTV was always a kind of unfortunate child: 'The quality wasn't great in terms of production. It was okay and innovative in many ways. People were not ashamed of it but it wasn't something they wanted to draw attention to particularly. A lot of the feedback from broadcasting peers, politicians, others was that "this isn't as good as it needs to be". The difficulty was, we can't put more money into it because it wasn't yet breaking even. So the question was, "how do we improve the production values in order that we can be proud of it?". WSTV was seen as something that loses money that isn't quite as good as it needs to be. That was the baggage it had to carry.'

Given such restraints, only one approach to remedying the situation remained: to install as deputy editor of WSTV a first-class broadcasting professional who knew what standards were required. I knew Rachel Attwell from her previous years as a BBC Radio 4 producer. Thereafter she had worked at Independent Television News (ITN). She was surely just what we and WSTV needed. It turned out that in luring Rachel back to the BBC, I did her no favours. Yes, she was originally from the BBC, but her years at ITN were held against her, as she rapidly discovered. She was encouraged to observe the Bush House newsroom at work as part of her induction. For Attwell, it was a revelation and a baptism of fire: 'The World Service newsroom treated me like the woman bringing plague in. Absolutely nobody spoke to me. I sat in a corner with my headphones on and listened to World Service. That was supposed to get me into the World Service ethic, which seemed to me a lot of people standing around with not very much to do and a lot of people in the bar. It was always brilliant but it wasn't television journalism. It wasn't in a competitive world and we were competing against CNN.'

Attwell knew from direct experience and observation that CNN was very good. Somehow she had to fire up the ambitions, the expectations and the standards of the entire WSTV network. She started at the top, on the screen. What did viewers see? What did WSTV look like? She started with the actual studio. They had, she acknowledged, performed miracles: 'They'd taken a storeroom and done incredible things to make it look like a television studio. But it looked like a storeroom. I looked at it and I thought, "oh my God, they do all know this is terrible, don't they? They do all know this is nothing to do with journalism?". But they didn't.'

Next, Rachel considered the journalists on the screen, the network presenters. These were the faces to whom viewers would or would not relate. There was no comfort here: 'The presenters were weak. I can understand why some of the people appointed were there because you had to put a face on the screen. In the end, someone's got to read the news. So the first thing they did when I arrived was say, "Sort the presenters out". And I said, "One or two of these presenters are really not capable." I thought we could waste some contracts and bring in two or three fresh faces. That was a battle.'

As if that was not enough, she found that those journalists from the Bush House newsroom who now worked at WSTV remained totally unreconciled to her and her agenda: 'Then there was the Bush House lot and they were impossible. They were polite, of course, but would not do anything that emanated from me. For instance, there would be a news story, a couple of really quite big stories broke, and we weren't kept updated as it developed.'

There was a gap of comprehension, philosophy, outlook, inclination and tradition. For Bush House, the hourly news bulletin, on the hour, every hour, had a verity and authority not too far removed from tablets of stone. That had made BBCWS great. For Attwell and Irwin, of course, there was something new and different in play – rolling news, news as it happened, news as it evolved by the minute, in the minute, actual, immediate, urgent, necessary. These were not tablets of stone but gobbets from the living frontline of life. Attwell found the culture clash vast: 'I wasn't even asking them to do rolling news. I was just saying, "This story has broken, we're a live news channel, can we please reflect this story has broken?" And they all treated me all the time as though "you don't know anything about Bush House, you don't understand our standards". When they set WSTV up, they made Bush House responsible for the journalism. But nobody in Bush House knew anything about television journalism. When an aeroplane crashed into Schiphol Airport in Amsterdam, a very able editor led the WSTV news on it. Not surprising. The Bush House lot came and complained and said, "They hadn't had a second source." The editor pointed out that they were putting out pictures of the actual event!'

It was a massive gulf which no more senior person had the authority, time or inclination to bridge. WSTV was never owned by any single individual. The BBC's complex structures and varied and conflicting funding sources saw to that. It should have collapsed under the weight of its deep organizational contradictions. Something else, believes Richard Sambrook, kept it going: 'There were enough people who believed in it. There was a strategic impetus because in the end, whether people thought it was a good idea or not, once it arrived, it was there. The competitive elements against CNN and then later Al Jazeera and other state channels launching became very apparent. We had BBC World there and people felt "we have to try and find a way of making this work". It really just took some people with the imagination to keep the plates spinning and to look at things from another direction. That business about saying, "This is the BBC's biggest TV channel" was a way of just shifting the perspective.'

They included BBC engineers such as Ian Troughton, who believed that it was their role to solve problems in the best traditions of that division. He introduced automated studio cameras and low heat generating studio lighting. Troughton and his team pioneered 'Hi8' lightweight cameras for use by foreign correspondents: 'This wouldn't attract the attention of foreign authorities. The BBC reporter looked just like a tourist.' These self-styled maverick engineers pointed out that since WSTV was a commercial service, it had to be economic. Flexibility was essential: 'You had to think on your feet to make it financially viable.' Their approach was an important part of the entire team's spirit and effectiveness. They broke no rules, they just bent and occasionally challenged those that existed.

By January 1995, the WSTV network was creatively refreshed with a reshaped schedule and regionally targeted daily current affairs. The essential first battles had been fought and some settled. They were only to be the first battles.

Long before WSTV settled into what proved to be its normal life pattern of changes to funding, threats of closure, reorganizations, restructurings, all expressive of deep BBC intellectual confusion about who it was for, who owned it and whether it should exist or not, there was a kind of last hurrah of the founding Irwin regime. If his deal with the Hong Kong-based Star TV was one of its high points, Rupert Murdoch's intervention looked like one of the lowest. Faced with objections from the Beijing government, on 17 April 1994, Murdoch, the new owner of Star TV, dropped WSTV from the northern beam of the satellite which covered China. This was a body blow to WSTV coverage and credibility. In taking this step, he had broken the original 10-year agreement signed with Star TV. Many would have accepted the power of Murdoch. Irwin took to the law. A comparatively junior member of staff, the 30-year-old Sharon Purtill, was told to fly to the Virgin Islands to issue a writ to Murdoch's lawyers. While another colleague flew to Hong Kong to another Murdoch head office, Purtill had to find her destination on a map while racing against the clock: 'Chris's colleague said, "Have you got your passport?" I said, "Of course I have." He said, "We need you to go to Beef Island." I was thinking, "Beef Island?" He said, "Yes, we're issuing a writ to Murdoch." I go, "Oh, okay." I had to look up the atlas to figure out where Beef Island was. I had no idea where it was. So we had to book my tickets. Then we went to the High Courts. We waited until four o'clock then the writ got biked from there to the law firm.

'I had to sign an affidavit to accept the writ. I took a taxi to Heathrow to run through the airport to get on a plane to go to New York. To find out when I landed that my plane nearly got diverted because of gale-force winds. Then I had to change to another flight to Puerto Rico. I arrived at 1 a.m., had four hours' sleep, got up, got on another flight that eventually landed me on Road Island, Tortola, in the Virgin Islands. Then I had to spend a very long day with the lawyers there chasing round for the main judge because I discovered I needed another affidavit signed by a judge. He had a day off, he was on the golf course and having lunch. I spent the whole day running around the island. Because the idea was that Murdoch couldn't counterwrit us if we managed to deliver it within a certain period of time. That's why we did it at four o'clock, because the writs are not listed until ten o'clock the following morning. I ended up in Murdoch's offshore business in Tortola, sitting there until they accepted the writ off me because at one point, they didn't want to accept it. So I sat there until somebody took it off me. I said, "I have to hand it over to the most senior person in this building."'

The almost cloak-and-dagger flight through the night worked. Murdoch had to honour the existing Star TV contract. It was worth £10 million to WSTV. Would anyone other than Chris Irwin and his team have fought it? Against the odds, the ingredients of Irwin's commercial and international strategies and Attwell's bitterly resisted journalism reforms had their effect. At an international gathering of news channels, the head of CNN, Chris Cramer, greeted Rachel Attwell in the most gratifying way: 'Chris came up very nicely and almost congratulated me: "There's some good stuff you know, you're a real competitor for us, we have to think hard." He was very envious of HARDtalk, which he thought was a very simple but successful idea, which is still running to this day. But the really bad period was that first year, the combination of bloody-mindedness, no money, the wrong people in the jobs, a terrible studio. I really didn't think it would survive but it did get better. By the middle of the period that I was involved, you began to feel intensely proud of it. We won awards and there were fantastic journalists working on it.'

Before that apotheosis, Irwin came across the ruthless face of internal BBC politics. It was only a month after Murdoch had switched off the satellite beam that covered China, a few weeks since the legal rush to the Virgin Islands, a month before the launch of BBC Arabic Television. Surely success beckoned? At an elaborate BBC farewell dinner for a senior executive, unconnected with WSTV, Irwin ran into the former, sacked BBC director-general, Alasdair Milne. Out of favour he might be, out of touch with internal BBC politics, never: 'It was an old-style Scottish piss-up basically at the licence payers' expense. At the end, Alasdair came up to me and said, "It's time to buckle your brogues!" And I said, "What the hell do you mean, Alasdair?" He said, "Buckle your brogues, they're going to get you." I don't know how he knew but within three months I'd been got.'

To this day, Irwin does not know why he was sacked. No reason was given. He has mixed feelings about the occasion and how he responded: 'When I look back, I behaved very weakly. I'm not someone who does contest being got rid of because I've always believed that once someone points a dagger at you, you're not going to feel the same about the thing after that. Although I felt very badly betrayed, it wasn't something that I wanted to turn around on!'

Irwin left on 10 May 1994. It had been an intense four years. They included the Arnold Baker moment of commercial inspiration, the Checkland coup over the BBC governors, the Irwin voyage of discovery to find international markets and audiences. The Attwell renovation of the network was still fully to come as she built on the deeds of the three pioneer founders. Their actions were each critical and decisive. Without them, WSTV would never have become the reality that it is today. Chris Irwin muses over its 500 million audience: 'I think it was an extraordinary thing. I wouldn't have thought we'd survive for over 30 years in those early days because I didn't think the wider BBC commitment was robust enough. I'm very proud of that. I still use "Founding chief executive of BBC World Service Television" when asked for a brief CV. That is one of the things that gets through. I'm deeply proud of it.'

The BBC's own commitment to its most-watched channel never solidified. As a senior news executive, Richard Sambrook witnessed at least two attempts to shut down WSTV altogether, a shuttlecock batted back and forth between the warring arms of the BBC: 'Nobody believed it was going to make money. BBC Worldwide wanted to wash their hands of it. The BBC governors and the BBC Trust were running wary of "cross trading" issues and "state aid" issues. This was not a channel that they felt was as strong as it could be. And they were hearing from the executive, "well, we can't actually find a way to make it stronger." So some of them said, "Well, pack it up then." It's easier that way. But the thing about imagination and innovation is to say, "Actually, we can find a way of keeping the ball in the air". And there were a number of people at different levels who had different ways of doing that.'

World Service Television was a great, often inconvenient idea. Unloved at least by most politicians, many BBC bureaucrats, too many radio and TV journalists, it was not tidy, it did not fit. It was too radical for a long-established institution set in its ways yet there were enough in its ranks who saw the value of the idea, understood its necessity and threw everything behind it. It gave the BBC a place in the world of television networks, a huge strategic step. The informal triumvirate of Arnold Baker, Checkland and Irwin was critical. Baker's imagination, Checkland's decisiveness, Irwin's vision and energy, each made a decisive contribution. It was a kind of informal, instinctual, group leadership. Sometimes things happen that way. The model is not in the rule books. When it works, it works. Collectively, all three helped to keep the ball of WSTV in the air. It was too good an idea to fail but it so nearly did. Those who made decisive contributions deserve recognition, they each made a difference.

Observations

- A big idea may not be deliverable by a single person, no matter how visionary.
- Such an idea may take years to find its time. Keeping it alive is not an idle activity.
- Rejection from many sources is a test of viability. It can be a source of learning and understanding.
- Responding to rejection involves a myriad of steps and actions.
- Events may be your friend, they should be recognized and seized.
- Opponents may be effective in opposing, undermining and delaying an idea. It is better to initiate than to oppose.
- Entrenched bureaucracies feel threatened by the new. That is why they are so hostile to it.
- Acts of managerial daring are often essential to permit innovation.
- The effective visionary takes risks that are not foolhardy.
- There's no point in having authority if you don't use it; the only true limits on authority are those that are self-imposed.
- Success needs to be claimed and voiced or many will choose not to recognize it as such.
- Success is not final and conclusive; it may need fighting for repeatedly.
- A big vision is always worth having; fulfilment is all.

References

Dudley Lynch, Paul Kordis, *The Strategy of the Dolphin: Scoring a Win in a Chaotic World* (William Morrow, 1989).

Ian Richardson, editor, *BBC World Service Television Timeline, 1968–2019.*

5

'Breaking the Mould': A New Kind of TV Journalism

Featuring interviews with:

Joan Bakewell, Arts Reporter, *Newsnight*; Labour Peer, 2011–present

George Carey, Editor, *Newsnight*, 1979–82

Tim Gardam, Producer, *Newsnight*, Chief Executive, Nuffield Foundation, 2016–present

John Gau, Head of Current Affairs, BBC Television, 1978–81

Robert Harris, Reporter, *Newsnight*; Author, *Act of Oblivion*, 2022

Lorraine Heggessey, Assistant Producer, *Newsnight*, 1981–83; Controller BBC One, 2000–05

Ann MacMillan, London Correspondent and Bureau Chief, Canadian Broadcasting Corporation (CBC), 1981–2013

Ron Neil, Deputy Editor, *Newsnight*, 1979–80; Editor, *Newsnight*, 1981–84

Peter Snow, Presenter, *Newsnight*, 1979–97

It was early February 1980 and at around 10.30 p.m. something different appeared on the screens of BBC Two. A new, brassy, confident signature tune, horns blaring, heralded the unveiling of a new studio set; somewhat long, with a curious church-like apse at its heart. The set was filled by no fewer than four people – journalists, presumably – seated at desks, whose actual functions and purposes awaited revelation. There was an atmosphere of expectation, a sense of purpose. The title of the new programme, *Newsnight*, promised an entirely new approach to television journalism, one where news events and issues would be presented in their entirety, not just what was happening in the world but what they might mean.

If this sounded a simple, even commonsensical proposition, the actual appearance of the programme on screens around the nation represented a story in itself. It had faced four months of delays while trade unions haggled over terms and conditions. Senior BBC management delayed, obstructed or avoided commitment and support, preferring to follow their own sectional interests. Colleagues predicted its speedy demise. Often, the entire project seemed on the brink of collapse, virtually friendless in the corridors of power. The fact that it did finally appear, live, on air, was principally the work of one person, editor George Carey. He had confronted a historic, seemingly unchallengeable part of the professional and bureaucratic fabric of television journalism. Most pronounced at the BBC, the lines between news and current affairs were old, deep, organizationally entrenched, culturally expressed, professionally justified and rigorously policed. Their existence and the practices and behaviours that ensued could not be overestimated. They were historic; they were institutional.

The nature and scale of the revolution in television journalism that Carey achieved with *Newsnight* can only be appreciated and valued if the situation that existed beforehand is understood. He himself states the proposition in disarmingly simple terms: 'It was evident to me that news people really focused on the facts. They were good when things were actually happening – there was a strike, there was a war. They were much less good when it involved straight politics, where someone sat speaking perfectly intelligently, straight to camera, over an image of Westminster. It didn't seem watchable and the agenda was too narrow. I thought what was particularly wasted was the huge resource of really brilliant journalists, mainly foreign correspondents, because all they ever really had was two-and-a-half minutes. They weren't regularly covering how the world is. News was stuffed full of journalists but not stuffed full of imaginative people for presenting events. There was a culture of no change. I'm painting it in primary colours, but news wasn't something you experimented with, you got it right.'

But getting it right, the essential and existential core of newsroom practice and discipline, was no longer adequate for explaining a complex and dangerous world. What Carey and a few others understood and analysed, those who had to work in the system as it existed were appalled by the atmosphere created by this culture. Lorraine Heggessey was a young trainee flung into this world: 'There was the equivalent of the Berlin Wall between news and current affairs. And George Carey had this idea of bringing together the two disciplines – the experienced journalists who were reacting on a daily basis to news stories and the more in-depth and more filmic approach of current affairs. If you brought these two together in one programme, you could go behind the news agenda. You'd cover fewer stories but do them in more detail. What was so exciting as a young journalist at the BBC was to be part of something new, marrying the two disciplines. When I joined, I was completely unaware that there were these somewhat arbitrary distinctions and it sounds ridiculous now.'

From my own experience in BBC journalism, I saw two tribes at play, for they were tribal in their loyalties. One I called the 'Roundheads' of news, austerely dedicated to things they could identify as facts. The other tribe were the 'Cavaliers', who saw events as just the starting point for examination, the signal for imaginative exploration and interpretation. The differences between the two were, as a seasoned professional like Joan Bakewell witnessed, real and intensely felt and expressed: 'It was a virulently antagonistic relationship, that news and current affairs each wanted to be the leading breaker of stories, coverer of stories, grabber of exclusives, scoops of celebrity, whatever it was. There were armed camps. You were not allowed to trespass from one to the other. All of us who cared about news knew it was damaging for the public because the public didn't recognize this difference. The idea began to grow that it was not serving what we all knew to be the best way forward. But how do you change things at the BBC? That was the problem.'

Deep cultural and social divisions were at play too. These were the 1970s after all. Ron Neil, a Scot by birth, was well attuned to picking up the nuances of English social distinctions. They were deeply embedded in BBC attitudes, amplified too by working in separate buildings in west London. The vast Newsroom was at the heart of the monolithic Television Centre at Shepherd's Bush. Current Affairs existed in a separate universe of shabbily converted cottages, half a mile away in Lime Grove. They might have been on different planets in Neil's experience: 'The difference between the news and current affairs was enormous. In many ways, completely different disciplines. News originally came from radio – a lot of the staff were newspaper journalists who moved into television news, where they were producing bulletins rather than making programmes. Nothing was more than a minute and a half or two minutes. It was its own discipline. In Lime Grove, on the other hand, there was a very strong Oxbridge presence: very bright people, young men and women, who came from the background of a top university. We saw the world not in terms of bulletins, but grassroots programmes and debates and arguments. The two sides didn't like each other. It was quite a hostile relationship. Suddenly, the BBC decided it wanted to bring the two disciplines together. The manifestation of that was to be *Newsnight*.'

George Carey, with a news background, was to be editor; he asked Ron Neil from current affairs to be his deputy. Such gestures were important signals to the suspicious tribes. Together, they would work to bring the two antagonistic disciplines together. The importance of their partnership should not be underestimated, as Lorraine Heggessey witnessed: 'If you wanted to categorize them, Ron was more of a populist, in terms of the popular news agenda. George was more of an intellectual. Ron was a very instinctive journalist, with a finger on the pulse of "what's the man in the pub talking about?" George was very much "this story is incredibly important and we need to make sure that the audience understands what's led us to this point and what is going on behind it". The two made a good counterbalance to each other and helped to make a richer programme.'

The complex web of resistance to any idea of innovation would not vanish or be abandoned just because of reasoned argument. Some of it came from longstanding and deep cultural and professional divisions. The fact that they were real and not fabricated made them harder to overcome. As a young researcher trainee, Robert Harris witnessed them at first-hand: 'There was more dedicated professionalism in news. You were properly trained. News was a law unto itself, it was a separate domain. The turf was jealously guarded. It was classic generalism in the television current affairs service. There was a sense of superiority in the Lime Grove current affairs culture, more akin to "gentlemen" rather than the "players" in news.

On my research assistant trainee scheme in 1978, there were 15 of us and 12 had either been to Oxford or Cambridge. It was overwhelming. I can't remember anyone who wasn't white on that course; it was probably the last gasp.'

This was the brew that George Carey had stirred up, a toxic mixture of class, education, tradition, inclination, aptitude, entrenchment, habit, skills and training. A wise person would have left it to stew or at least decided that there were easier ways of making their way in the BBC than challenging some of its deepest instincts and practices. He may not have been the only person reaching the conclusion he did about the need for change and the opportunities that would flow from it but he was special in a certain single-mindedness of purpose with a readiness to do something about it. If he was a pioneer, Carey often took people by surprise on first meeting, even experienced journalists such as Ann MacMillan of the Canadian Broadcasting Corporation (CBC): 'I was expecting a real sort of fireball to do something like he was planning to do, push two different strands of the BBC together against most of their will, someone rather loud and pushy. George was very gentle and thoughtful. He was passionate about what he wanted to do. But he didn't overdo it. He talked about the problems. He talked about the way he could see forward. I was very impressed by him. He wasn't a sort of superstar type guy, he just was a very solid, thoughtful man.'

Carey had to be more complex than that in practice, though the quietly insistently persuasive style he displayed to Ann MacMillan was an important part of his weaponry. Robert Harris spotted some of the deeper complexities and subtleties in Carey's character, aspects of which he himself might not have been aware: 'I got on well with George. He'd have made a brilliant cardinal in the Catholic Church, worldly, amusing. He was quite fearless in his way and quite an inspiring figure. He was also very amused by life. He wasn't a systems man at all. He was almost a perfect person to bridge what we now can see was in many ways a false cultural divide.'

One colleague recalled what they labelled Carey's 'persuasive leadership style'. Some characterized it as involving a tactic described as 'wheedling' to get his way. Others, like Tim Gardam, recognized his capacity to cajole and manipulate. He was, according to another colleague, a 'great tempter'. Such psychological manoeuvres were a necessary part of his armoury. Interestingly, Gardam, like Harris, sensed something almost out of time about Carey: 'He was brilliant. He's quite a medieval figure. You could have seen him in the church in the fifteenth century. In the Renaissance, you could have seen him in a court but he was always the radical.'

Occasionally, this underlying characteristic led Carey to overstate his case, to heighten the tone of his arguments, an approach that almost backfired as he himself recognizes: 'When I started the recruitment in 1979, trying to get people to join my band, I was probably rather incautiously saying, "We're going to change the news, we're going to revolutionize things, we're going to make it all different, come and join me". And this was filtered back to the bosses and I think they felt "what the fuck is going on?".'

If that was a rare tactical misstep on Carey's part, it did not diminish the scale or vision of the changes he was determined to put into practice and which he knew were needed: 'I had a very passionate view that it had to basically be news, but not the same news. There were two ways in which it should be different. The agenda should be different. The foreign news agenda was often dictated by where the TV crews were deployed, as opposed to being where what was interesting and what was important. And secondly, I wanted to beef up the political analysis, the argument, the exchange of opinions. News was not scared of opinions, but they wanted simply to display them in little snippets, 30 seconds of this view, 20 seconds of that rather than test the validity. They'd always try and balance – all perfectly praiseworthy, but it wasn't getting you anywhere. I think that the BBC's obsession with balance was terribly dangerous because it very often worked against truth.'

Carey's three-pronged agenda could be summed up as deploying TV news crews in an editorially dynamic purposive way; harnessing the full fire of political exchange into the studio and trusting his journalists to set out their conclusions without first corralling them in the iron claws of so-called 'BBC balance'. Each one would involve real change in the way a programme would behave. Together, they amounted to a massive agenda for change. That was why *Newsnight* was needed. These would be its purposes, but who would put them into practice?

Taken as a whole, BBC news and current affairs had many distinguished and experienced journalists and reporters. Were they exactly what radical innovation demanded? Carey took a brave, even risky step. He recruited his head presenter/reporter, the principal face of the new programme, from outside the BBC. There was no formal selection process as such, no evidence that he sought authority to do so. He approached Peter Snow from ITN, largely because he found him entertaining when he was on the screen with his famous studio 'sandtrays' for explaining wars and conflict zones. He loved Snow's flamboyance for sure but above all, Carey was looking for authority on the screen: 'This show was going out late at night. It was trying to be different. What I didn't want it to be was irrelevant. And if we were going to be daring on the agenda, it had to be daring on the presentation side too. I really wanted it to feel that this was something that people must listen to.'

There is no indication that Carey consulted widely or at all about his hoped-for main presenter. A more cautious editor would have done and risked opposition, objections, even failure. Carey simply lifted the phone to Peter Snow: 'I didn't know George Carey from Adam, I had no idea who he was. I got this call from George saying, "Look, old chap, we're thinking of starting this new programme, 45 minutes news in depth with a real difference to the style of news programme and we think you're the sort of chap we'd like to have on it!' He'd seen me do all sorts of things on ITN, everything from discussion to presentation and explanation and interviewing.'

Snow agreed to talk to Carey over a lunch with Ron Neil. George was at his most eloquent and persuasive, wheedling, manipulative even. Snow listened: 'They were golden words to me. This would be a programme when, instead of telling people about an issue, a war, a diplomatic struggle, in three minutes, we would do it in 10 or 12, or 15 minutes. Instead of having to just give the headlines with a quick graphic, you would be able to explain in much more detail what was going on. We would send camera crews abroad. Instead of having to fill a whole half-hour programme, we would just do that wonderful length 10–12 minutes, which would allow us to say enough but not too much about the subject. He made it very clear. He also tempted me with lots of money – I think it was almost double my salary at ITN, it was a lot. And that's attractive. The lunch was terrifically successful. I loved George because he was a great explainer and because he was clearly the innovator who was producing this new programme.'

Snow seems to have had one condition for joining; that ITN's foreign editor, the greatly experienced John Mahoney, should come too. It was a crucial appointment. Carey's entirely unauthorized financial deal with Peter Snow shocked his superiors including the generally supportive John Gau, head of Current Affairs. This was not how BBC staff, even quite senior ones, negotiated contracts, especially with outsiders from

ITN. Gau had to sort it out: 'A big contractual problem came with Peter Snow, of course. He came from ITN and wanted an enormous sum of money, or so it seemed. And you could imagine George was saying, "You know, he's just the sort of person we need." And I said, "Yes, he's just the sort of person we need. And then of course, add him to the bill and we can't possibly pay him that!"'

But he did. Gau's endorsement of Carey's freelance, almost buccaneering approach to hiring staff and setting contracts was shaped by two factors at least. He trusted him personally but his own commitment to the *Newsnight* project was almost as big. In fact, Gau fought for it with the crucial controller of BBC Two, Brian Wenham, for almost a year. His commitment and in effect protection of Carey from internal BBC negotiations cannot be overestimated, nor can the impact of Peter Snow's recruitment as main presenter of *Newsnight*. As an assistant producer, Tim Gardam felt the positive, almost physical impact of the appointment: 'The moment I knew *Newsnight* was different was when I met Peter Snow. One should not underestimate the sheer catalytic energy of him, coming from ITN, coming into the building. That was the absolute key thing. Then, ITN's *News at Ten* was so much bigger than the BBC *Nine O'Clock News*. *News at Ten* was half an hour long, not 20 minutes long. It had that signature to it. And Peter arrived; he had a contact book, he was leaping around like a daddy longlegs.'

Snow had another, deeper role on the nascent *Newsnight*. Carey may have only half-appreciated just how great his impact would be. Peter Snow proved an active – in every sense – ingredient in the inchoate, half-understood programme formula that Carey was working towards. This is how Gardam experienced it: 'George was a brilliant editor since he was incredibly permissive. It was extraordinarily unusual for someone who was driving a new programme not to have absolute grip and control over it. He didn't mind anarchy really. In many ways, *Newsnight* was chaotic. But he really didn't seem to worry about that. He was both hands-on and hands-off. Unlike any other editor I ever worked for, he was incredibly enabling. These are late twentieth-century management words. I'd never heard of any of them but that was what he was doing. And undoubtedly, Peter Snow was the catalyst.'

Snow brought with him another layer of complexity, another approach to TV journalism, another set of institutional awareness. Somehow, they would need melding into a new whole. But equally, this extraordinary melange of traditions became an element, in Gardam's view, in *Newsnight*'s evolution and ultimate success: 'It brought together totally different idioms in a world that is now almost medieval to look back on. It was like a world of separate monasteries, where Current Affairs was utterly different to News. As for the BBC and ITN, no one ever came from ITN to the BBC! The World Service was somewhere completely different too. They all had different idioms and all these melded together. George permitted all this to happen'.

My own recruitment to the *Newsnight* presenting and reporting team was also pure Carey. We did not know one another; he knew nothing of my then very slight television work. Chancing on seeing me on a mid-afternoon minority TV programme, he decided that he liked what he saw and was looking for, what he called a 'real sense of authority'. That was enough for him, there was no formal or informal BBC selection process. Our personal conversation was very brief. Carey took the executive and editorial decision in line with his vision for *Newsnight*, a vision to which I strongly responded. Instinctively, he created a subtle balance in what became the main presenting partnership of Peter Snow and myself. We were strongly contrasted, as people, as journalists: Peter the ebullient charismatic television personality, almost leaping out of the screen with energy, knowledge and enthusiasm. My own screen presence was perhaps more cerebral, in a lower key but fully in line with the fundamental programme philosophy.

Carey's innovation extended to those he recruited for the reporting team of journalists. They were disparate for sure, as Tim Gardam recalls, but they were all originals: 'There was a convention to current affairs reporting, just as there was a convention to news reporting. The interconnection of the two on *Newsnight* broke both. You would have never have got scripts such as David Sells wrote in traditional *Panorama* reporting. David Lomax was the master reporter and Mike Duttfield, his director, together were the masters. Vincent Hanna came from somewhere else again. He wasn't a BBC figure at all really, he was a politician. They didn't really understand rules, any of them. People like Charles Wheeler, who had spent a lifetime not understanding rules and not accepting them. Remember too that many of the people who George was given to staff the programme were people who were on the shelf. The news people who came to *Newsnight* were people who News department didn't understand. They didn't know what to do with Charles Wheeler anymore. In many ways, in liberating them, George also liberated himself into what he had always wanted to do.'

I regarded the journalists engaged by Carey, myself included, as a kind of *Salon de Refuses* – people overlooked, ignored or disregarded by established or conventional parts of the BBC because their styles, their approach did not fit the systems in place. That in itself was a revealing commentary on the orthodoxies operating in a large organization. There was little room for the truly original, the independent, still less the maverick: *Newsnight* was the beneficiary.

Carey now had the philosophy, he had the presenters, he had the reporters and journalists, he was accumulating staff. One thing was missing: formal bureaucratic permission to start broadcasting. The BBC unions did not accept that the very different working practices of two divisions of the BBC could be integrated without negotiation and without their agreement. Scheduled to start broadcasting in September 1979, the internal BBC union, the ABS (Association of Broadcasting Staff) insisted on delay until they approved of new terms of pay and conditions. Suddenly, the radical new vehicle of television journalism ground to an embarrassing halt. Some doubted it would ever recover. Others, notably those who always believed *Newsnight* was set up to fail, hoped it would never start. It looked like Carey's biggest challenge.

It was also a challenge for BBC management, one that objectively and in retrospect, it failed to meet. It was all very well to dream up a fancy new television programme, it had to find a home in the schedules of one of the two existing BBC TV channels. Each was presided over by a huge figure with absolute power. Each was, understandably, concerned about and responsible for the success of their channel in audience numbers. John Gau, as head of Current Affairs, found himself a helpless supplicant before the aptly named channel controllers. Intellectually, he thought he had a great idea. Might it have a place on BBC One? Gau's conversation with its no-nonsense controller, Bill Cotton, was brief: 'Bill said, "I can't have this show, it doesn't do me any good" or some such. And it became apparent that Bill Cotton wasn't going to have any sort of current affairs show on BBC One, mainly because there was already a half-an-hour *News at Nine O'Clock*. So he didn't need it.'

One door closed with a slam. Not that Cotton was being unreasonable. He had to deliver a successful, popular, mass television network with consistently high ratings. His personal preference would have been for a late-night chat show with, as he insisted, 'a band'. *Newsnight*, however clever, would not do for BBC One, or as he believed for the BBC. Personally, Cotton may have had little sympathy for and interest in the *Newsnight* type of programme but as a consummate television operator, he had no choice. That left the so-called 'minority' channel, BBC Two, as *Newsnight*'s best possible home. Surely a natural one? Gau set out his case to the Channel Two Controller, the mercurial Brian Wenham: 'If Current Affairs was to have a nightly show, having it on BBC Two would be an obvious thing. And the next obvious thing was it would need news in it, because there wasn't any news on BBC Two. And we should do it in the late evening as a way of summing up the day, summing up the week. We sent it forward to Brian Wenham. He was implacably opposed to it, not to the show as such but to doing it in the late evening. He wanted it at 7.30 or thereabouts. I resisted this and said, "Look, at the end of the night, you can certainly have some news and you can start really examining today and examining the week," and I wrote a piece saying we have to have this.'

Wenham was adamant: an early-evening scheduled slot or nothing. Faced with this impasse, the matter went to the BBC governors, the overall supervisory body of the Corporation. It was never clear why a non-professional body such as this should take decisions on journalistic editorial questions. They were wholly unqualified to do so. Such were the ways of the time. The governors wisely avoided straying into waters where they had no soundings and approved a late evening slot for *Newsnight* on BBC Two. A decision of a kind though it solved only a fraction of the problem. It did, however, represent a real bureaucratic and political success for John Gau. It took its toll and he almost paid a price: 'That's where I got into a lot of trouble. I was so relieved because this had gone on, back and forth, for the best part of a year. I dictated a long letter to Wenham – slightly triumphant, I'm sorry to say, and probably a bit sarcastic because I was just fed up with it – and sent it off. I remember writing something like, "At last we have got to the right place. As the Greeks say, 'you learn wisdom by suffering'". I was told afterwards that Wenham took this letter into a colleague and said, "Is this a sackable offence?"'

Throughout, Gau's concentration on managing the strategy surrounding the programme protected George Carey. For his part, he always understood and valued Gau's diplomatic and persuasive efforts at the higher BBC levels: 'I don't think I ever felt it wouldn't happen, I was so committed to it. And I knew that I did have some real supporters. I knew John Gau was on my side. He wrote some wonderfully funny ferocious memos to Brian Wenham, complaining about lack of this or lack of support.'

This official support was essential to allowing Carey to get on with the task of making and transmitting a ground-breaking programme. Progress had after all been made. Carey now had a programme, he had engaged presenters and journalists, he had a philosophy; he had a place in the schedules, however reluctantly agreed. What could go wrong? There was still no agreement with the BBC unions. Journalists in the newsroom worked to agreements negotiated by the NUJ (National Union of Journalists). Producers in Current Affairs worked to agreements negotiated by the ABS (Association of Broadcasting Staff). The agreements were different. The ABS demanded they be brought into line for those working on *Newsnight*. The programme was scheduled to start transmission in September 1979. The ABS demanded detailed agreements before it could start. Would it ever start? The September start deadline was surrendered; it was BBC management at its weakest in an abject surrender.

Five months of frustration and farce followed. Carey knew that while he negotiated with the ABS, 'Thirty people who had thrown in their lot with me were looking at a blank wall, with the whole thing collapsing into nothingness.' Even the optimistic Peter Snow felt 'frustrated, really quite upset and rather depressed by it all'. A kind of last-ditch solution to the frustration was to create pilot, dummy programmes in a gloomy basement conference room in Television Centre. There, equipped only with tables and chairs, the handpicked elite *Newsnight* team pretended to make programmes, to choose items, to create a running order, scribbled some scripts and even actively engaged real people to do interviews.

Peter Snow was present at moments of relieving farce: 'We managed to persuade Peter Barry, the Irish Foreign Minister, to agree to an interview: "This is our new BBC programme, *Newsnight* here. Very nice of you to talk to us." And he did his thing. At the end of it, the interviewer had to explain. Barry said, "When is the interview on?" The interviewer had to say, "Well, I'm afraid, Minister, it's not going to be on because we're doing a pilot for a programme." Barry didn't explode but he was extremely taken aback. He said, "It won't be another five years before I appear on your programme again."'

Undeterred, the production team kept on trying and were nothing if not ambitious. They even approached the British Foreign Secretary, Lord Carrington, for a dummy interview on a major international topic. Snow recalls Carrington's memorable reply: 'Peter Carrington said, "If you think I'm going to do a fictitious interview for a fictitious programme, with a fictitious person, it's out of the question so go away, leave me alone." So we didn't get him on the air.'

Some see a small benefit accruing from those fantasy programmes in a dank basement in Television Centre. The disparate team bonded in the atmosphere of shared frustration and impotence. Had each of us made a disastrous career turn? It was too a real test of Carey's leadership, as Tim Gardam witnessed, and of his partnership with Ron Neil: 'Ron Neil was actually very important, particularly for the current affairs people clapping people on the back and saying it was all going to be fine. And George's constant believing in the dream. Ridiculous things like insisting we rang up ministers to ask as if they were going to be on air, "would they come on the programme?" Some of them got the wrong end of the stick and made their way to the studio, but there wasn't actually a programme. George was extraordinarily optimistic and refusing to face reality.'

As Gardam observes, the whole experience of five months pretending to make programmes with no assurance about a future was borderline unacceptable, managerially and psychologically. It should have been but it wasn't: 'When I look back on it, to take a team of 30 or more and tell them to do nothing for four months is an incredibly unfair thing to do to a lot of people in their early twenties particularly. All these producers and presenters had been brought across to direct and to present. I'm amazed we all stayed actually but there were fewer career options elsewhere then.'

It is striking that the highest levels of BBC management took so few steps to support a supposed breakthrough programme like *Newsnight* and an innovator like Carey. In particular, Alasdair Milne, Managing Director of BBC Television, adopted a 'do nothing' stance that infuriated John Gau: 'The Association of Broadcasting Staff (ABS) was a joke union. Nobody took ABS seriously and suddenly they started making a fuss. Frankly, we'd never had anything to do with the ABS previously and at no stage had they ever crossed our bows. And I was really disappointed with Alasdair, because he just said, "Okay, we'll just wait." He should have said, "Okay, we'll go on the air and they can stop us." I suggested that ABS would have had to pull the plugs on the transmission and I don't think they would have done.'

Coming from ITN, Peter Snow was accustomed to strong, decisive leadership. He was dismayed by what he saw at the BBC. Every senior manager he observed seemed to be thinking about what was going on behind them – a classic 'minding their backs' approach: 'They're all soft, it was all squidgy. The contrast hit me so forcefully when I went to the BBC. The wonderful thing about ITN was the way David Nicholas, for whom I have unbounded admiration, a wonderful editor, would say, "Yes, go with it, do that, just go for it." Carey would tell me sometimes about majorly squidgy management with no clear point of reference. If George could have talked to the director-general and said, "I'm going to do this," and the DG said, "Good idea, go for it," that would have been fine.'

But that was never on offer. There were too many layers of power, authority and obstruction between the two. The most important, the most intractable, the most elusive was BBC Two Controller Brian Wenham. There was no communication with Peter Snow: 'It was an extraordinary way in which the BBC operated that had me completely puzzled. Brian Wenham seemed to represent that. I used to go and see him occasionally and he would talk rather like a politician talks. That awful expression, "Yes, Peter, I see where you're coming from" and that sort of thing. And it's like "Come on, Brian, here we are just waffling".'

But Wenham seemed, was, unbudgeable for months. George Carey is rather more charitable about him although he was at the receiving end of Wenham's complexities: 'I think Brian was a very subtle, interesting man. And he wouldn't commit. He was like that, he was kind of sceptical about the whole notion of television. I wouldn't say he was unsupportive. He just, you know, he had to make sure he didn't overspend.'

That is far too generous an assessment. In my experience, Wenham was cynical, lazy and evasive. Disinclined to make or take hard decisions, he viewed those who were attempting the new with amused indifference. He deferred decisions like a cat playing with a mouse. Robert Harris recalls him as a slightly menacing, very funny but still menacing, intellectual presence hovering in the background. I recognize this description. But he was one of the most senior and powerful executives in BBC Television. In my judgement, addressing, understanding and ultimately encouraging innovation should have been one of his main purposes. His resort to lazy politician weasel-words, as he did to Peter Snow, was characteristic.

Newsnight finally got on air in late January 1980, five months late. It was nothing to do with Wenham, nothing to do with the highest levels of BBC management and leadership. If so it seemed in the apparatchiks' view, *Newsnight* had never been worth actively supporting, now it was no longer worth actively holding it up. Let Carey and his enthusiasts get on with the job – and they did.

To understand what they did, Carey's complex character needs further examination. Tim Gardam concludes: 'Being absolutely impossible is often a characteristic of brilliant people. It could not be applied to George. Rather, he created *Newsnight* and stuck to it through its teething problems by taking no notice of, nor caring much about, what anyone further higher up the hierarchy thought. He never shared the pressure with anyone that I knew. No doubt he was also thought to be "impossible" by the management, but George's intransigence was brilliantly indirect. He didn't demand anything of anyone, rather he shrugged things off.'

It was not the case that Carey was indifferent to the problems of a five-month delay nor shrugged off the personal and professional strains involved. He could see through to deeper consequences, benefits even, though his rationale has a kind of Panglossian optimism: 'It may be the case that the long industrial fire through which we had to march in a way played into our hands because we were all on a sinking ship that we kept afloat and we rowed through.'

An entirely new programme, working on new assumptions, aspiring to project new purposes and practices into traditional ways of journalistic working might expect a clear direction from the editor. Carey was very ready to provide it but did so in a somewhat unexpected way. For some, paradoxically, it came over as almost evangelical: 'Evangelical is probably giving me more credit than I deserve but I felt passionately that people need to be given the freedom not to stick by the rules. There were some rules obviously to stick by but we had to think outside the box all the time. Otherwise, we would disappear without trace. If we just did a longer version of the same things that other people were doing, we were dead in the water. We had young tearaways from current affairs who were amazing. I tried to both be clear about what I wanted but leave it to people to find their solutions.'

There was no formula for the young tearaways who prowled the *Newsnight* editorial offices. There was huge opportunity mixed with personal responsibility. It was no accident, in Tim Gardam's recollection, that the young journalists and producers had a great deal in common: 'They had a signature. They could write, they had something to say. Yet they had something to say within what was then a much more secure sense of BBC impartiality. You were not pushing a line but people wanted to hear what they had to say, because they had something particular to say. There were a whole series of different voices within the *Newsnight* voice. The writing was different. It was thoughtful and energetic at the same time.'

They were offered a culture of demands and opportunities within a framework of personal and institutional responsibility.

A tempting and challenging combination, it was very grown-up. Peter Snow soon recognized that the team Carey had formed around him was capable of responding to both: 'It was instantly clear to me that George surrounded himself not with cronies who were yes men, but people who were brilliant producers with strong minds of their own, who would argue for their own thoughts and ideas in a meeting. They were young, very good producers and editorial geniuses at thinking up good ideas and ways to treat a subject or at least to make the subject right for *Newsnight*. They were absolutely brilliant at the use of graphics, an interview and clips of people talking and good film and so on – magical, actually magical.'

Opportunities existed for anyone on the basis of their ideas not on the score of their seniority or years of experience. Everyone from Peter Snow onwards was ready to listen to ideas because everybody on the production team felt they had a voice in the programme. One phrase in particular was banned: 'There's an interesting story in the *Guardian* this morning'. The very junior Lorraine Heggessey was caught up in this atmosphere and practice: 'It was a very demanding programme to be on. We used to have our morning meeting at 10 o'clock. No matter how junior or senior you were, you were supposed to come up with three ideas for that night's programme. It was very intimidating for somebody starting out, but also a huge opportunity because if you did come up with an item that got picked, then you would work on that item. It also taught you to deliver. If you didn't get an interviewee in the studio, which can be quite a tall order to persuade people to leave their sofas at half past ten at night and come to the studio to do an interview; if you didn't put your video package together, there would be a black hole on the screen. It was a very good discipline and training that stood me in good stead for the rest of my career. A very steep learning curve.'

Heggessey later rose to become controller of BBC One. Editorial responsibility on *Newsnight* was pushed down to what might be seen as very junior levels. That might have been regarded as a risk. It was not the only one. Studio and camera technology were evolving fast in what was a slowly emerging digital world. They too became part of the *Newsnight* world that young producers such as Tim Gardam relished. This was no time for caution: 'There was often chaos in the studio – it was always going wrong, things were breaking down. It was a world where we pushed the technology to the limits. It kept on breaking because we were trying to make it do things that it hadn't done before. It was itself a Petri dish – we didn't know what we were creating in it. We were allowed to do that probably because it was going out late at night and only half a million people watching. There were no pressures to take it off-air or change the editor. In a more prominent position, the pressures would have been much greater. It had that window in the first year to invent itself.'

Part of the invention certainly involved being open to other people's ideas. The arts seldom featured in the regular coverage and activity of news or current affairs. They were not one of Carey's own preoccupations, broadly curious as he was about them personally. It took a robust approach from the distinguished broadcaster and arts journalist Joan Bakewell to shake things up. She had taken matters into her own hands by going to see the controller of BBC Two, Brian Wenham: 'I said, "The trouble is, the arts really get short shrift here. On a newscast, you have sport but it's always at the end. You never have the arts." I churned out the old figures about more people going to the theatre than going to football matches. And he said, "Is that really true?" I trotted out more figures which I knew to be accurate about the number of people who took part in the arts in this country. He could see that was a good argument. If there were to be football results at the end of the programme, why shouldn't there be something like an opening of a star-studded production at the Royal Shakespeare Company?'

Bakewell then had to convince George Carey that the arts should – and did – feature in his brave new world of integrated journalism. Though the idea for regular arts coverage was not Carey's, he was certainly open-minded enough to test Bakewell's proposition: 'I talked to George a lot about his intentions for the programme, which were enormously focused on changing news. He said, "Well, it's your idea, you set out the argument for this so let's present it as you think we should do it." I put up lots of ideas. For example, "There's a show opening here, there's a financial crisis there, or a production of a programme at Aldeburgh starring famous performers". George liked some of those and not others so he said, "Turn up at the editorial meeting and we'll see where we go."'

There is more than a hint of the canny, calculating Carey in that exchange. He sounded slightly unconvinced but was content to leave it to the instincts of his daily editors and producers. For her part, Bakewell perhaps sensed that a rather more nuanced argument for regular arts coverage was needed: 'A story about the arts was refreshing because it had a completely different agenda, a different profile, a different spectrum. It looked worldwide – a visiting Japanese theatre company coming over, for example. It gave viewers a slightly oblique look at the world, different from the news and current affairs, and people liked that.'

In the end, the idea of arts coverage presented by Joan Bakewell chimed totally with Carey's sense of the innovatory nature of the programme's emerging agenda: 'George felt, driving to make a new impact, the arts would be a corner that would be so original because no one else had bothered to do it before. He would be able to say, "Look, it really is different. Joan's out there doing the arts. I mean, how weird is that?" So he got me on board. All the hard-nosed news and current affairs were a bit cautious, though not sniffy: "Why are we doing this? What's the point of it?" They would never have thought of it themselves but given it was there, they'd come along and see what I had to offer.'

Bakewell's persistence, knowledge and professionalism, not to mention sheer hard work, resulted in her achieving an astonishing strike rate of two or three eight-minute arts film reports each week. Sometimes Carey had to insist to a questioning editor of the day that a Bakewell story 'belonged to the programme, I'd like you to run it'. Her recruitment also allowed him to remedy to a small extent the gap he recognized of appointing too few, if any, women reporters from the start. But the Bakewell arts commitment added a further touch of distinctiveness and distinction to the *Newsnight* mix.

She recalls a certain exhilaration of spirit: 'It was a sense of "We're ploughing a new path here, we're changing the nature of programming. Nobody's done this before. And we're going to do it well". It felt like that, it felt very buoyant. And if they don't like it, which is quite tricky in the BBC, we're not going to adjust, we're going to go on doing it because we believe in it.'

A year or two later, Bakewell was not alone in being stunned when John Birt arrived as director-general and abolished her role entirely. She was sacked by phone call to her agent. Even a subsequent and joyous farewell *Newsnight* dinner could not undo the hurt of this brutality. By then, Bakewell had entrenched the arts in the agenda of a major television programme in a way which has never been followed since.

Carey was also ready to take what others would have seen as high journalistic risks. Robert Harris was a very young producer when he approached him with a story that most would have waved aside as 'too difficult': 'It was Winston Churchill and the use of chemical weapons. Robert had done some research to show that Churchill was quite prepared to use chemical or biological weapons in the Second World War, if necessary. He'd got wonderful research, documents about an island in the Hebrides, which had been used to experiment with Anthrax or something. It was a brilliant piece. And Winston Churchill Jr stormed into the Commons, attacked *Newsnight* and me and everything. The story went to *The Times*. I said to Robert, "Well, let's draft a reply." He said, "I'll do it." It was a brilliantly constructed reply.'

Carey trusted Harris's ability to handle the most politically inflammatory of subjects. The young reporter did not let him down: 'The story was correct and based on pretty exhaustive research in the Public Record Office that I had read. The chief of staff documents said the "Prime Minister has directed us to look at the use of chemical weapons and biological weapons against German cities". That was the document I based it on, it wasn't wrong.'

If that kickstarted Harris's later television reporting career, it also delivered a huge payoff to *Newsnight* itself journalistically. Some 18 months after the Churchill story, Harris produced something even more sensational. *The Times* was about to publish what they had been assured were Adolf Hitler's diaries. Harris had what he judged to be good evidence that they were forgeries. His source was the then respected authority on all things Nazi, historian David Irving: 'Irving said he was very fed up because he'd been in Germany for a week, having heard that Hitler's diaries had been discovered. He'd wasted a lot of time and a lot of money trying to track down these things. Then they turned out to be obvious forgeries. Then in April, one Friday afternoon, the story broke that *The Times* was about to publish Hitler's diaries. So I rang Irving and said, "Are these the ones that you were talking about at Christmas?" And he said, "Yes, they are. And they're fake, I can tell you that." And so I was in the story right from the start.'

Carey had by then moved on from *Newsnight* due to promotion. Without his support for the earlier story, it is unlikely that most BBC programmes would have taken this one on. It remained a big call for Carey's successor, then-editor Ron Neil. On one side, a brilliant young investigative reporter with a good track record. On the other, the weighty authority of the mighty historian, Hugh Trevor Roper, who had assured *The Times* that the diaries were authentic. Neil put *The Times* Editor, Charles Douglas-Home, in the *Newsnight* studio with David Irving. Events then unravelled in an almost farcical way, as Robert Harris recalls: 'It became the famous interview. Irving may have flourished his copy of the forgeries, which were done by the same man who *The Times* was paying all this money to. Charles Douglas-Home, the editor, said, "I'm a historian, I know the smell of old documents." These documents certainly smelled. Misjudgement. *Newsnight* was quickly out of the traps on that.'

It was a huge editorial call for the programme, a vindication of its whole approach of making and breaking news. Within days, *The Times*' story was in ruins. It was a vindication of the Carey approach to backing his journalistic talents. And Carey had also been capable of his own unpredictable ideas, seeming to appear completely out of thin air. He could even take Peter Snow by surprise: 'I can remember one item where George popped up, saying, "Peter, this is the anniversary, the centenary of the Battle of Maiwand in Afghanistan." I said, "I'm sorry?" The Battle of Maiwand, in which the British managed to lose rather badly in the middle of Afghanistan. I said, "Oh, really?" And George said, "I think we should make it not the lead item perhaps, but the middle item today." So I said, "Right."

'I think Tim Gardam as producer put together all these little models, the first time we used models, and it was enormous fun to do and quite captivating. Whether anybody took the slightest notice I have no idea but it was a sort of "George-ian" idea. We have a centenary. Let's just replay this battle which people have never heard of and make it interesting.'

In the end, Carey had two operating editorial principles. The first, repeated endlessly, was 'You cannot lead the programme with the same story as the *Nine O'Clock News*'. I remember a real sense of journalistic failure on the rare occasions when our lead story was the same as theirs. Very often, the *Newsnight* lead was close to or similar to that on ITN's *News at Ten*. We found that validating. Carey's second principle was just as important: 'Don't think of yourself as the last show of the day, think of yourself as the first show of the following day.'

The fundamental philosophy of *Newsnight* was that it was possible, even necessary, to combine the exactitude of newsgathering – 'what had happened?'– with the imaginative scrutiny of current affairs – 'what does this mean?' Once a daring presumption based on judgement rather than hard evidence, it had been steadily vindicated throughout the programme's first year. Whether reporting from the strikes in the Polish shipyards in Gdańsk, charting the implosion of the Labour Party under the impact of ultra-left wing 'entryism' in the Militant Tendency or the independence struggle in Zimbabwe, these events demonstrated that proper meaning could be explored within the framework of regular, sometimes continuous coverage rather than fragmentary interventions. It reached its climax during coverage of the Falklands War in 1981.

Newsnight started with certain advantages: it started late, an hour after the *Nine O'Clock News* came off-air; it did not have the burden of an official Ministry of Defence announcement to carry as the *Nine* bulletin did; its transmission was closer to the day's events in the south Atlantic because of the time zone differences; it could carry more current reports on the actual events of a full day in the conflict. These were big editorial advantages which the programme seized. It became a nightly programme – after all, the war did not have a weekend break. But its defining journalistic expression and achievement was unquestionably what became known as 'Peter Snow's Sandpit'. The centre of the studio had a scale model of the Falklands in some geographical detail. Snow could set out exactly where fighting was occurring, attacks were coming from, deployments taking place, landings were likely.

Clustered around the sandpit on a nightly basis were the cream of former British senior military commanders, all recruited from Snow's historic contacts book: 'They were thrilled to do it. Like us, they valued the opportunity to go into more depth and to speak in more detail about things. Not just say, "Jolly good show, chaps" but "Yes, this is a tricky one and I can see the Argentinians are up to this and up to that" so it was very important. That sand-table stuff is just one example of the kind of work you could develop in George's *Newsnight* vehicle. The combination of brilliant graphics, wonderful graphics artists and electronic news was brilliant. And of course the ability to get people. The military men all came rushing towards us when we wanted them to talk.'

Some criticized the detailed authority of the analysis as betrayal, as giving away national, military secrets to the enemy. Most saw it as a service to viewers. Those weeks cemented *Newsnight*'s place in the BBC Two schedules. Even Controller Brian Wenham grudgingly, if gracelessly, had to acknowledge this. George Carey had in fact already moved on from the programme to other appointments but Peter Snow's Sandpit and all its implications had been incubated in the depths of his philosophy, his work. When he left, no one suggested that a bold experiment was over, that it had been a nice try but the old ways were best. It is in fact remarkable that Carey's increasingly simple-sounding approach to editing and defining a programme became the bedrock of *Newsnight*'s journalism: 'I think there's no other way of running a successful programme because you can't take every decision in the minutiae. You can sometimes come in and say, "Hey, that's wrong, let's do this way." But for the most part, I tried to make people think it through for themselves and just laid out some guidelines and kind of watched their backs.'

In a world crammed with journalistic pontification and management theorizing, Carey's conclusions might have a somewhat disingenuous tone. Two of the 'young tearaways' who worked closely with him suggest additional perspectives – Tim Gardam, for one: 'George created *Newsnight* as its first editor and set an idiom that lasted decades. Not only was he not a dominant editor in the office – quite the opposite – but in the first seven years, the programme never had an editor following him that stayed for more than 18 months to two years. The programme had an immediate independent life of its own. Quite remarkable if you think about it. It was not a format that any individual could put their personal stamp on, its culture was self-generating.'

Permissive he might be, directly involved he always was. Carey was often seen running through the labyrinthine corridors of Television Centre clutching bundles of yellow-paged scripts to get an item on air. Robert Harris would be first to acknowledge that the editorial trust Carey put in him as a young journalist set him on his major writing career. In the record of BBC television journalism, what place does he see *Newsnight* playing?

'A big place. It was a transition point between two eras – the freewheeling, intellectual Hugh Weldon-ish kind of era, then the rigid John Birt era. It stands as a hinge between those two, it married the two traditions pretty well. The fact that it's still going 40 years later is proof that it worked. If you abolished *Newsnight* now, you'd only have to reinvent it.'

There is a paradox to the personality of George Carey. He is described by one close observer as 'a bit of a solitary underneath'. Adding that for all his electric connection in conversation, there was something quite self-sufficient about him, not exactly withheld but a little remote at times. He summed up his own passion as 'I love inventing new languages' of expression, of journalism. Managing bureaucracies would never have satisfied or interested him. Besides, managers would always have been wary of his darting, curious, restless mind. It would have been quite wrong and a waste of talent for this particular, distinctive, original, influential, elusive, daring innovator. Ideas he nurtured, talent he fostered.

Observations

+ Many people observe the need for change but do nothing about it. Even clever people like the familiar and the comfortable at work.
+ Acknowledging the strength of the argument does not mean support for its implications.
+ Delay may be a more effective way of resisting innovation than outright opposition.
+ The innovator's greatest weapon is the strength of the argument.
+ The effective innovator does not need to be a firebrand. The quiet innovator may take people off their guard by putting them at their ease.
+ To put innovation into practice needs like-minded people in support: a big vision will be a shared one.

+ Choosing a team to realize the vision itself demands daring and risk.
+ There are two kinds of loyalty. The first is loyalty to the person; the second, just as important, is loyalty to the idea.
+ A radical vision does not need to be run by rules. Just two may be enough.
+ Taking risks based on trust and responsibility is not foolhardy.
+ Being serious can involve having fun. It is an essential, if poorly recognized, ingredient of success.
+ A soundly realized and based vision will survive because of its own innate strength. A soundly based vision will not need its innovator to keep it going.

6

'Shakespeare in Gdańsk': The Four-Hundred-Year Dream

Featuring interviews with:

Zbigniew Canowiecki, Chairman, Theatrum Gedanense Foundation

Robert Florczak, Artist, Collaborator, Organizer of Events

Maria Gostynska, Head of International Relations, Gdańsk Shakespeare Theatre

Justyna Limon, Vice-Chairperson, Theatrum Gedanense Foundation

Anna Ratkiewicz, Head of Education, Gdańsk Shakespeare Theatre

Anna Reichel, Secretary, Gdańsk Theatre Foundation, Projects and Events Co-ordinator

Joanna Śnieżko, Festival Co-ordinator, Gdańsk Shakespeare Theatre

Boika Sokolova, Shakespeare Scholar, University of Notre Dame (USA) in England

Anna Szynkaruk-Zgirska, Head of Communications and International Cooperation, Gdańsk Shakespeare Theatre

Tadeusz Wolański, Translator of Festivals and Theatre Publications

The historic port city of Gdańsk lies on the Baltic Sea coast of Poland. A city of long defensive walls, imposing gates, a deep harbour, ornate streets of rich merchants' houses, elaborate municipal buildings, the largest brick-built church in Europe, Gdańsk was the most important port and city on the Baltic for centuries. In the twentieth century, the city of Danzig (as it was usually called in England) was at the centre of some of the century's more anguishing and dramatic turning points. In 1939, the Nazi-German demands over what was called the Polish Corridor with Danzig at its entrance were the prelude to the invasion of Poland and the start of the Second World War. Gdańsk was effectively levelled during that conflict, then painstakingly re-built.

In the late 1980s, after four decades of Communist Party rule, striking shipyard workers in the Gdańsk shipyards, led by the future Polish President, Lech Wałęsa, sustained the decade-long protests which led to the collapse of communist rule in Poland and ultimately in eastern Europe. Among the many other freedoms that resurfaced in 1989, Gdańsk was able to revert to and rediscover its far-older, far richer, far more fulfilling cultural and trading past. For at least 400 years previously, Gdańsk had been at the heart of that great mercantile trading network which interconnected northern Europe's cities, the Hanseatic League. This not only brought all the needs, goods and riches of the known world to Gdańsk. Between 1590 and 1660, Hansa ships brought a very special, human cargo from London. Bands of English strolling players, actors, the best in the profession, arrived to chance fame and fortune by performing the most modern drama available; they brought the plays of William Shakespeare and other English playwrights to continental Europe. By all accounts, they were well received, made good money, were well treated by local rulers and visited regularly for two generations.

In one respect, these London actors may have felt oddly at home in Gdańsk in those last years of the sixteenth century. From 1611, they certainly performed Shakespeare in what was known as 'The Fencing School'. A print from about 1650 shows a wooden, quadrilateral building with no roof. Contemporaries, it is said, would have seen a close resemblance to London's Fortune Theatre at the time. No wonder the players felt at home and returned to Gdańsk so regularly.

Today, a theatre once again stands on the exact footprint of the Fencing School just outside Gdańsk's old city walls. A striking, black brick, apparently rectangular building, actually more like a disguised cross, it houses a performing space which can be configured in three ways, a fourth when the roof is opened, a dramatic *homage* to its open-aired predecessor, The Fencing School. This is the Gdańsk Shakespeare Theatre, opened in 2014. It is a cultural, historical and architectural landmark.

We know about the venue and the Gentlemen of the Companies, as they were formally known, through the work of Poland's leading Shakespeare scholar, Professor Jerzy Limon. He researched and reconstructed the repertoire and itineraries of English players throughout north Europe in the seventeenth century. He recorded the reception they received on their travels too. These Gentlemen of the Companies travelled as far south as Bohemia and Austria. Limon was first and foremost a scholar; also, a person of restless energy and searching imagination. One day in 1989, he decided to set about building a new Shakespeare theatre in Gdańsk, reviving the 400-year-old historic connection. Twenty-five years later, the theatre was built and opened after an epic personal, political, psychological and practical battle against inertia, opposition, indifference, hostility and above all, fundamental doubt. After all, who was Jerzy Limon to dream such a dream? A lowly paid professor of Shakespeare, not a seasoned arts entrepreneur. The odds were stacked heavily against him, impossibly surely.

Limon was surrounded by sceptics. His wife, the highly practical businesswoman Justyna Limon, thought the idea was 'beautiful but crazy'. Close academic colleagues, such as Tadeusz Wolański, went further: 'It was absolutely crazy. I had lived through Sam Wanamaker's The Globe Theatre in London, which had taken years to realize. That's in a city like London, where there are lots of rich companies and sponsors with a tradition [of artistic support] too. In Poland, there was absolutely nothing like it. Few remembered that there had ever been a theatre here. The local bureaucracy too, the initial reaction whenever you went to see anybody in the town council, was: "No! What do you want?" You had to fight for absolutely everything.'

One of Limon's close artistic collaborators in organizing elaborate public events, Robert Florczak expressed his reservations in a very Polish manner, one that anticipated, almost relished, the prospect of failure: 'Crazy is not the right word. If you'd asked me if I was certain that he would achieve it, I had the impression that it was like the old Polish saying: "Chasing the rabbit and not catching it; it was a chase with a great idea". Poland at that time was so poor. Financially, it was a disaster. To think that you could be able to collect enough money to build a theatre was an absurd idea but a wonderful one. It was fun to participate but I was sceptical.'

But Limon was not merely a Polish Shakespearian scholar inspired by a particular project. Boika Sokolova, a Bulgarian Shakespeare scholar, suggests a much wider dimension to his thinking: 'Limon was a European through and through. A fantastic Renaissance scholar, yes, but something else, too. He was an East European who knew what Eastern Europe had done to people, what it had lost during communism. When the world changed, what he did was to restore not just the place of Gdańsk and of Poland on the cultural map, but to join the dots in a larger cultural history which had been suppressed. I felt a kind of Eastern European loyalty to him and in him. The place had become a backwater. This man published ground-breaking research and discovered important cultural connections, links and inroads into the heart of a much larger history. He connected people, culture was something connected.'

In his academic research Limon was increasingly dismayed to find that books about European theatre could omit any mention of Poland at all. Connection was certainly needed, so was reconnection. The impulse was intellectual, cultural and political.

If Limon's intellectual foundations were profound and well-based, how practical was the actual project? Leading Gdańsk businessman Zbigniew Canowiecki was invited to meet what he was told was a 'crazy man with a crazy idea'. He was however struck at the meeting by the impression of Limon as a 'go-getter, a doer, an achiever'. Then Canowiecki found himself becoming fascinated: 'This man was an outstanding academic. He seemed to be somebody with an unrealizable idea. He threw it into the ether, as it were, and said, "Maybe it seems unrealizable to you, but I'm going to realize it. And this is the kind of idea that could change the world". Jerzy was predestined to have an idea and to realize it. If it's possible in the areas of maths and physics, why not in the area of humanities? If it sounds crazy but you can do it, you find yourself in the process.'

Jerzy Limon devoted almost a quarter of a century to realizing his dream and to finding himself. Writing years later, Limon knew his family thought he had gone mad but it was a madness that never left him. Indeed, he celebrated it: 'Madness and dreams are made from the same material as frenzy,' he insisted. Jerzy invoked the ancient power of Furor Divinus, the Divine Wrath as an invisible influence. As a person who was intellectually creative, he insisted that 'building a theatre is a creative action'. That was all very well. The vision, the necessary vision, was there but fine phrases and great mythic invocations would not get his theatre built.

There was something else in the air of the time. Jerzy was dreaming his dreams just as Poland was emerging from almost half a century under Communist Party rule since the Second World War. It had been on the wrong side of the Cold War and the Iron Curtain and had become an economic, financial and moral mire. I was in Poland as managing director, BBC World Service, on the day the election results were declared in 1989. I sat in the office of a high Communist Party official in Warsaw as he told me that they had lost the election, a unique concession in post-war European politics. The following day, I travelled to Gdańsk to join in the celebrations for the 60th birthday of the striking shipyard workers' leader, Lech Walesa. At a Walesa family lunch the next day, Walesa was not triumphalist. Rather, he felt a certain human sympathy for the defeated Communist leaders: 'They want to be included in "my family"!' he told me. 'It is as if they want to lay their heads on my shoulder and be loved!' I could not dare to imagine that 30 years later, I would visit Gdańsk to celebrate the creation of a stunning theatre dedicated to William Shakespeare.

If Poland was stunned by the fact of its democratic overthrow of communism in 1989, the painful awakening of economic reality was still to come. First it was a time when political and personal freedom could and did reappear. With freedom came a heady hope. As Anna Reichel recalls it, Limon's otherwise crazy idea of rebuilding a Shakespeare theatre came wrapped up in the intoxication of the political moment. It was music to the ears of a young postgraduate student: 'The way the Professor was talking about it was amazing. It was the nineties. That was a very particular period in Polish history, because we thought that everything was possible. It was just after the collapse of the Berlin Wall and the end of the communist regime. We were so enthusiastic. I was young and what a great idea.'

The sense of limitless possibilities in the hoped-for 'new' Poland affected people of all ages. Justyna Limon set up a school for teaching English with two friends from university. Hope and opportunity seemed everywhere and available for everyone: 'Nineteen eighty-nine was a very important year for Poland because this was when we had the first partially free democratic elections. The Communist Party didn't expect that the opposition would win such a vast majority. We were ecstatic about this result without any bloodshed. We could have the transformation of the political system after so many years after the war. Our grandparents and our parents, their professional life was really marred by communists. My parents couldn't achieve what they would have liked under communism. All of a sudden, we were still young, in our thirties, and this happened. Everybody got in some kind of frenzy and started thinking, "what can I do now?". I set up my School of English and my husband immediately thought of setting up a foundation to reconstruct an Elizabethan Theatre in Gdańsk. Jerzy often repeated in his interviews; he really believed that since we were going to build a democratic state, everything would change.'

Years later, in happy retrospect, Limon could laugh at the way that his naive dreams and those of others about the way the new Poland would act and behave were dashed. For instance, habits of giving philanthropically, let alone having enough money to give charitably, would take decades to develop. Civil Society, as it came to be known, did not exist. In a later YouTube video, Jerzy recounted an early fundraising event in 1991 that demonstrated the scale of the problem. It became one of his favourite, bittersweet memories: 'We thought that during

185

democracy, we would have enlightened politicians and with the new economy, generous capitalists. Everyone would think the theatre was a good idea and money would fall like manna from heaven. Nothing like that happened. At the event, instead of reaching for their cheque books, people were putting bottles of sparkling wine into their pockets to take home.'

In Justyna Limon's memory, the entire fundraiser received just one cheque in support. There was a long way to go. It would be a lengthy learning process for him. Fortunately, Jerzy had a shrewd businessman like Zbigniew Canowiecki to school him: 'Jerzy had a kind of naive, childlike faith that, because he had an idea, business would come running to support it. It took me several years before I could convince him that's not how business works. Business might bring money for a one-off event like a concert, but certainly not to rebuild a theatre. It was my own interest in culture allied with business acumen which brought Jerzy down to earth from the naive and childlike idea that business will just give money and things would happen.'

The theatre was years away from happening, the gap between the idea and the actual still huge. Even the skills and disciplines needed to bridge that gap were yet to be identified, still less learned and put into practice. Probably Jerzy himself was unaware of what still needed to be done to make the idea something that people might take seriously. All he had was the vision – a beautiful vision, but only a vision. His university colleague, Tadeusz Wolański, believes that Limon's vision had another dimension: it was deeply grounded in the politics and atmosphere of the time. That helped to keep him going: 'I think he saw it as being a bridge between the past because there had been a theatre once and so there was something there to build on. But it's a huge stretch of the imagination, building a bridge where you don't know where it's going. If you see a river, you can see both banks and you think, "we'll link those." But you couldn't see where this was going to go. He thought it was going to happen and he was mad as well. If he had any idea of the problems that he would encounter, persuading people, finding money, I don't know whether he would have thought about it seriously. He really had no idea what was going to happen. But he never gave up. That was the amazing thing.'

Being a man of the theatre and unafraid of the grand theatrical gesture, Limon made the really big one: he knew he needed to enlist a big name as a supporter. At home together one day, Justyna saw him writing, hardly an unusual situation: 'I asked him, "What are you doing?" And he said, "I'm writing a letter." "Yes? To whom?" And he said, "To Prince Charles." "Yes? What about?" "Well, I would like to ask him to be the patron of the theatre foundation." And so he sent this letter, just by post, by ordinary post to the wrong address, because all we knew was Buckingham Palace. It was the time of no internet so you couldn't check where you should address letters to Prince Charles. I was just laughing.'

Jerzy recalled that this time Justyna thought he really had lost his senses completely. Months of silence followed then an official acknowledgement of Jerzy's letter from the Prince of Wales' office appeared. The letter had got to the right address and the right person. Jerzy was not surprised: 'The English Royal Mail is very good.' (It was after all the Royal Mail, he observed naively.) More astonishingly still, a letter from Prince Charles himself then arrived, accepting Jerzy's invitation to become patron of the Gdańsk Shakespeare Foundation. Even Justyna suspended her disbelief: 'We know exactly the date this letter was written. It's 28 August 1990. It was absolutely amazing. The Prince said that he would be "honoured" to become patron or something like this. So polite, you know. I thought, "Oh, this is amazing. This is wonderful." Here people didn't believe in us and there in Britain, Prince Charles believed in this project.

It gave credibility to the whole project. Everybody thought, "Well, if Prince Charles thinks it's a serious idea, there must be something in it. Maybe I don't believe but it must be a serious project." So this letter was very important.'

Why did Prince Charles agree to become patron of a distant foundation devoted, so it said, to rebuilding a Shakespearean theatre in a country of which Britain 'knew nothing'? Of course, he was known to love Shakespeare and the Royal Shakespeare Company in Stratford-upon-Avon. But Gdańsk? Then, recalls Justyna Limon, the Prince actually met Jerzy Limon: 'Jerzy had this great charm. He charmed everybody. The first person was Prince Charles. About this first meeting with Jerzy, he said: "Being incurably romantic, I fell for this idea" or something like that. It says a lot about Charles.'

The meeting was important at many levels. The Prince and the Professor were much the same age, in their forties; both were idealists. Prince Charles had a political awareness as well as his romantic one. Poland, he believed, needed bringing back to the cultural image of Europe. At all events, the Prince followed through on his romantic impulse. He even visited Gdańsk and did what he perhaps does best in supporting one of his adopted causes: opening his houses for use as receptions, where the case for support could be most persuasively made by others. St James's Palace in London and the Prince's country residence, Highgrove, were the scenes of more than one occasion where influential and wealthy Polish citizens were actively cultivated for support.

Zbigniew Canowiecki, by then chairman of the Theatre Foundation Board, attended more than one: 'Jerzy understood people's needs. In 1989, Poland was slowly waking up, slowly coming to life. People wanted something that wasn't grey, something that needed to be exceptional and it would be for exceptional people. These people flocked to this idea and he knew how to gain support from the patron of the whole undertaking, the Prince of Wales. Every two years or so, the Prince would invite people to one or other of his residences. I attended almost every one of them. Once at St James's, once at Highgrove, he wined and dined the Marshal of the Region, the Lieutenant Governor, the Mayor of Gdańsk, business people and so on. In the 1990s, people were just creeping out of communism, throwing off the shackles. To be invited by such a person to such a residence, they would come not only for their own personal gratification, but to meet the Prince. And he referred to "My Friend, Jerzy Limon".'

Jerzy had an intensely pragmatic side, even a blatantly opportunistic side. At Highgrove in 2002, a declaration was signed in the form of a Letter of Intent, where local and national Polish politicians supported the idea of creating the theatre. This was countersigned by Donald Tusk, later chairman of the Council of Europe. Once signed, thought Limon, they couldn't back out of supporting it. Limon was adept at pulling every string, emotional, social, intellectual, historical; every theatrical trick. He began to understand that the whole project depended on the persuasiveness of its deliberate theatricality. It needed glitz and celebrity. Justyna Limon recalls one of the receptions at St James's Palace to set up the Association of British friends: 'Every time during these receptions, there was an artistic event. For the first one, it was Emma Thompson and Alan Rickman, who gave a performance of reading old letters, the letters that the English actors wrote to the Senate of Gdańsk in the seventeenth century, asking for permission to perform here. It was absolutely great.'

So simple, so apt, so persuasive. Somewhere along the line, Limon became a cultural entrepreneur, a suave politician, a supreme networker and a hard-nosed realist about the nuts and bolts of international cultural diplomacy. Prince Charles provided the highest international endorsement. US First Lady Laura Bush hosted a fundraiser in Washington with Poland's First Lady, Jolanta Kwaśniewska. The legendary Polish film director, Andrzej Wajda, became a festival president. Something more was needed. Zbigniew Canowiecki observed Jerzy at his persuasive best: 'Jerzy did not neglect the European Union and many events were held in Brussels for Euro MPs, the European Commission, the European Council. Possibly the most important thing that he sold to people was the idea of building the theatre without having a theatre building. Because artistic events were taking place. In 1993, the first Shakespeare Days were held. In 1997 the first festival took place to mark the millennium of the founding of the city of Gdańsk.'

So far, so good. The political, diplomatic strategy of persuasion had one stage further to go. Canowiecki was nominated to make what was a cheeky, even unlikely request: 'Poland had joined the European Union in 2004. In 2006, the Polish Minister of Culture came to Gdańsk. Jerzy was abroad so he asked me to meet him. I proposed to him the idea of building a theatre from European Union funds. I told the Minister that, in a sense, we already have a theatre: "We have events, we have a festival, we have the spirits, we have the people. All we need is a building." A year after that, in 2007, at the request of the Polish government, European Union funds became available for the building of the theatre itself physically.'

It is extraordinary that a Shakespeare scholar could operate and persuade at such high international levels. Jerzy knew there was a job of persuasion to be done at home in Gdańsk itself. Many people needed persuading, convincing of the project; more than the rich and the powerful had to be involved. Having a personal vision was not enough, it had to be communicated to the citizens of the city. He sought help from his long-time artistic collaborator, Robert Florczak. Gdańsk itself needed to be wooed with Shakespeare Days, otherwise why would they know what was going on? 'This was his idea with his Shakespeare Days to let the people of Gdańsk and Poland know that there is such a thing as the Shakespeare Foundation, which wants to reconstruct the Shakespearean Theatre in Gdańsk. In Poland, theatre-goers are not 90 per cent of the population and Jerzy wanted this Shakespearean theatre to be a project open to as many people, as wide an audience as possible. He was very keen on conveying the message. This is why he wanted to open Shakespeare Days with theatre performances in the main street of Gdańsk. He asked me to help and I did, of course.'

Dluga Street is the main artery of Gdańsk — a great civic space, lined with grand public and private buildings and redolent of the city's history and standing. Every year it was the scene of the St Dominic's Fair. Made for great civic and public events, in 1993, Dluga Street got a new one. Shakespeare Week showcased the visit of the Oxford Stage Company, underlining the Anglo-Polish connection at the heart of Jerzy's dream. It also included other companies, workshops and conferences. But the public had to be involved.

Dluga Street became the venue for a never-to-be-forgotten street pageant, which Anna Reichel recalls vividly: 'You have to understand the context. In the early nineties, it was the first time that we saw these kinds of colourful, joyful manifestations of culture, of togetherness on the streets. Before, life under the communist regime was quite grim. This was like an outburst of festivity of abundance. There were these half-naked sirens on these carts and flying angels and things that were never seen before. That was really quite spectacular. And it was like, "The actors are coming!"'

That hardly does justice to the pageant that Robert Florczak mounted to meet what he always acknowledged was Jerzy's concept. He laid out quite a specific plan, but then gave an open hand as to how it was realized. Robert found him open to what some would see as wild ideas, certainly the courageous ones. But Limon always took responsibility. Florczak knew he was not shy of doing that: 'The Oxford Stage Company were on a float with six cold-blooded stallions. They were enormous animals, pulling this cart with the Oxford Stage Company on it. I don't know if they would allow us to do this nowadays, it would be absolutely too dangerous. Of course, five or six men were attending these horses but they were real stallions, enormous animals, six of them, going down the main street of Gdańsk for the crowd. Jerzy conveyed his idea and was quite specific: where it's going to be, the time that he wanted the Oxford stage company and so on. He was very brave because what we did was not 100 per cent safe. Later, we had people walking, painted gold, and almost naked. There is something that beauty makes so easily acceptable because the people accepted it. There were no comments about the nudity. We did quite courageous things in these parades.'

Many of Limon's public events throughout the evolution of the theatre were strongly connected with Shakespeare, both personally, intellectually and even opportunistically. On 23 April 2012, Shakespeare's 448th birthday anniversary, Andrzej Wajda directed open-air performances by every Polish actor who had ever portrayed Hamlet. Four years later, on the quarter-centenary of Shakespeare's death on 23 April 2016, Limon cast and costumed 400 mourners to parade through the streets, wailing and howling with grief. No one wept for Shakespeare in Stratford-upon-Avon.

Anna Szynkaruk-Zgirska, Limon's head of communications, first heard of the plan from him: 'And we were like, "Four hundred mourners? How? This is not going to happen. This is impossible. We've never made that, we'll never make it." And we did. And it was a great success.'

The apogee of Jerzy's public concepts came later at an important stage in the construction process. For complex technical reasons, the theatre site was to be handed over to the construction company. Far from being something to hide, Jerzy insisted that it was a great landmark and had to be properly marked and celebrated. It would convey the vital message that the theatre was going to be built.

Szynkaruk-Zgirska had to fit it into the communications plan, if that wasn't too precise an idea: 'We were doing events that were communicating the whole idea of building the project. When the actual plot of the site was given to the builders, there was a big event with cranes. We were still communicating through events that were associated with Shakespeare, were associated with building the theatre, that were bringing interest into people. But we were not talking about the theatre itself. We were just communicating through art. This was a very good way around it.'

'Communicating through art' sounds a very Limon-esque approach. It was wholly his, says Szynkaruk-Zgirska: 'This was completely Professor's idea from the beginning. Most of the great ideas were his because he had a lot of ideas. We were laughing because sometimes we called it his "illuminations". He would be walking down the street and have this "illumination". Then he would come to us and he told us something. We would say, "This is impossible," and then we made it.'

The Ballet of the Bulldozers in 2011 must count as one of Limon's most ambitious, improbable ideas. Naturally, he turned to Robert Florczak, his collaborator-in-chief. There wasn't much to work with just an old parking lot, an excavated site surrounded by fencing and very little in the way of budget. But Florczak wasn't Jerzy's comrade for nothing: 'I said, "Listen, if you have a building company, then they must have these bulldozers, these diggers." I was always fascinated with these guys who worked these machines. They're artists, what they do is fantastic, the agility with which they pick material up. So I thought, "Maybe we can do a dance of these diggers and a bulldozer, of course." And I had a great musician friend, Wojtek Mazolewski. I built a special little box, it was like a roadside container but made out of plastic. It was transparent so we could see him. But the little roof and three sides meant his musical instruments weren't rained on. Then I had a stage on which we had this Viennese classical dancer dressed as a white swan. I also put microphones in the engines of the diggers and I had a DJ, who was mixing Wojtek's music with the sounds of the engines. Also, there was the voice of Maria Callas remixed. When she went "Awwww", the diggers went "Ahhhh" and they lifted their scoops.'

Florczak was not interested in mere colourful chaos. He wanted order, system, even choreography, some discipline and control: 'I bought two flashlights and two white, transparent plastic plumbing tubes. I was the conductor but we had no time to practise. The diggers came at 3 o'clock — the idea was that they were going to follow my conducting. The thing that they were really scared of was I wanted them to spin around with the scoops in the air. They were scared that if they hit each other, we'd have a catastrophe. I convinced them. The mechanical diggers did this spinning, scoops in the air, to the music with the engines and the bass guitar and the Maria Callas, the swan dancing and all the remixes, and it really worked.'

It is Robert Florczak's almost English understatement to say that they 'had great fun'. If Limon had only been interested in showy gestures, however much fun they were, it is doubtful if the theatre would ever have been realized. He proved to be highly practical and a quick learner in the necessary skills of cultural leadership. Businessman Zbigniew Canowiecki was especially struck by this ability: 'Jerzy Limon had the gift of translating his concept into reality, the gift of selling his idea. He took advantage by meeting a whole range of incredibly enthusiastic people, people that Jerzy talked into accepting his crazy dream. His strategy was to spread the idea. He was a humanist with a superb PR marketing technique. He could have written a book about it if he'd wanted to.'

Some of this must have come naturally to him. Charm and the ability to persuade were in his DNA. Those qualities alone would not have delivered a successful project. Even he did not know how much there was still to learn. To fulfil his new role of a visionary he had to stop dreaming and become ruthlessly practical. Of course, he was a cultural leader; now he had to become a cultural manager as well.

Justyna Limon saw her husband evolving in new directions: 'He had no idea about business. He was an academic, also a writer – in his heart, he was an artist really. From the time when he got this idea, he started learning. He had great intuition but not the actual knowledge. He didn't take a book of advice, *How to Run Your Business*. What we now call "networking" became fashionable in the last 10 years or so. He did it without naming it. Wherever he went, he approached absolutely everybody – he realized that he must build a really broad front of supporters.'

This included identifying people with money who would support cultural projects, an idea and practice that had to be built from scratch in the post-communist years. This too, as Anna Reichel saw, was something new for all of them to learn: 'Sponsorship didn't exist in Poland at the time. That was a completely new concept. We didn't know how to write sponsorship bids. What was amazing about Jerzy was that he knew that we have to learn and he knew how to do it. The moment I joined, he immediately sent me on two different secondments. I spent three months in London at the Association for Business Sponsorship of the Arts (ABSA). I went for another three months' secondment to The Prince's Trust.

'As a professor, Jerzy Limon was a very humble person
– he knew what he knew and he knew what he didn't know.
He was really excellent when it came to sponsors and writing
applications for grants. He was inquisitive, not only when it
came to scholarship and theatrical issues, but also when it came
to opportunities of what could be done, which were the avenues
we could apply for.'

Marketing, networking, sponsorship, politics – all were
skills that had to be learned and practised in the service of this
huge cultural project. Nobody taught Jerzy Limon, nobody
warned or advised him that cultural leadership involved all
these activities and disciplines. He never undertook a course
in arts management. Jerzy largely discovered them for himself
and understood that they had to be mastered. He made sure
his colleagues acquired the necessary skills to manage a major
cultural project. He never found the process easy or indeed
congenial and once described the world of management as:
'For me, a violent departure from safe and peaceful isolation.
Also, a collision, often a painful one, with the world that is
governed by its own rules, with nightmarish bureaucracy,
with disinterested hostility of officials, with backstabbing, with
common negligence. It was an encounter with a world which,
as Hamlet has it, is governed by "the proud man's contumely"
and "the insolence of office".'

But he did it. Jerzy's sheer intellectual curiosity took him even
further into the fields of management, into the very idea of the
nature of the audience he wanted to attract to his theatre. Who
were they? How did they act and behave? Maria Gostynska
experienced his response during a visit to the Silk Road
Festival in Shanghai: 'He got very interested in the reaction
of the audience there. They were just sitting eating, drinking,
chatting, doing all these things. And he said, "You see, it's like a
city audience, an ordinary audience who feel that they can come.

They are not restricted by any rules like Europe. It resembles very much Shakespearean times." He was not asking, "How come that they eat, that they drink, that they use the mobile phones?" He was looking from the scholarly perspective and said it would be beneficial for our audience too. I remember our ladies working in our box office, seeing spectators arriving in shorts, perhaps just from the beach, and they said, "No, we shouldn't let them in the theatre." And Jerzy said, "No, they are our audience. We can't make theatre only for the elite or elegant."'

Characteristically, Limon was thinking of building audiences before there were any. Beyond that, he certainly understood where real power lay and with power, came money. It was in the European Union. The historic 2007 decision to fund 75 per cent of the theatre's construction costs was a tribute to his personal advocacy. It also reflected the EU's belief that one of Europe's emerging democracies deserved practical support through a major cultural landmark. Curiously, raising the money for the actual building costs proved to be the least of Limon's problems. The balance of the 25 per cent came from the regional government and city authorities. Jerzy's political instincts told him not to take all these institutional backers for granted, especially the EU. How could he recognize and pay them?

Maria Gostynska was part of the scheme to give the Gdańsk Shakespeare Theatre an international dimension which would also project the EU's influence: 'There was this great event in February 2008 that our local and central authorities came to Gdańsk and signed the act of creating the Shakespeare Theatre as a cultural institution. It was also the time when Professor Limon decided that we need to thank the EU for financial support for building the theatre and not only by writing official letters. The idea was to thank the EU by showing the most interesting, intriguing theatrical phenomena from around the world. We started with the British Festival in 2014 with the theatre's grand opening. We continued with presenting the theatre, music, visual arts – a different spectrum of artistic activities from Lithuania, Georgia, Germany, Estonia, 14 different countries. But Professor wanted to extend these international relations throughout the year. It also was the answer to our audiences' needs, actually. They said, "We know that you're a Shakespeare Theatre, but we are fed up with asking 'To be or not to be' all the time. We want to see something different." And Limon said, "Yes, we are to be an artistic think tank."'

Of the many striking perspectives that he offered, one of the most striking may have been that Shakespeare was not just the great 'English' playwright. As Boika Sokolova points out, the Bard was culturally European, to his bones, though people didn't think in such categories back then: 'Just think of how many of the plots that Shakespeare used for his plays are from continental sources, or are travelling international plots. You could perform these plays in other countries in Europe without much text. Because people would know about Julius Caesar, or a story like Romeo and Juliet, or that of the slandered, murdered wife, which is in *Othello*. The taming of a shrewish wife, too, you find across the board.' Yet the fact remained that despite the intense activity, the sometimes crazy merry-go-round of ideas, the shafts of illumination, the official support, the theatre as a tangible project was years away from becoming a reality.

No one was better placed and able to witness the problems and the struggle than Justyna Limon: 'It was like a war really. It wasn't like him going to all these people and charming them and they all saying, "Oh, wonderful, wonderful, we will help you." It was a war, you had to fight. I divide the history into periods of fight and then the victories. So the fight for the land, the actual site which was crucial. Without the land, without owning the right to this plot, we could never ever do anything.

This took almost 10 years. And we got it at the end of the decade of the nineties. Then these piranhas, the archaeologists, arrived (my husband called them piranhas). The plot was fenced, they started the excavations and it went on for five years. And at that time, my husband was always bringing very famous visitors like the great theatre director Peter Brook to what we called a big dark hole in the ground, where they were digging.'

Limon would stare down into the seemingly never-changing hole and talk eloquently about the beauty of the theatre to come, the quality of its productions. Others, say Justyna, could see only the hole: 'There's one famous Polish actress who always supported us, Krystyna Janda, and she said, "Well, I went to this hole with Professor Limon twice and it always drove me to despair. Because there he was, one year after another standing at this black hole, talking about his beautiful dreams and I could see no progress. The archaeologists were still there, digging and digging, and we could see no end to it." And she said, "If I were him, I would pay these archaeologists with my own money just to go away." But he kept calm. He knew there was nothing they could do about it, these were the rules of the game.'

True, the archaeologists unearthed a seventeenth-century toilet and dildo. More valuably, they found timbers from the original Fencing School (now subtly incorporated into the Professor Jerzy Limon Library within the theatre building). There could be no possible doubt about the accuracy of the site; the time had come to decide what to put onto it.

Oddly, in all the merry-go-round of activity, very little thought seems to have been given as to exactly what the theatre might look like, what the performance space would be, what kind of performances would be mounted. Was it really just to be a reconstruction of the seventeenth-century Fencing School with its pleasant echoes of the Fortune Theatre in London of the same time? Could this be more than a piece of historical sentimentality? Was this the great Professor Jerzy Limon's big idea? It was not only his idea but the assumption of everyone involved. It is faintly comic but the sheer political, financial, economic, psychological and diplomatic complications of keeping the 'crazy idea' moving forward meant that the fundamental matter of what kind of theatre should it be seems never to have been addressed. The main stipulation was that the building must be made from brick, it should be contemporary.

Holding an international competition in 2005 soon provided a host of answers. The first conclusion from every one of the 40 or so competition entries was that none were interested in pastiche, historical reconstruction. The theatre had to be, to look new, of the time, of its time. All the submissions were modernist using a lot of glass. Jerzy had insisted from the beginning that the design decision would not be his, suggesting either a real uncertainty on his part, real openness of mind about the possibilities or genuine hope that others might have better ideas than himself. At all events, says Justyna Limon, he passed the decision to others: 'My husband gave all the power of the decision making to the commission. He asked an international commission of architects, one of them was sent by The Prince's Trust as well. There were seven of them – Andrzej Wajda as well, our famous film director, who always supported us. It was up to them to decide, it wasn't up to Jerzy. He said, "No, it had to be architects, it must be specialists. There must be theatre people as well."'

What followed was not the theatre's last crisis but certainly a major one even by the standards of its then 15-year odyssey. Following their deliberations, the jurors of the independent commission arrived at the Limon house in a state of confusion. Yes, they had a wonderful project by an Italian architect, Renato Rizzi, but it spread physically far beyond the limits of the available plot of land, filling an entire block. More than a theatre, it was a complex. This broke the terms of the competition. There was no way that the City of Gdańsk Council would, could accept and fund it. With heated argument continuing over drinks, the deadlock was broken by one jury member from New York, recalls Justyna Limon: 'He made a speech in defence of this Italian project. He said, "Look, guys, this Italian architect had the courage to design this, even though he knew he would be rejected, because he broke the rules of the competition. So now, you must have the courage to accept it."'

Jerzy and his colleagues were right to be impressed by Rizzi's scheme. What he gave them was not a single theatre space but a space which could be configured in three different ways. It could have a thrust stage in the Elizabethan manner; it could be a totally flat floor space for theatre in the round; or it could be a box stage with proscenium and facing seats like an Italian theatre. It was wonderfully flexible and adjustable. And it had a roof of 420 square metres, weighing 90 tons, which could swing open in just minutes. No wonder Jerzy wrote about it later in such glowing terms: 'It does not pretend to be ancient, it presents itself as a post-modern creation; it has the ability to reflect the past and comment on it.' Limon added: 'The Gdańsk Shakespeare Theatre originates in the past and at the same time uses twenty-first-century technology. Evoking past centuries, it is also "specialist" in the language of the present era and present aesthetics.' What particularly delighted him was the opening roof, a spectacular *homage* to the original open-roofed Fencing School. For Jerzy, 'it opened the treasure chest'.

More metaphysically, Limon mused: 'The theatre as a building has its own hidden agenda, a kind of text but not one written in words.' That implicit text would have been for everyone who worked there to discover for themselves. My guess is that he could not have been more amazed and delighted by Rizzi's design. (The story of how the competition rule-breaking design came to be accepted and built is for another time and another place.) Construction began in 2011 and finished in 2014, a 25-year journey in all from its inception. As a first-time visitor myself in 2022, I was filled with admiration.

The Gdańsk Shakespeare Theatre (GST) stands alongside a stretch of the city walls. They, like most of the rest of the city, are made of reddish-brown brick. GST is built of black bricks, giving it a look of connection with the city, from the nature of the shared material, and keeping a certain distance too because of the choice of colour. Was Renato Rizzi keeping these two tensions in play, connection/distance? A three-storey rectangular shoebox, rather longer than it is wide, well proportioned, offering a presence without being assertive. The exterior makes no flash gestures, offering rather a quiet, undemonstrative seriousness. The first-time visitor recognizes it as a building, a place, from some distance. It does not need to shout its presence, it has its own. The outside consists mainly of walls, real walls. Perhaps this is Rizzi's most daring trick. The external walls are not the structure of the building; they are walls flanked by open corridors as though the inside of a castle or fort – very odd indeed. The GST is about connecting Poland with Shakespeare, with the world, with fellow scholars and performers, with audiences. Why should it exist within a protecting – excluding – wall? I cannot answer my own question. It may not matter. That may be the wrong comparison. Jerzy called it a treasure chest. It had a roof that raised, a lid for the chest. On this understanding the external walls are the containers for the treasure inside, the theatre. Less a chest, more a casket of precious objects – Shakespeare would surely have approved.

It certainly matters, may not matter, once the visitor enters. They are greeted by light coloured wood surfaces, well-proportioned spaces and a feeling that theatre, however experimental, does not need to be housed in eagerly sought or deliberately manufactured grunge. As for the performing space? On the night I saw it, the layout was conventional, stage, stalls seats facing, with Globe-type galleries at four levels, a permanent feature. Generous, harmonious, atmospheric, intimate but not claustrophobic.

During one of the very first performances at the opening in 2014, there was behind-the-scenes drama. For the occasion, the Bulgarian National Theatre were giving their production of *Hamlet*. As always in the theatre, there was something to worry about. Would the promised opening of the roof actually happen? Boika Sokolova will never forget the moment: 'The atmosphere of the opening was electric. For me, there was an added taste of excitement because the Bulgarian National Theatre was performing, (an invitation I was quietly involved with, on Jerzy's request). That night, it was hoped that the roof would open for the first time in a performance. The huge structure is controlled by very sensitive electronics. If there is wind, it won't budge. But lo and behold, as Claudius, who stood on a ramp over the heads of the front rows, reached the line, "But 'tis not so above", and pointed up, the roof started to open. It was absolutely stunning. The director, Javor Gardev, told me afterwards he was hearing in his earphones, "No, we're terribly sorry, too windy, the roof is not opening" – until it did, almost on cue. Sheer magic.'

Limon would have regarded this as divinely ordained or at least due to the benign intervention of fortune. My own conclusion is simple: any theatre company, any city, any government, any nation would be overjoyed and blessed to have such a theatre even if it was capable only of the one configuration that I witnessed. To have a three-theatres-in-one space is riches beyond the asking. Jerzy's Dream undoubtedly did not conceive of what he finally got. But without having a dream in the first instance, he would have got nothing. Daring to dream was the greatest risk he took. In his own words, as he contemplated GST in all its functioning glory: 'I am not sure if what I am seeing is real or perhaps just a dream. I ask not to be awakened from this dream because I would like it to last forever.'

Jerzy need not have worried. In Shakespeare's *A Midsummer Night's Dream*, the weaver Bottom's dream is disrupted by the intrusion of reality. It proved to have 'no bottom'. In real life, Jerzy's Dream had a real bottom, actual sides and an opening roof. It could not be more real. How did it stay alive for him? Justyna Limon lived with it for as long as he did: 'When he started it, I don't think he thought that it would take 24 years. He was an optimist, a born optimist. I think he thought at the beginning, "Maybe it will take five years," and then maybe 10 years. If somebody had told him at the beginning, "Look, Jurek, it's going to take you most of your lifetime. You won't be able to write your novels, your books because you wouldn't have time for it," I don't know what he would have said. But once he started it, there was no way that he would even hesitate. I haven't seen a moment of hesitation that he would stop.'

Finally, GST opened its doors on its festival on 19 September 2014. Gdańsk had celebrated St Dominic for centuries. Now it had another dimension, one that connected time, people, places and art across the centuries in the most extraordinary ways. An explanation is needed. Who was the person who had the vision and kept it alive to the point of completion, 24 years later? Most of the senior team of executives were chosen by Limon and have worked with him for 15–20 years. Loyalty there was in abundance, of course, but also a clear-eyed understanding of his weaknesses.

Joanna Śnieżko was festival co-ordinator for 20 years. How good was Limon at keeping them informed of what needed doing, of what was going on? 'During all these years, I just realized that even I didn't know about everything because he was dividing his communication to different members of the team. Some of us knew this and some of us knew that. Sometimes he went to the person responsible for sponsors, then he went to the accountant and made some decisions. Not everything was communicated to me. I didn't feel I was in a position where I could ever ask that I should know everything. He was the boss and he was deciding about it. I didn't have the feeling that he totally failed with something, he always found the solution.'

This opaqueness should have been unacceptable to a key executive – Śnieżko should have been in possession of all the facts. It was not made easier, she recalls, by a superstitious streak in Limon's make up, playful in part, but also perfectly real: 'He also believed in miracles. He used to say: "Remember, 'fortune' takes care of us." Because one name of the building that was here before us was the Fortune Theatre. He used to say quite often, "Remember, fortune and the Goddess of Fortune are taking care of us."'

Others were less able to find comfort in such instincts. Limon liked numbers to which he attached a quasi-mystical significance. He loved jokes, usually his own frequently repeated. These very human traits compensated for the inevitable volatility of his reactions. Anna Szynkaruk-Zgirska, engaged in communication and international relations for two decades, witnessed several of them: 'He was sometimes cross and disappointed because not everything went smoothly in this job. There were times that he was angry with us and he communicated it very clearly. Sometimes shouting, but sometimes just saying what we had done wrong and how he saw it from his point of view. I had moments when I said, "This is too much, I can't take it any longer." But then the moment passed and I continued. He was definitely a person that you would look up to.'

No one ever accused Limon of asking things of them that he was not prepared to demand of himself. Maria Gostynska ran his international relations for 15 years: 'He was a workaholic. He sent us emails at 2 a.m., expecting a response because of his being full of ideas. When the theatre was being built and so many things were conducted at one time, we were working really hard. Was he overwhelming us with his ideas? No, it was rather the feeling of "Okay, I want to be part of this enterprise, I want to help him". Sometimes from the physical point of view, you needed to go and get some rest. But they were fantastic times.'

But Gostynska also witnessed the limitations of Limon's approach to working and the price he was probably paying: 'Passion is the most important driver in our lives actually. You need to have passion in your life, otherwise you will just get burned out. He was shining with his passion and his knowledge and his eloquence and it attracted people. He came across many difficulties, especially office rules or things that he was always complaining about. Sometimes, passion is not enough to overcome these difficulties. He was angry about that. But my role was to see what's possible and what's not.'

Yet another longstanding colleague, Anna Ratkiewicz, has run GST's education programmes for 20 years from the time when such activities hardly existed at large in the arts world. She catches something of the subtlety of the way Limon managed activities and people: 'He was very demanding. You had to do what he wanted, what he asked, but he was also very open. If I had an idea, I could come and say: "Professor, maybe we could do something different?" He always said yes, he was open. He didn't say that would cost a lot. He said okay, the sky is the limit: "Anna, dream and we will try to get funds." He trusted people, he was always optimistic.'

In Anna Ratkiewicz's experience, Limon often got closely involved in the practical details of projects. As he did so, he shared the responsibility for decisions and what was and was not working: 'He was observing, he was seeing the troubles. He was giving you directions: "Okay, Anna, maybe you should do it in a different way." We talked a lot after and during the event, but it was always optimistic. When we decided to end something, it was both our decision, not just his. He was, "Okay, Anna, maybe we'll stop this one because it doesn't work." But it was always sharing. It was not, "I said it and you have to do it." It was "Anna, what do you think?" And the sentence "The sky is the limit" was his everyday sentence.'

As an academic colleague, Tadeusz Wolański was never subject to such human minutiae of management. He was strongly aware of the way Limon behaved towards his team, many of whom had been his students: 'He looked after them incredibly, he was charming to the nth degree. He really was polite, never an unsuitable word. He used to give people their head as well: "This is your job. I want it done, how you do it is up to you. I'll support you anytime you want anything." But he wasn't looking over people's shoulders.'

It was a combination of detailed understanding of what was needed combined with a deep trust in people. Viewing it from close up but removed from the actual operational front line, Justyna Limon expressed Limon's working style as 'This is the task, it's up to you how to do it!': 'They felt such enormous responsibility that they would do everything not to let him down because of this freedom that he gave them. It was the same with the artists. That was the secret. All of them called him "Professor" or "Prof". They said, "We had to do the best because we couldn't let him down because he had such faith in us." They felt this trust. He praised them and they just did everything for him.'

In one respect at least, Limon was utterly conventional. His wife, Justyna, was a highly successful businessperson, her earnings made his role as full-time campaigner for the theatre possible. Jerzy always said he could not have done it without her financial support, but he did not consult her on practical matters or at least admit that he did and might even have followed her advice. Justyna recalls: 'Jerzy didn't like any advice from me. I would say, "About marketing, I would do this and that." He listened to me but he didn't like to admit that. Because I was critical and I often criticized this and that and of course, he didn't like that.'

There were at least two further dimensions to Jerzy Limon, the 'Professor', the respected academic, the translator of Shakespeare into demotic Polish, the student of theatre productions, the scourer of obscure archives. He loved Shakespeare but, according to Anna Reichel, he was no snob: 'He never approached Shakespeare on his knees. He wasn't praying to Shakespeare. He understood very well, there was a "Bethlehem period" of educated people who came to the theatre. There were also the "groundlings". He understood very well the different layers of humour of the text in Shakespeare so that it could be understood. He was never elitist in his approach and wanted to show it to as many people as possible. He wanted to make people believe that they belonged and could come and see Shakespeare. Basically, Shakespeare was very funny, sometimes a little bit obnoxious and it could be conveyed to different types of people. It was very open to everybody.'

Limon was so steeped in Shakespeare, his characters, his thoughts, his approach to life that it mediated his own responses to behaviour, life and to other people's actions. Sometimes, thought Anna Reichel, it even made life easier for him: 'He was the least judgemental person I've ever met. Even when there were times when people cheated on us because they said they would give money and they didn't. He always said, "It's human nature, Shakespeare wrote about it in this play or in that play. He acts exactly as that person or that character." It was because he lived Shakespeare in a way, he knew him so well. It was all blended in and was very coherent.'

Limon's generosity and curiosity of mind showed itself in many ways. He loved thinking up projects and especially ones with fancy names. It is not clear what he would have included in a venture called 'Shakesploring Europe' but it was a brilliant title for something that would not have been dull. Project collaborator Robert Florczak always saw him as far more than a Shakespeare scholar, a man of the theatre: 'Jerzy was a man of great ideas. I am certain he was a great conceptual artist. But he was too modest and he just didn't want to convey this. He gave these ideas like cuckoo's eggs. Artists are very keen on using somebody's idea and treating it as theirs and they often forget that it's not their idea. So he used to give us these cuckoo's eggs and we treated them as ours and we'd nourish them. And unfortunately, we're out of these cuckoo's eggs.'

Jerzy Limon saw his vision of theatre and theatre productions realized for six years in his finally realized GST – 'Gdańsk Shakespeare Theatre' – from 2014. I had one experience of the GST summer festival experience in July 2022. That year, the festival staged 19 productions from nine, mainly European countries. Anyone expecting or perhaps hoping for text-based versions of Shakespeare would have been surprised, even disappointed. High reverence for the text is not the hallmark of European Shakespeare. How could it be given the language and translation question? What I saw was an intense, physical, dance, sound- and movement-based interpretation of *Titus Andronicus*, perhaps Shakespeare's bloodiest play. As a theatrical experience, regardless of the source material, it struck me as brilliantly conceived and superbly executed. Were the moral questions addressed? Probably not by relying on Shakespeare's text. Probably 'yes', judging as far as I could by the physicality of the action and the professionalism of the company.

Was this the kind of approach that Limon intended and hoped for? Boika Sokolova has few doubts: 'A precious jewel set in the silver sea might be a good tag to describe the theatre. Jerzy referred to the overall structure as a treasure box. In the centre of the box is that precious, wooden, historical and very modern space, where you can do practically everything. What the opening of the theatre did was that in this space, you can do modern theatre, you can do happening, you can do very cutting-edge theatre work, you can do Shakespeare, you can do renaissance drama. The space, which is also so beautiful, is so full of symbolic layers because everything in this theatre is very carefully thought through. This is a place which is really exceptional.'

In February 2021, Jerzy developed a cough. Though Covid was still raging, there was no reason for linking his overt symptoms with the pandemic. Besides, he always had bad throats at this time of the year because he talked so much. The symptoms grew worse, Covid was diagnosed, he was taken to hospital and died a fortnight after first falling ill on 3 March 2021. The shock among colleagues was huge; the level of despair, according to Tadeusz Wolański, 'unbelievable'. Perhaps Jerzy could have summoned up a Shakespearian parallel of a hero struck down in his prime. He might have thought that too vainglorious.

Boika Sokolova returns to a word Limon used about the theatre itself: 'The intense reaction from all over the Shakespeare community just showed what a treasure of a person Jerzy himself was. He created a treasure of a theatre, but it takes a treasure of a person, a person of a particular kind to do that. So it was an immense sense of loss and devastation. His work meant more than it matters in purely scholarly terms. It was a kind of rare gift. It showed that the impossible could be attained, that these

Europeans could do it. And they have been doing it, despite everything. He was a trailblazer.'

In the summer of 2022, at the 26th Gdańsk Shakespeare Festival, at its organizational height, I discovered a variety of ways of coming to terms with Jerzy's death. For some, like Joanna Śnieżko, it was the projects he conceived but will in fact be realized, such as seminars on the 'Helplessness of the Philosopher' based on Shakespeare's works. For Robert Florczak, the memory and the legacy are something even more playful: 'One of his last ideas was the "Smallest Theatre in the World", which would be in one of those advertising columns, the round ones. We had architects already working on this, I was also the consultant. Whether it's going to have two floors or one floor and two artists, or one artist, the smallest theatre in the world. It was going to be on wheels so that you could put it in different places and it was supposed to be first in Dluga Street in Gdańsk, one of the advertising methods of the theatre. But it was also an incredible concept to have.'

The level of despair at Jerzy's sudden death has been followed by the sense of utter loss. He left behind a fully realized version of an impossible dream which he pursued to the point of obsession and exhaustion over 25 years. His devotion to Shakespeare was total. It was also, as Maria Gostynska once discovered, utterly confident, utterly undogmatic and utterly commonsensical. She was often asked by journalists about the very existence of Shakespeare: 'I said, "Professor, everybody says that Shakespeare has never existed. What should I answer? Was he living or not?" And he replied, "Even if he wasn't, so what? We have his legacy, his literature, whether it was Ben Johnson, Marlowe or whoever."'

Jerzy Limon cannot be awakened from his final dream but he lived to realize a dream that everyone but he thought was either impossible, unrealistic, impractical or actually mad. And the theatre is a treasure.

Observations

+ A dream may be dismissed as impossible but can still come to fruition, and a dream may be dismissed as mad but may still be realized.

+ Even the dreamer can recognize the madness of his dream but believe that the madness is the factor that leads to its success.

+ There is actual madness, sheer irrationality and divine madness, truly a gift from the gods. Determining the difference between the two types of madness is in the gift of the dreamer.

+ Keeping a dream alive over 25 years requires a refusal to look failure in the face as a possibility.

+ Fortune may well favour the brave but no one should count on it.

+ Many skills are needed to devise, manage and run a cultural project. If they are not known, they must be acquired.

+ Big visions require and deserve big gestures. Having a big vision may attract a fellow dreamer.

+ Winning local support involves fun and entertainment. Earning international support needs calculation, flattery and charm.

+ Loyalty is the glue that binds a team together. Loyalty and authority are the key elements of the network of trust.

+ Leaders move on or pass away. The vision endures. A great vision calls for a great leader.

+ Not every leader is illuminated by illuminations. If they are, they shed a special light for all to see. When leadership and scholarship are worn lightly, they are irresistible.

References

Marta Gibinska, Malgorzata Grzegorzewska, Jacek Fabiszak and Agnieszka Zukowska, *This Treasure of Theatre: Shakespeare and the Arts from the Early Modern Period to the Twenty-first Century: Essays in Honour of Professor Jerzy Limon* (Slowo/obraz terytoria, 2020).

Jerzy Limon, 'A Theatre of Two Times: A Stroll around the Gdańsk Shakespeare Theatre'.

Robert Florczak, 'With the Help of the Muses: 25 Years of the Gdańsk Shakespeare Festival: Retrospective, Recycling, Remix'.

Twenty-sixth Shakespeare Festival catalogue, 2022.

7

'A Decent Attempt': Sharing Knowledge with Russians After the Great Collapse, 1991

Featuring interviews with:
Andrei Allakhverdov, Radio journalist and presenter
Neil Cameron, TV documentary director
Elena Cook, Radio producer and presenter
Fiona Cushley, Radio and TV producer and director
Corinna Furse, Executive Director, Marshall Plan of the
    Mind (MPM)
Natasha Groom, audience researcher
Tim Grout-Smith, Executive producer, TV and Radio
Nik Abu Haidar, Radio and TV producer
David Morton, Head of Russian Service, BBC World
    Service
Guy Pugh, Radio producer
Tim Williams, Head of MPM, Moscow Office

The fall of the Soviet Union in 1991 is rightly called the 'great collapse', carrying with it implications of political, economic, societal and institutional destruction causing a void of almost unimaginable dimensions. Would the former Soviet Union become akin to a cosmic black hole whose intense destructive energy would drag into it anyone unwise enough to approach too closely? The great collapse of a nuclear super power could not be overlooked, ignored or still less dismissed. This is the account of how a randomly assembled group of journalists and broadcasters came to face up to the black hole. They saw it less as a cosmic style phenomenon with its malign gravitational pull towards annihilation, rather as a mere (albeit huge) void which might be filled, should be filled, even demanded to be filled. The material they would use to fill it would be knowledge of how a post-Soviet, post-authoritarian society could run itself better, needed to be run better in the interests of its bewildered citizens, adrift in an unknown sea of freedom and personal responsibility. An enormous undertaking, it is also an account of how high-level leadership can be expressed by a group. Sometimes, leadership, it seems, does not require a single leader.

Furthermore, the story of the Marshall Plan of the Mind (MPM) demonstrates that the person who conceived the idea is usually not the one to turn it into actuality. I should know. As managing director of the BBC World Service in 1991, I was very aware of the importance of Russian and English language broadcasts over a generation or more in providing listeners in the Soviet Union with knowledge about the world and their own country which their own broadcasters denied them. We knew that these broadcasts were valued, especially by the KGB – after all, they really needed to know about what was going on around the world.

It was a City businessman who first suggested to me that the BBC's status, reputation and influence should be deployed to provide information about how to live in post-communist Russia. On the back of this casual conversation, I made a hopeful speech on the idea to the Prince of Wales's Business Forum in October 1991. I was not prepared for the positive response. A working party to explore the idea was set up, a funding request to the government's Know How Fund (KHF) submitted in March

1992. The MPM project, with KHF funding, was launched at the Banqueting House, Whitehall, in January 1993, just 15 months after my first exploratory speech. How can this speed of response be explained?

MPM Head Tim Williams captures the mood of the time. By moving fast, he points out, we were well ahead of our competitors in the aid/development/consultancy field: 'Seizing that moment was important. There was a need and immediately there was this response. We weren't sitting around thinking about it, committees discussing, limiting everything. It was just "let's get on and do it". It was the spirit of the organization. There was a general sense of racing, a very fast direction of movement. We all got into the flow of that stream.'

Personally, I shared the excitement of the sense of need, opportunity and speed of response. Thereafter, I kept a close watching and supporting brief, encouraging but no further. Others though went beyond enthusiasm and followed through in practice over the next decade. They turned an idea into a project, the merely possible into the dramatically actual. It lasted for a decade, some elements of it rather longer. It ceased when politics at the highest level changed decisively in the new Russia. The fact that MPM stopped does not mean that it was a failure. It demonstrated the novel experience of a kind of group leadership based on shared understanding and purpose. Such shared leadership is rare. For it to happen and succeed in any degree is rarer still.

None of it can be fully understood without recollecting the reality of Russia as it emerged from the ruins of the Soviet Union, freed from the shackles of the Communist Party. David Morton, then heading the BBC Russian Service, insists that no one then knew what might happen and that if change was to come, no one knew what direction it would follow. For the immediate present in 1991, all that was clear was that everything

217

was different: 'Everything fell apart. Nobody knew what was happening. The institutions carried on but the lifeblood had been sucked out. Universities continued, as did prisons, schools and workplaces, but they had no funds. They had to try and get money from somewhere. They were all constantly looking for sponsors so that they could do the things that they'd been doing before. The same experience was echoed across everything you looked at.'

Executive producer Tim Grout-Smith could not altogether believe the lack of knowledge in the former Soviet Union about how the routine practicalities of life in a non-authoritarian society were practised. The knowledge gap was huge and with it an even bigger deficit of understanding about how an open pluralist society – if that was to be the alternative – might operate. He lists a catalogue of ignorance instilled by three generations of centralized communism, a vast litany of misery: 'How does a civil society work? How do you run a small business? How do you manage a farm now that the collective farms are broken down? A so-called culture "belief system" collapsed. How did they earn their living? What was insurance? How did NGOs work? Within the agricultural system, a huge dislike of private farming and misunderstanding of what it meant.'

In the actual experience of everyday living, David Morton recalls, the great collapse was personal, puzzling and painful: 'Suddenly money didn't have any value. In the days of the Soviet Union, you were on a salary of some kind, earning perhaps 150/200 roubles a month. That sum suddenly meant nothing at all. You could hardly live on 150 roubles. Pensioners who were on 50 or 60 roubles were in a worse situation. It was perhaps not as shocking as we might think in the sense that Russian pensioners and people outside the cities had lived extremely badly in the Soviet Union for years and years. There was nothing unusual even in the Soviet period of old ladies living on tea and black bread for decades. There wasn't much in the shops in the Soviet period. And there wasn't much imagination to do anything with it. It was a very, very poor society.'

This society abruptly got even poorer after 1991 and no one had any idea of what would come next. It wasn't as if nothing was working but as Grout-Smith was to discover, any business activity that did take place was riddled with contradictions: 'Some lovely people who were setting up a clothes business said, "Look, if we were totally legal, we would pay 100 per cent of our profits back to the state." There were punitive laws that still regarded capitalism as inherently corrupt. Everybody was working slightly illegally, which benefited all sorts of corruption. You could always get something for something. The laws were wrong and that's what corrupted the system. How did you get food from the farm to the shops without it being hugely damaged? I remember people sweeping peppers out of an open bed truck with brooms at a shop in Kyiv, that was how primitive it was.'

Into the wide open spaces of institutional collapse, private destitution, social and economic ignorance, something worse than opportunism was quick to move in and show its face. As Radio and TV producer Nik Abu Haidar found, it went beyond mere corruption – it was the mafia: 'I was in St Petersburg and called a guy who was setting up a pizza place – revolutionary for St Petersburg at the time. Saying, "Can I come and see you for an interview?" He said, "Of course, what time?" I said, "Three o'clock." His words were: "I can't see you at three, I've got the Mafia coming at three". Being young and stupid, I said, "Do you mind if I come anyway? Can I try and interview the Mafia?" When I got there, I found two guys whose knuckles were dragging on the floor. And I went up to them and said, "Hi, I'm from the BBC and I'm really interested in what you're doing. Is it alright if I interview you?" For a split second, I thought I might have asked my last question in life. They looked at me, they just laughed and thought, is anyone really this stupid? They said, "No, we're not going to talk to you." They concluded their business and left. When I spoke to the entrepreneur afterwards, I said, "What are you going to do? Are you going to pay them?" And he said to me, "Look, Nik, you don't understand. I'm not rich enough to be able not to pay them."'

The situation of the new Russia was in a sense worse than a void, it was a nightmare. Into this seemingly unpromising environment, BBC MPM launched its first three series of programmes in January 1993. Financed by the British Know How Fund and corporate sponsors, the programmes covered 'How Business Works', the 'Free Market Society' and, inspired by the educational, outreach work of the BBC Radio 4's legendary drama *The Archers*, a Russian daily soap opera, *Dom Syem, Podyezd Chetyre*.

Writing in March 1993, less than three months after the start of broadcasting, Corinna Furse, MPM's executive director, could say: 'We started out idealistic but we had no idea of what we were facing. Secretly, in the early stages, we did not really believe we could achieve what we have. In the last three months, we have gone from talking about ideas to having three programmes on Russian airwaves. It's like getting from nought to 60 miles an hour in 4.3 seconds.'

The new and special ingredient lay in the fact that MPM programmes were carried on domestic Russian broadcasting air waves. President Boris Yeltsin had set up a new independent national broadcaster, the All Russian Radio and TV Company (VGTRK). Its visionary director, Oleg Poptsov, took what must have been a real risk: he decided to co-operate with MPM, to partner even. For 70 years, BBC World Service broadcasts had reached Soviet listeners solely through the medium of shortwave radio transmitted from outside the Soviet Union. These were often jammed. Now MPM programmes, independent of the BBC, guided by a significantly different agenda, became part of the fabric of domestic Russian listening, thanks to the arrangement with Poptsov and VGRK. It is impossible to overestimate the importance of this relationship. MPM programmes would go into every Russian domestic kitchen, thanks to the built-in *tochka*. Millions of homes had it on the whole time, especially those in the countryside.

There was no contradiction with BBC World Service, which in all its languages from Russian to English had always provided open news and information. But MPM offered something importantly distinct: knowledge and skills. On the first night of transmission of 'Free Market Society' in January 1993, Radio Russia's phone lines were jammed with calls from across the nation.

Crucially, Russian listeners would not have tuned in, still less paid attention, had they suspected the motives or the message of the broadcasters. It was an article of MPM philosophy, there was no 'message'. Information provided in the programmes was there for listeners to use or not as they personally decided. MPM's approach had to be built on seeking trust and deserving to be trusted. Few understood this better than a former Russian radio broadcasting anchor, Andrei Allakhverdov: 'We were making information available. At that time, everyone discovered everything. Things were introduced in society and the economy that people really did not understand. At the same time, there were social institutions that no one understood how they worked; insurance in healthcare or how education would work in this new society. Everyone was used to the fact that everything had been owned by the state. Now we needed to do it ourselves and we needed to understand how it worked. It was absolutely invaluable information, absolutely openly given. It was not just a theory.'

MPM programme makers above all came face to face with people who ran businesses but knew all too well that abnormal new conditions meant they had to learn new methods fast. The approach of the broadcaster to this situation and to such people was, as producer Guy Pugh learned, crucial. Openness was key: 'We were trying to spread the word. It's about changing but also just trying to find positive messages and say, "This is what you can do. And this is the way life can be led". That was the mission statement we had, "creating good by doing good, inspired by the best". We also tried to find homegrown examples where all people had to do was tell us about what they were doing in their environment.'

Every programme maker was aware of the possibility of misunderstanding MPM's intentions and purposes. Worse still, misrepresentation of intentions was a real danger. It would have been all too easy to fall into one of several traps. Was this not just capitalist propaganda, a neo-imperialist plot? Documentary director Neil Cameron always faced up to the potential dangers of such accusations: 'We were concerned about it. I don't think we really experienced much ourselves because we were cautious. We approached with an attitude of "We're here to find out, we're not here to tell you stuff". There was a very open attitude on the part of the people we'd gone to see. We weren't outsiders going in to tell them how to do things. We had to be very careful not to say, "You're doing it all wrong" or anything like that. We said, "We're here to look at how you do these things and to look at how other places do these things."'

Cameron summed up the approach as 'permissive rather than didactic', adopted in large measure because much of the MPM team had a background of common experience of life under the former Soviet Union and the attitudes inbred by the system:

'People had always been told how they should do things. They'd been directed from on high. That annoyed them, but there was nothing they could do about it. We could encourage them to think, "No, you don't have to rely on people from on high, you can do this for yourselves". We were going into places that had operated in an authoritarian regime for a long time. We wanted to be very gentle to say, "Let's ask you questions, let's find out from you," but encourage them to think that they could do things better.'

Despite this, wariness, doubts and caution were bound to appear. When Tim Grout-Smith met suspicion about MPM's motives, he could reply on the basis of personal experience: 'I know people say, "Oh, international aid can be imperialist". I didn't think we did that at all. We found very willing, eager recipients of the kind of information we were giving them. We did a whole TV series with a workbook and a radio series on agriculture. In Ukraine we gave them free to both independent and national state broadcasters. The independent broadcasters came to us months later and said it was so popular, "Could we run it again, please?" The posters advertising our series became something of collector's items. They were taken down from bus stops almost as soon as they could get them.'

That easy accusations failed to stick says a great deal for the basic underlying philosophy of MPM: 'Here is information that you may find useful in the circumstances in which Russia now exists. Do with it what you will!' A lesser charge could easily be levelled; that the enthusiastic band of MPM producers and programme makers were just idealistic 'do-gooders', a suggestion rebutted by Nik Abu Haidar: 'It's a very easy term to throw, unfounded abuse. With my hand on my heart, nobody in that team was a do-gooder. Everybody was driven by a desire to do something positive. We have to remember the context of the time. No one knew what the hell was going on. No one knew how things were going to develop. There were no rules. Everybody was driven by a belief that there was something positive to be done here. Whether we did it correctly, whether we made mistakes, that's a completely different debate. But if anyone is saying there were a lot of do-gooders who wanted to sound good in social events in Islington, that is not the case.'

It helped that the MPM team were all highly aware of Russian feelings about their own country. Poor they might be, misruled they had been, controlled they were, confused they had become, but, as David Morton points out, in Russian minds outsiders had no business to judge them: 'Russians are highly sensitive to any notion that they weren't any longer a very great country. It's always been true that if you want to make a speech in Russia, the best thing to do is to make a few references early on to "your vast country". They love the idea. They've been told for years that it's the greatest country in the world. Deep down, they believe that. When you were dealing from the BBC's perspective, or from MPM's perspective, anything which sounded patronizing raised hackles in the most terrible way.'

Perhaps the worst error in judging the Russian response to MPM was made by me when choosing the very title of the project – 'Marshall Plan of the Mind'. I was inspired by memories of the historical Marshall Plan of April 1948 when vast quantities of US funding literally put Western European economies back on their feet after the ravages of the Second World War. It was described as the most disinterested act in modern history. It seemed to me that the comparably disinterested process of providing information and skills to a nation in acute transition 50 years later merited invoking the 'Marshall Plan' name. I was well-meaning historically, naive psychologically. There were at least three assumptions in my thinking that were incorrect. Soviet Leader Josef Stalin had totally rejected any Marshall Plan aid. Then, the very word 'mind' evoked 'thought control' in most Russians, a controlled world from which they were just escaping. Finally, as BBC World Service's David Morton heard for himself, Russian officialdom hated it: 'They thought it was dreadful. I remember Boris Pankin, the ambassador in London, gently telling people in the BBC that it wasn't a good idea to call it "Marshall Plan of the Mind" because it made it look as if his countrymen were begging for charity from the West. In some ways they were but the idea that that's what they were doing was completely unacceptable.'

The fact that the very title did not unseat the entire project at the first hurdle may be due to three factors. Most Russians had long forgotten about the historical Marshall Plan, let alone Stalin's rejection of it (his rejection might have counted in its favour!). The new programme quickly became known as 'MPM' and few Russians bothered to question what the letters stood for. Above all, the MPM team seldom fell into the trap of thinking themselves better than their audience and Russian collaborators.

Their background and outlook were crucial. Most spoke Russian, most had lived in the former Soviet Union and knew it for what it was. Some were Russian and had married Englishmen, some were Russian nationals recruited to the MPM programme-making teams. They shared several characteristics, they were very different from previous generations of Soviet experts. These, while fluent Russian speakers and authoritative in Soviet politics, had seldom lived in the country. Besides they had been too involved fighting the Cold War and many became out-and-out Cold Warriors. They saw the Soviet Union through the prism of ideology, the battle of ideas, the existential conflict with Western democracies.

For their part, the MPM cohort were dealing with Russia, with problems of material wellbeing, of everyday living, with matters of skills, knowledge and information. Most of them, not merely those born Russian, loved the country, the nation, the culture, the very idea of Russia. Having often lived in the former Soviet Union made a huge difference in their perceptions. Young, often recent graduates, they were not the children of the Cold War and could not have been further from the assumptions and inclinations of the Cold Warriors. They did not join MPM to defeat communism, they got involved because they wanted to help Russians.

It helped that the Russians on the team, such as Andrei Allakhverdov, smelled hope in the air of the early 1990s: 'For us young journalists, it was the time of hopes, the time of where and when we could realize everything we were thinking about. It was a time of intensive learning about everything, of the life around us in the country, outside the country. We discovered that we could travel, we could discover the world, understand how things work in the world, the economy, politics, everything. Just everyday life and it was very exciting.'

That sense of optimism, of almost infinite possibility even in the chaos of post-Soviet Russia, was shared by his fellow Russian on the MPM team, Elena Cook: 'All these ideas floating about, doing things creatively, doing things in an unbiased way without any state propaganda, having multiple voices, all of it seemed to be extremely exciting. For me, it was really revolutionary. There was absolutely no precedent and nothing I could think of which was similar to it. I was really overwhelmed.'

Such intensely personal and Russian perspectives were an essential part of the MPM mix. Putting together the team of broadcasters, documentary filmmakers, radio producers, writers and organizers, keeping it coherent and working to the single, though simple, line would never have been easy. Doing so from a London office while teams spread out over the whole of Russia and Europe was difficult, may have seemed impossible. The later move to Moscow scarcely made such problems easier, given the super continental size of Russia.

For a good decade, MPM stayed remarkably consistent in its approach to programme making, did not break up into factions or cliques and suffered no ideological ruptures over purposes and content. This may be explained by at least three factors. For a start, the Mission Statement was very simple: 'To further the understanding of a pluralist society and market economy; to provide individuals with the knowledge and skills to enable them to determine their economic and political future; to foster greater understanding between East and West.'

This mission statement was the lodestar of the senior management team of two people: Executive Head Corinna Furse and Editorial Director Kari Blackburn. They were a well-balanced and harmonious team, Furse a calm and capable administrator well-versed in bidding for funds, negotiating with supporters and funders and showing the production teams that she knew that her responsibility was to keep the project active and alive. She was the calm centre of something which could have spun off into confusion, even chaos. Order and purpose had to be maintained and Furse provided it.

On the programming side, Kari Blackburn was a brilliant intellect, a questing and imaginative mind, who understood the magnitude of both the MPM task, the opportunity it offered and the creative programming through which those purposes might be realized. Colleagues recall that she knew what was being made but never interfered or micromanaged. Together, Furse and Blackburn offered and provided common sense, consistent and unified direction, efficiency and devotion to the MPM project.

The two of them were after all running a new project for a new country in a previously uncharted and undefined way. There was no management model for what they were doing, no example to follow and no lessons from previous experience to turn to. That they achieved what they did as a joint leadership was a considerable achievement. Neither, however, claimed to be the totemic, perhaps charismatic figure who personified the project, provided public profile and whose single-minded belief, determination and commitment kept it going. Neither would have wanted that for themselves, still less for MPM. If Elena Cook saw Kari Blackburn as 'charismatic, creative, responsible and encouraging, like a mother' that did not diminish the deep harmony and co-operation between Kari and Corinna.

Yet was there a certain leadership absence at the very top as a result? Didn't a project such as MPM, continental in its range, ambitious to a fault, risky beyond measure, require, demand, the charismatic leader that so many other analogous projects of this kind had in practice? Wasn't the single-minded leader almost a necessary condition for success? The experience of MPM suggests that in certain particular cases, leadership can evolve its own form shaped by specific circumstances.

Each member of the MPM team had a different way of describing what occurred in practice. For Nik Abu Haidar, unity emerged from shared practices: 'The reason that MPM was able to function without a charismatic leader is that different production teams were doing different things in different projects. They each had within them, if not a charismatic leader, strong individuals with a fierce dedication to making the best programmes they could. There was camaraderie at the team level. The level of charisma was to some extent provided in each of the teams. Everybody needed to be driven by a single vision, not necessarily a single clearly set out vision. There was a level of conviction, which might have been interpreted in slightly different ways, but the direction was still the same.'

For Neil Cameron, the essential words that made up the experience of collective leadership among and within the production teams were 'collegial, collaborative, exploratory, innovative'. He added a characteristic of the whole MPM project was that no one ever said 'things must be done this way'. In Tim Grout-Smith's experience, the key description was of a leadership practice as 'a diverse sort of autonomous set-up', informed by a 'collective spirit full of ideas, drive and enthusiasm'.

Guy Pugh's attempt at defining how the MPM project held itself together through the team's collective sense of purpose was less lofty, rather more practical: 'It was a commitment to a core identity. We had a lot of MPM whole group meetings. We were all conscious of what the other teams were doing. We had this shared background. It was very easy for us to have friendship relationships with all sorts of people. There was a lot of support between projects. If you could help an author, or you needed to find a story, you could always approach colleagues very straightforwardly and get help if you were struggling.'

Perhaps the actuality of how MPM kept its sense of direction and purpose is best caught by Elena Cook's simple-sounding observation: 'It was like a beehive, but we didn't have the "queen bee".' This pointed to the fact that everyone worked tirelessly to a common purpose, shared and understood beyond the needs of regular instruction and direction.

These observations may explain how the MPM project evolved to a situation where those who made the programmes became in practice its intellectual leaders as a group. That does not make it less remarkable. The only explanation may lie in the extraordinary nature of the intellectual challenge they had been given, they had accepted and that they then set about solving in practice. Nothing less than to create a picture of Old Soviet Union morphing into New Russia and no fewer than 14 other countries besides, it was a huge redrawing of the geo-political landscape. For the MPM project, it was an epic challenge.

Phase One of MPM funding with £1.5 million from the government Know How Fund started in January 1993. On the basis of its performance Phase Two followed 18 months later in 1994 with doubled funding of £2.6 million. Phase Three in July 1996 attracted even more Know How Fund backing, of £4.1 million. In that time MPM made a series of programmes on business, democracy at national and local level, agriculture, personal finance, management, charities, economics, culture, law and the media and the radio 'soap opera' about everyday life in modern Russia, *Dom Syem*. That bald catalogue cannot begin to capture the intensity of the lived political and social experience the MPM teams found as they traversed the nation, as wide as two continents.

Few plunged into a wide range of projects more extensively than Guy Pugh and Nik Abu Haidar. It might have been ambitious in a Western country accustomed to the ways of television documentary crews but it was almost unheard of in Russia, no matter how seemingly freed from communist shackles. They dreamt up four areas of Russian life and business to examine: 'One was about aeroplanes because the Russian manufacturer, Sukhoi, makes fighters and bombers but also some of the best piston-engined aerobatic planes in the world. And this is a sideline, an enthusiasm which they had developed. They gave us the most tremendous access to factories where they were developing fighters. We interviewed the top man at Sukhoi, he was a hero of the Soviet Union. I also worked on a programme about fashion. We filmed in Moscow, Kostroma and Novosibirsk in Siberia, different fashion houses. We did a film about agriculture, a guy who was privatizing a farm near Krasnodar in the South of Russia. And football. Vladikavkaz. Nik Abu Haidar is probably the most passionate supporter of Barnet Football Club. We made a film about Spartak Vladikavkaz, the top team in Russia, even though it was in North Ossetia, more or less in the middle of nowhere.'

This would have been ambitious anywhere, at any time. In evolving Russia, it should have bordered on the reckless. But it paid off. The organizational effort needed is hard to capture. A decision was made to run seminars on business in five centres, not just the easy ones such as Moscow and St Petersburg, stuffed with Western bankers and consultants but business seminars in the regions. Nik Abu Haidar took it on: 'We had to organize travel around them at a time when there was no clarity as to whether the local airline was flying. You arrived in a town and had to work out whether the timetable was still on Moscow time or local time, that level of anarchy. I travelled around with thousands of dollars in cash on my person because you couldn't use a credit card. Trying to recce hotels to see is this a place where our business trainers can come? Somebody saying, "Well, we've got everything, we've got hot water, we've got cold water." That was the level. We went to five different cities in the provinces at a time when they were not developed. The further you got from Moscow, the less the changes had hit. We filled five business centres, three days each in five different places. Normal people, unassuming people who were trying to work out how to set up a business. They were thinking, "Okay, this is now legal. Let me think about this." Were we pushing on an open door? There was a huge desire for it and a need.'

Halfway across Russia, deep in Siberia, Elena Cook found herself in a meeting with the local mayor and governor. They couldn't wait to talk: 'We went to a sort of regional parliament, who were sitting for the first time, and all these members of the Parliament were openly talking about their ideas. We had this live recording of what was going on. We also had an interview with the mayor of Irkutsk and the governor of Irkutsk Oblast, about local and regional democracy. Then we all went to the *banya* [bath house] of course after the broadcast, in minus 30 degrees, to be lashed with *veniks* [birch bath brooms], rolled in the snow and shared shots of vodka.'

Closer to the centre, Guy Pugh too met an adventurous local mayor with a highly modern personal agenda for change: 'We made one film about a mayor who was pushing strong, democratic ideals in a satellite town outside Moscow. He was eloquent and a very impressive character, very welcoming, because we wanted to make a film about him. It was interesting to see him in operation and how he wanted to generate some levels of democracy, which were unheard of in Russia. He ruffled some feathers and of course, he ruffled so many feathers that he eventually got murdered.'

A stark reminder that the dark side of Russia was never far away. But the headiness, the exhilaration of hope and freedom could not be damped down. The further from Moscow, the greater the exuberance, the exhilaration. Elena Cook found it erupting in the Russian republic of Tatarstan on the River Volga: 'Boris Yeltsin was the one who addressed Russia's regions with the textbook phrase, "Take as much sovereignty as you can swallow". Tatarstan was a model for it. We went to Tatarstan, met the advisers to the Tatarstan President Shaimiyev, an innovative thinker. Some had trained in the West, clever, intelligent, professional. Just being able to go inside the Kremlin in the capital, Kazan, was unbelievable. We also went to a restaurant with one of the President's advisers and spent four hours talking about everything freely, no bounds on any topic. How Tatarstan was going to develop, what ideas they had, what autonomy meant to them.'

In the event Tatarstan's attempt at full sovereignty was rejected by Moscow. In these heady days almost everything seemed possible, however briefly. The former Soviet Russia would not vanish that simply. Travelling widely from Siberia to European Russia, Tim Grout-Smith came face to face with the realities of the old Soviet industrial system and practices: 'I went to Novosibirsk in Siberian Russia then to Tolyatti, the headquarters of Soviet car manufacturing. They had bizarre economic practices under which they sold an enormous number of cars to Finland under a formal agreement. The Finns then sold them back again because the vendors didn't want them. But they had to have them under some ridiculous political treaty they'd signed. We were coming across some very weird practices.'

The extent of the MPM team's travelling across and throughout former Soviet Union/new Russia cannot be overestimated. It is hard to imagine any other institution undertaking, let alone carrying out, what was almost a vast research as well as teaching project. The producers and programme makers could never have fully anticipated the unpredictable variety of what they found, politically, socially, culturally. Like Guy Pugh, they had to be ready for anything and were seldom disappointed: 'We did one film about a metal and jewellery factory in a godforsaken town called Zlatoust in the Urals, a real backwater. Somebody else had previously tried to make a film about Zlatoust and the Mafia had literally taken over the town. We made a film about a theatre in Magnitogorsk, which was a great story because the guy who had taken it over was a refugee from Tajikistan. As a Russian speaker in Tajikistan, he was a film director in jeopardy who had to get out very fast. Magnitogorsk, a city built around a massive steel, copper factory is not the most awe-inspiring place for theatre but he made it work and it was good.'

Such experiences painted the big picture of former Soviet Union/new Russia – contradictory, confused, inefficient, wasteful, random. The need to know about the modern business ways of the world outside was on a vast scale. In a sense that was hardly surprising. Elena Cook was to discover something else, more ordinary in one sense, more important in another. How far the vital threads of connection that constituted civil society as generally understood and practised did not exist at all: 'We did a series of programmes called *The Town Where I Live*. We went all over Russia with Russian producers. We recorded people who were experimenting for the very first time with neighbourhood schemes, mini local councils, where people elected their neighbours to run the borough. It was extremely experimental. We recorded in the jury courts for the first time. In the Soviet Union, there had never been any jury. In Saratov, I recorded a trial with jury present. All these jury people were sitting there, thinking something extraordinary was happening. It seemed to be the beginning of the real justice system, the foundations being laid.'

In another radio series, *You and Your Money*, listeners who had never had a private bank account had their financial hands held as the process was explained. There was so much that the Russians did not know. Elena Cook discovered that the whole notion and practice of the charity sector was hardly developed: 'We would come to a place and contact all the charities we had learned about from different sources, mostly from Charities Aid Foundation. They would meet for the first time; they would be living in the same city and would never have heard of each other. They wouldn't have a single idea that somebody else existed or that they were trying to set up a charity or self-help group too. They were saying to us, "Thank you for bringing us together".'

It was a cardinal principle of MPM that programmes would capture as much of the essence and nature of the whole of Russia. They would not be the creations of the atypical, unrepresentative Moscow/St Petersburg elites. To fulfil this objective, they travelled. Producer and director Fiona Cushley remembers just how far they travelled as she looked through MPM newsletters of the time: 'We went to Irkutsk, we went to Yekaterinburg. They got as far as Vladivostok. We were really trying to get a real sense of "We are covering the whole scale of Russia, not just the European part". The cities! Chelyabinsk! Kemerovo! A really dreary and sad place. Wherever we went, we made a proper connection with the people there. We made broadcasts with them.'

These journeys were almost invariably fraught. They called for adaptability, resilience and humour. Cushley recalls one which while appearing almost ludicrous speaks eloquently of the actual condition of Russia in the 1990s: 'We were stuck in Samara airport for 13 hours because no one had paid for the aircraft fuel. Nik and I were complete coffee addicts. The café had shut. So we went into the airport shop and saw that you could buy coffee beans and a coffee maker. We bought a coffee grinder as well, ground up the beans, got some water from somewhere, jumped over the counter into the café, plugging in the machine and making our own coffee. It's always been emblematic of the sense of possibility – we won't let anything get in our way, brewing up coffee in the middle of the airport. That was the sort of Russia it was.'

Almost certainly no member of the MPM team ever quite experienced a crisis similar to that facing Nik Abu Haidar in October 1993. The task was simple-sounding: to get a team of three British business trainers and three Russian interpreters to Saratov for a training seminar. The problem was that the trainers landed in Moscow on the day of the Yeltsin's armed coup against the rebels in the Russian White House.

'There was a revolution going on. I remember driving through Moscow to get to the airport. There were people fighting on the streets, no one knew what was going on. I picked up the business trainers off a flight from the UK. We put our guys in a van, drove again through near-riots to Vnukovo, the Moscow internal airport. We had a kind of council of state where I was saying, "This is a situation, no one's got a clue what's going on. We're flying out of Moscow now. We don't know what we're going to fly back to." I was the youngest person, but it was up to me to make the decision. The business trainers helped me and said, "We'll go with your guidance, but it's the interpreters here. They're all Muscovites, they need to decide." And the Muscovites said, "We think we should keep going. We're doing something good here." So I said, "Okay, I'm going to ring the first city we were going to," which was Saratov. I rang the guy there and said, "Look, this is what's going on here. You can clearly see." He said, "Yeah, there's a few tanks on the streets here, but don't worry, we'll hide you, please come." So we boarded our plane and kept to our plan, even though none of us had any idea how it would play out. Ultimately, we made the right decision – there was a civil war going on around us. But it was the Russian interpreters and the Saratov people who said, "Please, let's keep going".'

One of the most difficult parts of the entire MPM project was finding out what impact, if any, the programmes were having. Governments wanted to know; funders wanted to know; the programme makers themselves wanted to know; the entire MPM team was desperate to know. Were their extraordinary efforts and total commitment achieving anything? Was anyone out there listening, still more acting on what they heard? Anything approaching fully developed Western-style consumer marketing research hardly existed. Actual research into what listeners and viewers heard and watched was still weaker, though Andrei Allakhverdov found market research projects which MPM could tap into: 'There were quantitative and qualitative polls. We collaborated with several companies. The biggest were running omnibus polls and we were adding some questions for us. The bulk of their own questions were about detergent, yoghurt and other things. And we were asking, what radio stations do you listen to? Do you know this name? Have you ever heard any soap opera on Radio Russia, already a very big success? We also worked with the company that ran qualitative research. They made focus groups for us so we could understand what exactly people understand, what they do not understand, what they wanted to know. We also had a huge privilege because our programmes were broadcast by the national broadcaster. The audience was really enormous, perhaps 14 million. For the country like Russia, with 140 million people living there, 10 per cent is a huge portion of the population.'

Elena Cook also tapped into the experience of the listening habits of Russian audiences. In the past, the working assumption of the state-controlled communist society was that every Russian listened to the radio for one very simple reason: 'Everybody just assumed that the whole country was listening because the radio was on everywhere. You went into a home, you went into the collective farm, you went into a company, the radio was on, whatever it was broadcasting. But nobody was taking any notice. Everybody assumed because of that the audience figures were enormous. But that wasn't the case. Whereas in our case, special surveys were done in order to see what the listening figures were. And what shocked them was that there were such good listenerships for MPM, we had really good figures.'

In practice, the MPM team singly and collectively also assembled a variety of often random information to give them a passing idea of what effect their work might be having. Inevitably, it became a personal pick-and-mix approach but none the worse for that so long as it was recognized for what it was. Tim Grout-Smith constantly used the face-to-face approach as they toured the nation making programmes: 'We asked ordinary people for their opinions. That in itself was quite new. It used to be top down – you spoke to the collective farm boss, you didn't speak to the swineherd or the man trying to grow his parsnips. We were able to go in and talk to people about their own problems and what their situations were.'

Researcher Natasha Groom conducted scores of focus groups throughout Russia, leading discussions and assessing the effect of programmes: 'We searched for the holy grail of attitudinal change in Yaroslavl, Voronezh, Perm, Moscow and many other places. On one occasion I took Kari Blackburn and we sat in a collective farm in -20°C while participants discussed our agriculture series and surreptitiously drank vodka, which they had put in a teapot in the middle of the table hoping we would not notice.'

Occasionally, a single experience revealed astonishing evidence of the extent to which there was a real, live and engaged audience in the experience. Tim Williams found such a case while working in Albania, on a project spun off from MPM in Russia. The management for the programme had been trained and a board of trustees for the new MPM-style soap opera was formed. Its membership was predictable enough in the form of experienced journalists and a politician or two but something, said Williams, was missing: 'We all agreed what was missing was a listener so we had a competition. At the end of the programme, we said, "If you want to become a board member, write us a letter and say why." And we got something like 6,000 letters in a country of around one million people. That was really incredible.'

What MPM had to offer its paymasters was some quantitative research, some qualitative analysis, a good deal of hearsay evidence and some dramatic individual cases. Fortunately, the core funder, the British Know How Fund was very aware of the difficulty, perhaps near impossibility, of providing incontrovertible evidence of the impact of MPM in a country the size of Russia, still less one emerging from totalitarian control. Corinna Furse found the funders very pragmatic, realistic and accommodating in their responses: 'We were very respectful of our funders. We took a lot of trouble to do what we said we were going to do and report back. I spoke to the head of the Know How Fund. He said, "You were our best project" because we actually delivered what we promised. Masses of the other KHF programmes didn't deliver.'

The official approval should not have been surprising. By 1997, the soap opera, *Dom Syem*, promoted as being akin to a Russianized version of BBC television's celebrated *EastEnders*, was getting a weekly audience of 14 million. The number of local radio stations carrying MPM programmes had reached 115 across Russia. These were astonishing numbers which nobody in MPM would have dared set as targets from the outset. Politicians were noticing too. In July, Foreign Secretary Robin Cook visited MPM's Moscow office and was interviewed for *How Business Works*. Better still, in October, Prime Minister Tony Blair appeared in voice in an episode of *Dom Syem* while visiting Moscow. When the fifth anniversary of BBC MPM in 1998 was marked at Lancaster House, London, in the presence of Secretary of State for International Development Clare Short, warm words flowed. As chairman of the BBC MPM Trust, I responded in kind. We had political recognition for what we were doing, what could possibly go wrong?

None of us perceived that whatever the politicians might say or do, the bureaucratic winds of change in Whitehall were starting to blow against MPM. Worse still, nobody anywhere could have forecast that the internal politics of Russia were about to enter one of their most malign and closed periods.

The change in bureaucratic mindset in Whitehall was the first proximate cause for the erosion of the original MPM vision. MPM was funded by the Know How Fund from the start. KHF was part of Overseas Development Aid (ODA), a programme jointly led by the Foreign Office and Defence Ministry. ODA then turned into DfID (Department for International Development), which became the first major development ministry in the world. This apparently bureaucratic shift was to rebound heavily against everything MPM had done, how it behaved and what it stood for. Tim Williams is convinced that the true shift was one of approach and fundamental philosophy about the very idea and nature of development: 'Development people are social scientists, they're not people who studied the humanities. By contrast, all of us in MPM were humanities specialists. We understood how people work. We understood the quality of broadcasting, the quality of production, the quality of messaging. But DfID really wanted only numbers. How many people have taken the injection because they listen to a social advertisement telling them inject yourself? Really dull, not subtle, not trying to get underneath the skin of people. Especially in Russia, you are dealing with all these complexities. You're not just saying do this, do that. It's like getting this reluctant person on side to do something they've never done before.'

This transformation of approach from the top of governmental policy revealed itself in a greater insistence on numbers, on what they would call methodology. In this some detected a deep DfID discomfort with dealing with Russian society at all. For many in the MPM teams, like Tim Grout-Smith, they were now asked to do what they were not good at doing. Far from playing to MPM's special, perhaps unique, strengths of understanding people, the new DfID approach of demanding measurement of behaviour went totally against them: 'We suddenly had to produce time and motion studies and monitoring and evaluation, which we didn't really understand. It was very difficult to do for a lot of the kind of mind changing we were trying to get over. We were constantly irritated with the monitoring people sent to work with us. It wasn't just DfID from Whitehall, we were working with the EU and they were perhaps even worse, demanding to know how much we changed this society. Monitoring, evaluation is very important. It's just how you adapt to it. How do you sensibly find methodologies to quantify what's being done? In the situation we were in, it was very difficult to bring those things together. That's what changed MPM.'

Such a policy switch by the funders effectively saw the end of MPM's golden age, or perhaps even an age of innocence and idealism. It is an interesting question whether the social scientists of DfID were aware of the alteration they were imposing on the humanities-based culture of MPM. If they did notice, did they care? Probably not, convinced as they would have been at the validity, even the necessity, of their numbers-based approach. Guy Pugh experienced the transformation of the guiding policy in practice. He could see both what had worked before the changes and the problems of what followed: 'One of the joys of working with the original KHF funding is they did leave us alone, they trusted us to get on with doing what we promised to deliver. They gave us editorial control. When we were pursuing funding for various projects, especially from Europe, there was much more editorial interest that these funding organizations wanted to have. There was increasing tension about that. The glorious thing about the golden years of MPM was that we got this considerable amount of money and we were allowed to be editorially in control – that made a big, big difference.'

The gap of understanding between the two approaches cannot be overestimated. MPM could provide change, DfID demanded proof. MPM sought understanding, DfID demanded evidence. MPM offered trust and responsibility, DfID demanded control and accountability. MPM offered change over time, DfID demanded transformation now. Never the twain could or would meet. Such evidence as there was strongly suggested that MPM was having impacts in many places and in many ways. But it was the wrong kind of evidence for DfID, perhaps even the wrong kind of impact, and they held the moneybags.

But the BBC too was evolving its position. The entire structure of MPM had always sat uneasily within the BBC, using its name and reputation but somehow appearing to operate outside it. MPM was independently funded from the BBC, separately governed. It was a hybrid, perhaps a necessary hybrid but an uncomfortable one too. Some might have regarded it as an anomaly at best, an aberration at worst. In what was presented as a tidying-up operation, MPM was merged with BBC Education and World Service Training into a new BBC World Service Trust between 1999 and 2000. The game was up. MPM was seen and felt to be like a bastard child of the BBC. It needed bringing under control. Here too, BBC bureaucratic orderliness and sheer conservatism trumped collective inspiration.

Above all, the social and political atmosphere was changing inside Russia too. Not everyone wanted to know how business worked, or democracy functioned or how civil society could operate or how honest juries should behave. Many Russians reverted to old habits of pre-revolutionary behaviour – they were easier to exploit, they made more money, they were harder to control, they were more fun. Fiona Cushley smelled the mood changing in the air in the late 1990s: 'It began to be clear that it was becoming a bit Wild East / Wild West. What we used to call the wheeler dealers on the street, the whole racket of the street kiosks. It's very hard to remember whether you sensed "actually this is going a bit wrong, this is all going a bit too fast". We were so full of hope and probably a bit naive. We were so trying to push the positive. We were always aware that there was this parallel world out there in Russia which wasn't necessarily conforming to our little programme saying, "This is how you should do business". They were doing a whole different thing. This was growing and the oligarchs were being made. It was a real reminder of how things were becoming more out of control.'

There were worse signs to come. One of the most constructive relationships struck by MPM had been with Radio Russia. MPM contributed a wide range of increasingly popular programming from its portfolio. Radio Russia made its airwaves available; MPM programmes broadcast directly into Russian homes without editorial interference of any kind, a priceless connection. Even more significantly, in 1999, MPM set up the Foundation for Independent Broadcasting, a grouping of all its radio partners in what was a true legacy project. All went smoothly in that relationship too until, recalls Andrei Allekhverdov, the year 2005: 'The editor called me, I was at the time the editor-in-chief. He said, "You know, in your social programme, you're using the interviews with Valeria Novodvorskaya." I said, "Yes, what's wrong with that?" He said, "It's very wrong because she's persona non grata on Radio Russia." This was the first time when they said that not all the people who are speaking in our programmes are welcome on Radio Russia. Then they established a very strict system. Before putting programmes on air, they listened to them – they had never done this before. For about a year, we were sending them programmes in advance. Then something was wrong with the "soap" because some episodes were in Chechnya. The editor-in-chief of Radio Russia said, "No, nothing is wrong. Can we see the script?" We thought a little and decided yes, they can. They didn't say anything but after a few months, they said, "Thank you. It was a very, very fruitful collaboration for 14 years. Now we would like to run our own programmes."'

In another country, at another time, that might have seemed a natural progression. But this was Russia 2005, Putin's Russia, elected for the first time in 2000. For 15 years, Russia had been open to new ideas or at least more open than for at least two generations. Now the days of hope, experimentation, learning, openness of mind and approach, risk taking, innovation were to end. In their place came restored, centralized control, intense nationalism and resistance to outside influences and ideas. All the ingredients that had made the MPM project possible, to be welcomed with a sense of openness and possibility vanished from Russia.

In the UK, new rules prevailed, different systems took over. A project based on the humane attempt to assist people to adapt or alter how they acted and behaved was set aside in favour of methods which demanded demonstrable evidence that change promised would actually be delivered. With numbers. With specific outcomes. With certainty.

As individual members of the MPM team discovered that they were being forced to change from being innovative programme makers to report writers or project funding applicants, they started to peel away. For the better part of a decade, the first decade of the new post-Soviet Russia, a small-ish group of young, daring, mainly Russian-speaking programme makers were, in effect, given the continent of Russia as an arena of discovery. What they captured may well amount to a unique record of a society in radical transition. They were not indulging themselves for their own interests and purposes. They knew Russia and loved it, but without sentimentality. The intention was to assist those Russians who were so inclined to make the transition from the world of Communist *diktat* to one of individual responsibility. It was idealistic of course, but generous and selfless. The fact that anything was achieved was largely due to the cohesion shown by the MPM group, individuals of course who seemed to find themselves capable of common action towards a shared, understood goal. They did not need formal leadership to achieve this end, they had been their own leader. No one had predicted such a model of leadership might develop, nor consciously fostered or encouraged it. But it occurred, it was real and it worked. That it might be impossible to replicate does not diminish the fact that it once existed. One day somebody, somewhere, will try and replicate it.

Evaluating a project to which you may have given years of life and considerable quantities of intellectual and emotional commitment will necessarily be subjective. It will also be reflective. It has its own validity based on judgements shaped by time. As a comparative outsider to the MPM project as such, David Morton of the BBC Russian Service believes that MPM ceased not because it failed in any sense but political circumstances in Russia changed. He has no doubts about what MPM achieved: 'MPM gave us at the BBC the opportunity to do a lot more for people inside the former Soviet Union than we would have been able to do if we stayed within the constraints of Grant in Aid funding and BBC Russian service. That seems to me to be a quite adequate justification for the effort that went into MPM. Some very good programming was done. I think some very good people cut their teeth on it. That was pretty positive.'

For Nik Abu Haidar, MPM tapped into an existential debate within Russia about politics and economics which was central to future directions in Russian society. His strong belief is that some of the ideas offered by MPM programming remain, even if dormant, waiting to be taken up: 'What is quite clear is now you have people who are no angels saying "business and democracy have to work hand in hand". An equitable capitalism requires democracy. Everything else is what we're seeing played out in Russia today. I think it's clear that there was a crossroads and the wrong road was walked down. But some of the tools that are needed, some of the structures needed, some of the skills needed are still there. Huge amounts of resources and time have been wasted, but some of those things are still there. In that sense, yes, I think it's still possible to believe.'

Neil Cameron thinks of the projects that were never started, all the ideas never developed, all the follow-on programmes that might have deepened understanding of new ways to act. Now he looks back at what MPM actually did: 'I suppose it was an act of faith but it seemed quite a reasonable thing to think that you have a society which has completely changed. You can go in there and try to analyse it and make suggestions about how they might move forward. We found plenty of people who wanted it so I think it was more than an act of faith.'

It is hardly surprising that Russians like Elena Cook look back on MPM with a degree of fatalistic acceptance. She perhaps typifies the thoughts of many: 'It coincided with the best years in Russia. There was this coming together, this renaissance, this opening up in Russia, combined with doing something so innovative. Together, I thought it was unbelievable. Everyone I've spoken to who worked for MPM and who listened to MPM programmes in Russia, says "Wasn't it amazing?" But looking at Russia today, I rather think, "Weren't we stupid to believe it could ever last?"'

There is another strand of specifically Russian thinking about MPM expressed by Andrei Allakhverdov. You might call it the 'prophetic' strain in the Russian mind: 'I'm absolutely sure it wasn't a waste of time. Many things that we built were then ruined, that is true. But the journalists who live in Russia, unfortunately many of them had to leave and they live abroad. But they work and I daresay we contributed much to their understanding of what radio is. But it was not in vain, that's for sure. At one point I had a feeling that everything we had done for 20 years was ruined. Then I thought a bit more and understood it was not ruined and was not in vain. Unfortunately, I don't think anything like this is possible at the moment but when times change, I am absolutely sure there will be a necessity for this kind of project.'

In the meantime, all can reach their particular conclusions as to whether the decade or so of MPM activity could have left anything behind. If even one person learned something that changed their life, believes Fiona Cushley, then the work was not wasted. But these are the darkest days for any kind of optimism at a time when in her words, 'a greater evil took over': 'This is the worst possible time to be asking this question. It is so important that one has to say, "There was all the hope. And then it's totally deliberately extinguished. If you want to have an opinion, you're in jail at best." So to say, "Did it achieve anything?" This is the most difficult time; maybe in 10 years' time, people will say something completely different.'

But for now? Cushley insists that just because MPM stopped its programming, it wasn't any kind of failure. Even if it was only an attempt at social transformation, it was at least a decent one: 'It was absolutely the right time to do something. I've thought about it a lot. It was definitely the right time and we did our best.'

It was a decade-long journey from the emergence of a good idea to the then managing director, BBC World Service in 1991. None of us will know if the seeds of skill, curiosity, knowledge, information sowed by the plethora of MPM programming will ever break through the political permafrost that is Russia today. Russian history has always gone in surges, in cycles and so it will again. When the next perhaps humanistic cycle appears, who knows what elements from the MPM years might emerge too. What is clear is that a mere idea in an office was turned into an intense, living, lived-in reality. Those who picked up the idea and built the MPM in practice took responsibility for delivering it. Failure was not an option, they owed that to their Russian audiences. The MPM group owned the project. They took ownership because they believed in giving it away. It took a special kind of leadership to do that. It could not be taught, it could only be experienced.

Observations

+ Provided an idea is good enough, it requires only light direction thereafter.

+ A team project requires discipline, order and good management as well as inspiration. Once a team has adopted an idea through choice and shared understanding, it may start to own it.

+ Ownership involves a deep commitment and engagement, it cannot be ordered.

+ An effective team bases its strength on knowledge and real expertise in the project's subject area. Having strong feelings is not enough.

+ Doing good may be the outcome of an effective project but this may result from not being a do-gooder.

+ Talking down to those who are the intended beneficiaries of the project defeats the purpose of the exercise.

+ The teacher is not superior to the listener, they just happen to have more knowledge and information of a certain kind.

+ Just because you cannot prove that change results from a project does not mean that it does not occur.

+ Validation by measurement alone is dogmatic, arrogant and ultimately destructive. Even in the name of accountability.

+ Taking and accepting responsibility is morally superior to being merely accountable.

+ Just because a project ceases does not mean that everything has been lost. Change occurs in several different time scales, not all of which are immediately visible.

+ Success does not involve succeeding in every detail. Any success against impossible odds remains success.

+ Anyone who cannot be patient will never deliver a great vision.

References

MPM newsletters: March 1993, June 1995, November 1995.
MPM report, September 1997 (kindly made available by Fiona Cushley).
BBC MPM timeline, Timothy G. Williams, October 2022.

8

Lessons and Warnings

If anything emerges from the preceding stories, it is surely that no set profile exists for the visionary leader who realizes their dream against the odds. Experience does suggest they are a strikingly varied set of people, dramatically different from one another. Perhaps this is just as well — if there was an identifiable profile, let alone anything approaching a model, it would be imitated to the point of banality, reduced to a mere formula. Many would believe that following a certain model was all that was needed to achieve success in realizing a big idea. Quite the opposite is true. Yet the originator/achievers, to construct a label, do demonstrate some, perhaps several, qualities and characteristics in common and these are worth serious consideration.

They do not necessarily have to be the absolute expert in their field. If they were, pure expertise would almost certainly disable them from venturing into places judged to be impossible by others. Ignorance of detail, disregard of precedent, avoidance of convention are not barriers to success, they may be the very conditions demanded for radical innovation. The innovator never succeeded by accepting the rules and limitations built up by others over time but by going beyond them.

Yet neither is ignorance of the activity being challenged exactly a qualification. The desirable combination, varying according to the individual and the occasion, is one of real knowledge, expertise and experience larded with a fierce belief that things can be done better than by following existing rules and practices. Often the existence of an unsatisfactory situation provides the challenge for engineering radical change.

In one degree or another, the originator/achiever will be an innovator, a revolutionary, a questioner of the status quo not for its own sake but because they believe in the opportunity for change, the need for the new to be created. They are not in the market for gestures or showy initiatives but for true transformation.

None of those described in the book opted for a quiet life, nor expected it. All found that the path they took tested them, psychologically, even physically to the limit. Nor was the precise path pre-determined or easy to discern. How did they survive a profound challenge that they set themselves, that they chose more or less freely? What characteristics do they share?

Sheer bloody-mindedness is essential, a refusal to accept the judgement of others that their dream is just impossible. This might express itself in the form of quiet determination or the more noisy variety. Each can work and stem from the temperament of the individual.

A strong sense of ego is usually in play. Self-belief fortifies the determination needed. There is a vast difference between the selfishness of the pure egoist, the individualist in it for their own satisfactions, and the altruism of applied egotism. The difference is fundamental; the latter puts itself at the service of an idea and purpose rather than serving a private shallow satisfaction. It is possible to be a selfless egotist, an unexpected mixture. In practice, it makes a powerful combination.

The originator/achiever will possess the temperament that overcomes setbacks, often huge ones. They will do so by facing facts, often uncomfortable ones, but refuse to be broken by them. To do so involves possessing and displaying certain characteristics: persistence, of course, but combined with

252

adaptability, flexibility and perseverance. This business is a long-run game, never a quick fix and a clever one too. Other essential qualities include taking risks to the point of daring. If they border on existential foolhardiness, as they often may, that is not because doing so might be amusing but because not to do so could risk total failure. The corollary of taking risks is accepting full personal responsibility for any failure and never blaming others.

Any great idea or project must be personified and publicly expressed in the character and personality of the leader. Projecting the idea through their personality is a condition of its acceptance by the world and society. Without such conscious projection, recruitment of staff and supporters will be difficult or near-impossible, certainly at the desired levels of ability.

Leaders must deserve to be followed. Loyalty to the person cannot be commanded, loyalty to the idea will be earned. Without very public leadership, any project cannot move to the next, highly precious stage where colleagues, almost like disciples, recruit themselves because they have already identified themselves as followers.

Charismatic leaders secure real benefit from flaunting their public personality. Arrogance may be part of the mix too, a necessary belief in self not unattractive in the right measure. Not unattractive to the young too, always dedicated, often incredibly well qualified, already expert and prepared to commit wholeheartedly to a cause and a person with which they have identified. Self-selection is the best kind of recruitment. The clever young are a precious and valuable resource. They should not be underestimated, underappreciated or under-used. Their existence and commitment may represent the difference between success and failure.

Few of those described had a blueprint for success, any kind of formula. Few had more than some general objectives in pursuit of their dream, the implicit ones usually being the more persuasive. None was driven, motivated or aided by systems and formal planning. All were strongly instinctive and trusted their instincts about the direction they were set on following.

Success itself comes in different shapes and forms and needs to be recognized in all its variety. Even if it does not last very long, it may remain a unique example of a certain kind of achievement. Some success may appear to last but will not be validated by duration alone. Success is not defined by the number of its followers. In parts it remains success especially in any project of great ambition. Success in any part is never failure and will almost certainly have broached new boundaries of thought or application somewhere.

Recognizing where original innovation has dwindled into mere longevity is also vital. Knowing when to halt, no matter how original the beginning, is part of wisdom. An idea that has lost its savour becomes a mere habit, a formula. By the same token an originator who has lost their fervour becomes a token, a mere figurehead. Knowing when to stop and when to step aside are necessary features of the role of the innovator. Leaving with good grace involves style and demonstrates wisdom.

It remains a puzzle as to why the idea and practice of pursuing the original is so often unpopular, or if not actually unpopular is felt to be threatening. Of course, the new, the different, is almost always uncomfortable or inconvenient. It declares that what already exists is wrong or at least ready for massive improvement; it challenges the status quo, subverts it. This can be disturbing and rather than accept change, it is often easier to resist it. Most do.

Organizations, people, groups are far less good at assessing the true cost of failure to change, or admit the real benefits of accepting the chance of acceding to the new. Organizations are bad at recognizing that just as there is a reward for success, there is a cost associated with failing to take risk even when it fails. The cost of some failures may be the price of future success. Because it cannot be quantified, it is ignored.

Far easier to pigeonhole the originator/achiever as a maverick, a soloist, not a team-player; to dismiss their achievements as marginal, limited in application, restricted in scope, not capable of widespread, general application. The status quo and its comfortable defenders are many in number. Their strength is in depth and in ignorance. They prefer not to know what they are losing by not engaging with the originator/achiever. What they miss, what they turn their back on, is surprise, substance, new directions, fresh purpose and fun. Do they realize what they are missing, or how much they are missing? These stories should act as a constant reminder and as a goad to do better: the only thing they have to fear is the fear of being original.

INDEX